Derek Fell's
GROW THIS!

Derek Fell's

GROW THIS!

A GARDEN EXPERT'S GUIDE TO

Choosing the Best Vegetables, Flowers, and Seeds
So You're Never Disappointed Again

TEXT & PHOTOGRAPHY BY

Derek Fell

RODALE.

© 2013 by Derek Fell
Photographs © 2013 by Derek Fell

Rodale books may be purchased for business or promotional use or for special sales. For information, please write to:
Special Markets Department, Rodale Inc., 733 Third Avenue, New York, NY 10017

Printed in the United States of America
Rodale Inc. makes every effort to use acid-free ∞, recycled paper ♲.

Photographs by Derek Fell

Book design by Christina Gaugler

Library of Congress Cataloging-in-Publication Data is on file with the publisher.

ISBN 978–1–60961–826–1 direct hardcover
ISBN 978–1–60961–827–8 trade paperback

Distributed to the trade by Macmillan

2   4   6   8   10   9   7   5   3   1   hardcover
2   4   6   8   10   9   7   5   3   1   paperback

We inspire and enable people to improve their lives and the world around them.
rodalebooks.com

To the memory of all the plant breeders who worked to create flowers and vegetables the likes of which the world had never seen: people like Florence Bellis, for her hardy 'Barnhaven' primroses; Dr. Orie Eigsti, breeder of the first commercially successful seedless watermelons; Pauline Henry, for her 'Siloam' series of hybrid daylilies; Ted Torrey, breeder of many milestone home garden vegetables including 'Ambrosia' cantaloupe; George Russell, for his sensational 'Russell Hybrids' lupines; Henry Eckford, father of the modern sweet pea; Charles Weddle, eminent petunia and zinnia breeder; Leslie Woodriff, who took the pioneer lily-breeding work of Jan de Graaff to new heights; Professor A. P. Saunders, pioneer peony breeder; Mulford Foster, who trekked the jungles of Brazil for bromeliad species to hybridize; New Zealander John Eaton, who died soon after learning that his 'Bright Lights' chard had been honored by All-America Selections; also Claude Hope, who left government employment in Washington, DC, to establish a breeding facility in Costa Rica for the production of hybrid flowers, notably coleus, impatiens, and petunias; Charles Grimaldi, a San Francisco nurseryman who developed new honey-scented, repeat-blooming angel's trumpets; Walter Joblonsky, a Polish immigrant living in Indiana, who gave the world the most widely planted daylily of all time, the everblooming 'Stella d'Oro'; and, before him, Professor A. B. Stout, who hybridized hundreds of early daylily varieties at the New York Botanical Garden; plus the many other people you will meet in this book or whose work has influenced the decisions you make at seed racks and in garden centers each year.

And, of course, we must never forget Luther Burbank, the plant wizard, who bred the famous 'Russet Burbank' potato and more than 800 new plant varieties.

CONTENTS

The Importance of Variety Selection

Selection is the beginning and end of plant breeding.

—LUTHER BURBANK,
American botanist and horticulturist

Gardening is one of the most pleasurable activities known to mankind, full of expectations of a bountiful harvest of tasty, garden-fresh vegetables, or of dazzling color and sweet fragrances from drifts of flowers outdoors, or of armloads of flowers ready to be made into beautiful arrangements. The garden can be a quiet sanctuary where all the troubles of the world seem to disappear, and where the miracle of germination and growth can yield continuous harvests through all four seasons, not only by succession planting but through various kinds of storage for fruits and vegetables and through dried arrangements of everlasting flowers.

The garden can also be a place of bitter disappointment, unfortunately—where the time and energy we invest in planting and nurturing can produce meager results. Perhaps it is the consequence of planting an unfamiliar tomato variety that ripens too late, or a pathetically small crop of peppers as a result of a prolonged cold spell early in their development, or a starchy-tasting sweet corn that the seed catalog claimed to be supersweet and delicious. Even easy-to-grow annuals can disappoint. Most seed packets won't warn you about the mildew that attacks certain zinnias, and you may not know that certain flowers, such as seed geraniums, shatter after a downpour, leaving you with 2 weeks of a weak floral display as the plants struggle to recover.

Even when you have good soil, perfect growing conditions, and generous amounts of time to care for your garden, you may have disappointing results because of the variety you choose to plant. And that's the reason for *Derek Fell's Grow This!* I want to share the information I've gleaned over the years about vegetable, annual, perennial, herb, and lawn grass varieties, providing very specific reasons why one variety is recommended over another. I also want to provide the names of varieties that are poor performers or obsolete but that still find their way onto seed racks and garden center tables because they are cheap to produce or because they look good for a few weeks in a six-pack. It is often difficult for merchants to strike a balance between salesmanship and honesty about plants, but I believe that by learning the pros *and* the cons, you can make informed choices about what will, and won't, work in your garden. Ultimately, all of us want plants that grow and thrive and remain easy to care for, and that's the whole reason that plant breeding and hybridization exist—to continuously improve a plant's habit, bloom time, hardiness, and health so that all gardeners have success when they grow it.

Author Derek Fell in a planting of *Rudbeckia* 'Indian Summer' at Cedaridge Farm

I hope you'll find helpful—and vital—information and advice for more than 600 plant variety recommendations and cautions to ensure that you make the right plant choice every time. While all of us want every plant to grow beautifully and yield bountifully, few of us have the time to evaluate plant varieties by growing them side by side or by visiting test gardens and making notes on comparison plantings. And so we buy, plant, and nurture varieties in our own gardens, using trial and error to see what grows and tastes best in any given year. And that can be time consuming and frustrating, not to mention expensive.

I believe you can trust my variety recommendations because I've spent a lifetime in the garden and built a career around plants and growing, and I'm anxious to share what I've learned. I began gardening at the age of 6 when my grandfather gave me a packet of peas to plant in our backyard during World War II, and at the age of 17, I wrote my first garden article, interviewing champion growers of vegetables and flowers at the Shrewsbury Flower Show in

England. At age 19, I worked as catalog manager for Europe's biggest and oldest-established seed house, interviewing plant breeders and presenting their new varieties of vegetables and flowers to the general public. At age 25, I was appointed catalog manager for Burpee Seeds, America's largest mail-order seed house, and I had an office that overlooked Burpee's Fordhook Farm test plots. I introduced to the world Burpee's 'Ambrosia' melon, 'Burpee's Golden' beet, and Burpee's 'Lady' series of compact, large-flowered American marigolds, as well as other outstanding varieties bred for home garden performance (as opposed to commercial field production).

At age 30, I became a US citizen and was appointed director of All-America Selections, the national seed trials. I supervised the test gardens, the judging, and the subsequent publicity of award-winning plants, and I traveled the world visiting plant breeders to encourage them to enter their best new varieties for consideration as an award winner. I was responsible for introducing milestone award winners, such as the 'Sugar Snap' pea, 'Melody Hybrid' spinach, 'Snow Crown' cauliflower, 'Premium Crop' broccoli, 'Yellow Baby' watermelon, and other superior vegetables, plus superior flowers such as 'Magic Charms' dianthus, 'Butterfly' snapdragons, 'Redskin' dahlia, 'Southern Belle' hardy hibiscus, and 'Summer Carnival' hollyhock. I introduced to America from Holland the first commercially successful all-male asparagus and the amazing "Tomato-Potato," a graft that grows red ripe 'Sub-Arctic' tomatoes on the vine and 'Red Pontiac' potatoes in the soil. I am helping to save the heirloom stringless snap bean 'Lazy Wife' from being lost to cultivation by growing seed of the original variety every year for the past 45 years.

I also served as director of the National Garden Bureau, an information office sponsored by the American seed industry, and worked as a garden consultant to the White House. I've been writing garden books, consulting with industry leaders, and photographing the most beautiful and productive gardens in the world for some

Derek Fell with a harvest of 'Trombone' zucchini squash at Cedaridge Farm

time now. I visit local and national plant trials, such as the California Pack Trials, annually; they are now the best event for evaluating thousands of varieties sold by mail order and through retail establishments like garden centers and chain stores. I conduct my own tests on flowers and vegetables at my home, Cedaridge Farm, in Bucks County, Pennsylvania, a Zone 6 garden where the climate is like much of North America—freezing winters, cool during spring and fall, and hot summers. I also cultivate a test garden on frost-free Sanibel Island, Florida, growing annuals and vegetables during winter when much of the rest of the country is in the deep freeze, even experimenting with growing tender perennial crops year-round, like papaya, mango, and bananas.

I share all my experiences not to boast but to provide substantiation for my claim that the varieties described in *Derek Fell's Grow This!* have been thoroughly tested, not only by me under home garden conditions but by professionals like plant breeders, trial grounds managers, organic growers, and organic truck farmers whose livelihood depends on a quality product.

My greatest hope with this book is for you to experience the same satisfaction I feel when a variety of pea or pepper or tomato or marigold or zinnia performs so well that you can't wait to grow it next year and to tell all of your gardening friends and neighbors about your success. I am confident that you will experience the same pleasure I do from cultivating a successful garden when you choose the right varieties, whether your preference is growing vegetables, fruits, herbs, flowers, or a picture-perfect lawn. The right plant choice makes all the difference.

Derek Fell

GROW
PART 1
IT
RIGHT

Want satisfying yields and beautiful blooms? Strive for the best possible growing conditions in your garden and yard. It's as simple as that. While you can't control everything (like rainfall, frost, and drought), you can take advantage of your site's positive features and plan gardens that will thrive in adverse conditions. Gardens aren't effortless, though, so take the time to improve your soil with amendments and compost, gauge your garden's water requirements, learn about pestproofing and safe pest controls, and, above all, keep an eye on the garden so you can recognize and react when changes occur. When you're paying good money for quality seeds and transplants, you'll want to give them a great start when you bring them home.

CHAPTER 1

BE INFORMED BEFORE YOU BUY

The local garden center or your favorite mail-order catalog can be a bewildering place. Internet shopping for seeds and live plants is even more complicated. How do you choose among so many vegetable varieties that promise to be the tastiest, the earliest, the highest yielding, the most disease resistant, the most nutritious, or the biggest? Can ornamentals really deliver on their promises for long-lasting bloom, drought tolerance, or intoxicating fragrance when they're described in terms that make them sound all alike? And can you trust plants labeled an All-America Selections winner, a Proven Winner, a Perennial Plant of the Year, and other designations?

I wrote this book to help you understand that variety selection is one of the most important factors for garden success. Top-performing varieties will make gardening easier because they will deliver a benefit we value, such as extra-earliness (for example, 'Cherry Belle' radish—20 days to maturity), tenderness (such as 'Bright Lights' chard), or heavy yields ('Better Boy' tomato) and, in the case of flowers, longer-lasting floral displays (such as 'Wave' petunias).

BE INSPIRED, NOT CONFUSED

Garden catalogs start to arrive in December and January, with colorful photographs and descriptions that are meant to entice us into buying seeds or plants on good faith. The same kind of enticement happens at Easter, when garden centers load up with seed racks and tray tables heavy with healthy-looking transplants begging to be taken home. Often we are influenced to buy a particular petunia because it is already in flower, or we choose a six-pack of tomatoes on the strength of an attractive plant tag, or perhaps an herb labeled "tarragon" reminds us to enlarge our herb garden. But when you transplant all this promise to the garden, you discover that the first heavy rainfall destroys the petunia display because it isn't rain resistant, and the tomatoes are a variety that needs a long growing season, and the "tarragon" turns out to be the tasteless Russian variety and not the more desirable French.

What most of us need is guidance so that when we leaf through a catalog or wander the garden center aisles, we can make intelligent decisions. That's the goal of this book. Here you will learn about vegetable varieties that can perform the way you want, or flower varieties that produce long-lasting displays under adverse conditions, or lawn grasses that suit your region. You will also learn about varieties *to avoid*, for various reasons, even though these are the varieties you'll find in a seed rack or on a garden center table—because they are cheap to produce or look good in a six-pack, or simply because they have an appealing name or look enticing in a photograph.

Gardening is one of life's most pleasurable activities, but only when we see results that justify the time and expense spent on planting and nurturing our gardens.

This book aims to help you experience the most enjoyable garden possible, full of beauty from seasonlong flower displays or, in the case of edibles, from higher yields, earliness, tastier flavors, and other desirable factors. In other words, I want to help you distinguish between plant hope and plant hype.

New Names and Old Favorites

Seed packet descriptions and transplant labels can be confusing. Different companies often feature photos and descriptions of what appear to be identical varieties, but the names are different. And where is the explanation for paying extra for a plant labeled as "all-female" in the case of cucumbers and summer squash, or a "triploid hybrid" in the case of marigolds and watermelons, or "day neutral" in the case of strawberries? Is the cost really justified or not? In most cases it is, and I will explain precisely why (or, in some cases, why not). I'll explain why two identical varieties can be sold under different names, like 'Greenbud' broccoli and 'De Cicco' broccoli or 'Rainbow' chard and 'Five Color' chard, in the case of vegetables. The heirloom tomato 'Big Rainbow' is the same as 'Striped German' because a mail-order marketing company decided that 'Big Rainbow' was a better-selling name than 'Striped German'. The same is true of many flowers, where two different companies will sometimes call the same plant by different names: For example, I can't see a difference between the heirloom French mari-

'Grandpa Ott's' morning glory is an heirloom variety brought back into cultivation by Seed Savers Exchange.

gold 'Harlequin' that dates back to 1870 and the more recently introduced 'Mr. Majestic', or the heirloom morning glory 'Grandpa Ott's' and the more recent 'Star of Yalta'.

Also, it's useful to know that the market for live plants and seeds is always changing. A small army of plant breeders from mostly the United States, Japan, Holland, Germany, Israel, and the United Kingdom is constantly working to improve garden varieties of flowers and vegetables. As one breeder introduces a worthy new variety, another breeder may immediately try to improve it. Throughout this book, I often name the breeder responsible for a particular variety, like Johnny's, Pan American, Sakata, Syngenta, and Takii. Most of these names are not familiar to the public, since these breeders distribute their varieties through other companies better known to the public, such as Burpee Seeds, Harris Seeds, Park Seed, Stokes, and others. These are all reputable

Author Derek Fell evaluates marigold trials at Syngenta Flowers in Gilroy, California.

companies, but be aware that even a well-established company can change ownership and start to take shortcuts.

Another remarkable aspect of the seed and plant industry is the small army of amateur gardeners and farmers that's responsible for saving heirloom vegetables and ornamentals from being lost to cultivation by saving seed and sharing it through seed-saving exchanges. Many times, these are plants that grew in your parents' or grandparents' yards and have been dropped from commerce for many reasons, such as a succession of crop failures that made seed production too costly, or the introduction of an early (though not necessarily more flavorful) variety. Luckily, some gardeners valued a disappearing variety so highly that they saved their own seed and passed it along from one generation to the next. 'Brandywine' tomato, 'Lazy Wife' pole snap beans, and 'Dr. Martin's' limas beans are good examples.

The best plant varieties become popular by word-of-mouth recommendation. Who can argue against the popularity of Vidalia onions, for example, except that true Vidalias can be grown in only two counties of Georgia, and many onions sold as Vidalia may actually be 'Granax' or 'Walla Walla Sweet', which are more widely adapted for home gardeners? Among perennial flower varieties that became popular from word-of-mouth recommendation are 'Barnhaven' primroses, 'Siloam' hybrid daylilies, and Saunders tree peonies. Some varieties have become favorites among home gardeners through heavy advertising. 'Wave' petunias became popular after an aggressive publicity campaign, and 'Profusion' zinnias became a hit after they were seen in the California Pack Trials, an annual show-and-tell event run by leading plant breeders. Hibiscus 'Southern Belle', 'Bright Lights' chard, and 'Sugar Snap' peas enjoyed overnight success as a result of awards from All-America Selections, the national seed trials.

Generally speaking, home gardeners take a lot of convincing to try a new vegetable variety, because a familiar name conveys trust. But the person who is cautious about trying a new vegetable will readily try a new flower variety.

Disappointment with the performance of a new flower, it seems, is less traumatic than disappointment with a new vegetable or fruit.

SUBSTANTIATION FOR "THE BEST"

A recent poll revealed that many inexperienced home gardeners rely on garden center personnel for advice in choosing varieties. While many garden centers do employ a trained horticulturist to advise customers, in the busy season, the centers are staffed with seasonal help, who may or may not be qualified to offer advice.

One of the best places for nursery owners and garden center buyers to evaluate annuals and perennials is the California Pack Trials (also known as the California Spring Trials), an event that takes place the first week of April along the Pacific coast of California. More than 40 plant breeders have production facilities here and put on a display of their products for evaluation by garden center buyers in particular. The California Pack Trials started in 1966 when Glenn Goldsmith, founder of the plant breeding firm of Goldsmith Seeds (now a part of Syngenta Flowers), began a tradition of showing his customers comparisons between his breeding lines and those of his competitors. He displayed these in "packs"—the traditional six-pack plastic pots used by most garden centers and nurseries to sell live plants to the general public—and also in other

These propagation greenhouses are growing perennial calla lilies at Golden State Bulb Growers in Moss Landing, California.

popular transplant sizes, even gallon containers and hanging baskets. Soon, other breeders followed his lead, and the California Pack Trials became *the* place to make comparisons on plant performance. Collectively, the California Pack Trials have become the greatest flower show on earth, with more than 100 acres of flowers exhibited in outdoor display gardens and in greenhouses located between San Diego and San Francisco, with the greatest concentration of displays around Santa Barbara, Lompoc, Gilroy, and Salinas.

The California Pack Trials cover a much wider selection of plant families and varieties than some of the other trials and display exhibits, such as state universities, but the main objective is to show what a particular plant looks like on the sales bench in a small pot even though the best way to really determine the value of a variety is to see how well it performs out in the garden *after* it has been transplanted. Some of the growers involved in the California Pack Trials, such as Pan American Seeds, Sakata Seeds, Syngenta Flowers, and Takii Seeds, do have outdoor display gardens so garden performance can be evaluated.

This plant tag shows that the annual *Rudbeckia* 'Prairie Sun' won an All-America award for superior flowering performance compared to other black-eyed Susans.

Another important source of information about superior vegetable and flower varieties is All-America Selections, an institution started by the late Ray Hastings, a seedsman who in 1932 organized a network of test gardens with qualified judges to grow and evaluate new seed varieties from all over the world and make awards of recognition for the best. The test gardens are located in most climatic areas of the United States, with the judges drawn from universities and the seed industry. The new seed varieties are grown next to comparison plants already available here; the judges' scores are tallied at the end of the growing season, and the best performers are given awards: bronze, silver, and gold medals.

Some outstanding gold medal winners among vegetables include the 'Sugar Snap' pea, bred in Idaho by a professional pea breeder, and 'Bright Lights' Swiss chard, bred by a New Zealand home gardener. All-America Selections then uses its promotional expertise to introduce the award

Fordhook Farm's vegetable test plots are part of the research arm of Burpee Seeds, located near Doylestown, Pennsylvania.

winners. When European seed companies saw how successful the All-America Selections were, they started their own award system known as Fleuroselect.

Many retail seed and nursery companies also run trial gardens, such as Burpee Seeds at their famous Fordhook Farm in Pennsylvania, and Ball Horticultural, a wholesaler headquartered in West Chicago. The Seed Savers Exchange—a nonprofit organization dedicated to preserving heirloom varieties—also runs extensive trials to evaluate the performance of seed varieties in danger of being lost to cultivation.

In the academic world, many state universities run tests of annuals and vegetables and make awards of recognition for superior performance in their region. The University of Georgia, for example, names its Best of the Best annuals. Pennsylvania State University, Ohio State University, and Michigan State University run similar programs. These evaluations are mostly for the benefit of local nurserymen and garden center owners, but the public can visit the trials and obtain lists of award winners from Web sites.

There are also plant associations that grant awards. The American Iris Society gives its Dykes Memorial Medal to the best new bearded iris introductions; the American Hemerocallis Society has an award system for daylilies, and there is even an All-American Daylily Awards system as well as All-America Rose Selections. And the Perennial Plant Association names a Perennial Plant of the Year. All of these awards, winners lists, and judging criteria can be found on the Internet.

Shade-loving annuals are evaluated in test plots at the Landisville Flower Trials in Pennsylvania, run by Penn State University.

Some public parks and botanical gardens have comprehensive display gardens where new varieties are evaluated. In particular, Longwood Gardens in Pennsylvania labels many plants in its flowerbeds a Preferred Plant. Obviously, the average home gardener cannot visit all these facilities or keep up with all the garden industry improvements, so I've gathered as much information as I could by visiting these test and display gardens and plant trials, conducting interviews, and making comparisons to help you choose the best of the best for your home garden.

Keep alert for local specialty growers who often sell plants at a farmers' market or roadside stand. In my immediate area, in season, I can buy major perennial classes from local enthusiasts, including bearded irises, daylilies, hostas, chrysanthemums, and peonies. Remember, not all varieties find themselves in the main award programs, but that doesn't mean they should be overlooked. The benefits of Oregon-bred 'Barnhaven' primroses, for example, can be appreciated only by growing them (even though they are now available only from a remote breeding facility in Brittany, France). I discovered the charms of daffodil 'Gardenia' (a late-blooming, heavily perfumed, double-flowered white heirloom variety also known as *Narcissus albus plenus* 'Odoratus') after I acquired it from an heirloom bulb catalog and grew it myself at Cedaridge Farm; it may not have won an award, but it's surely a plant of distinction in my opinion.

BUYING SEEDS AND PLANTS

The decision to buy seeds or pay extra for plants depends on several factors. Some plants like sweet corn, peas, beans, radish, beets, and carrots are best grown from seed, as they resent transplanting. Others, like tomatoes and peppers, can take 6 to 8 weeks to reach transplant size, so you may prefer to buy small starter plants or even larger specimens, such as ready-to-bloom perennials in containers. Otherwise, a good general rule is: For instant results, buy plants; for economy, try seeds.

The Importance of Quality Seed

High-quality seeds will yield high-quality plants (given the right growing conditions, of course). A problem with buying seed is that you cannot tell if it is viable simply by looking at it, so it pays to buy from a reliable source and avoid using seed leftover from a previous year. The most reliable companies have their own test plots and offer only seed grown on organically improved soils.

All seed packets—whether purchased at a store or by mail—give the date of testing for germination. And all seed sold commercially must comply with federal germination testing standards. The most common reasons for loss of germination are heat and humidity. Some seed packets are made of a moisture-resistant material, as compared to a traditional paper packet, to preserve germination for a longer period.

How can you be sure whether a seed company or nursery is a reliable source? If you're not familiar with a particular seed company (or even if you are), you can search the company's name online and read the reviews. There will be a mix of positive and negative comments, but if there are more than a few complaints, think about choosing another supplier.

Know that there can be huge differences in cost between seed companies, largely based on the prestige of the company. Seed of a 'Better Boy' hybrid tomato, for example, comes from one producer irrespective of the brand name on the packet, and therefore a packet selling for $2 and another selling for $3 for the same amount of seed is likely to have the same origin and therefore the same quality. In other cases, seed of a particular variety can come from several sources. For example, several primary growers offer their own versions of 'Rainbow' coleus. When you see a seed offered as "originator's stock," that is an indication of quality, since it means the source is the actual originator of the variety and not a nondescript grower who may not maintain the same quality standard.

Seed packets sold from a garden center seed rack are generally old, established varieties because most garden center customers and supermarket shoppers look for familiar names and buy on price. The majority of the seed pack seeds are open pollinated (by wind or insects) and cost less than hybrids to produce, but the selection offered in a seed rack is generally not as good as from a catalog. When buying seed packets of vegetables and flowers, look for "mixtures" that are generally a better buy than choosing varieties or colors singly to mix yourself. With vegetables, generally the best mixtures use an organic dye to color the seeds to show the different varieties (for example, a three-color mix of green, yellow, and gray seeds for three colors of pattypan squash). With flowers, a "formula" mixture is better than a haphazard mixture that is produced by growing a mix of colors in the field, because in a formula mixture the colors are grown separately and blended in equal amounts so no one color dominates. The packet description will usually say "formula mixture" or say that the colors have been grown separately and mixed in equal proportions.

Seed life varies among varieties. For example, bean seeds can hold their germination for 3 years under cool conditions, while lettuce seed can lose its germination rapidly when exposed to high humidity. Before using leftover seed, test for germination by starting 10 seeds on a moist paper towel. Some seeds (especially hardy perennials such as primroses) germinate best after exposure to frost. Ten weeks in the crisper section of your refrigerator will normally provide the necessary cold period.

Buying Starter Plants Locally

Even though buying transplants costs more, many gardeners prefer to buy transplants from a local garden center because it saves time. Also, buying locally is more reliable than buying plants by mail because mail-order plants can be delayed in transit and arrive dehydrated or damaged. However, packaging methods today do allow most plants to be shipped safely *providing* you buy from a reliable source that will refund your money if you're disappointed.

When you buy starter plants from a garden center, look for short, stocky plants with dark green foliage, showing no yellowed leaves or signs of stretching or legginess. The leaves should be free of blemishes, such as spots or clusters of aphids, and should have leaves in various stages of growth. In general, a transplant should not already show fruit or large flower trusses; this helps avoid stress at transplant time.

With bedding plants, such as marigolds, zinnias, and impatiens, it's wise to cut off the first flush of flowers (if they've formed) before transplanting because this allows the plant to branch sideways and create a stocky, bushy habit. A transplant with its first flowers removed will soon overtake a transplant that has been allowed to keep its first flowers.

All starter plants should be adequately hardened off before they're planted. Hardening off helps the plant adapt to colder and windier conditions and reduces transplant shock when starters are planted into the garden. If the garden center has not already done this, you can harden off plants by placing them in a coldframe for several days if the weather is still brisk, or you can keep the plants in a sheltered location (like on a porch or under a shrub or evergreen branches to protect them from the wind).

Be aware that factors other than garden performance can influence the selection of varieties offered at a garden center. Growers who supply mass marketers like chain stores have their growing operations completely mechanized, and so a seed variety that has a 90 percent germination rate will be favored over one with a 70 percent germination rate, even if the latter is a better product. Also, mass merchandisers favor varieties that look good on the sales bench, either in six-packs or individual pots, irrespective of how the plant will perform after it has been transplanted. This "pack performance" explains the meteoric rise in sales of mini-petunias (*Calibrachoa*) and New Guinea impatiens—beauty queens at the point of sale but not so beautiful when home gardeners subsequently find them difficult to keep alive. In a maritime climate like Long Island, New York, they do better, but breeders continue to work on *Calibrachoa* to make them more durable. In my experience, the celosia series known as 'Century Mixed Colors' is a better plant for home garden performance than the 'Kimono' series from the same breeder; because of mass-merchandising outlets, sales of 'Kimono' are greater because 'Kimono' produces an early flower spike that allows the box stores to display more racks in a designated space and encourages a strong impulse purchase among its customers. Among tomatoes, garden centers often offer short, compact plants covered in fruit, like the variety 'Tiny Tim' or 'Patio'. But all you see in the way of fruit production is all you are likely to get, since they are determinate varieties that stay compact and ripen their fruit at one time. A much better choice for continuous production would be an indeterminate variety like 'Sweet Million' or 'Sun Gold'.

Some live plants come with hefty price tags, even though they are almost identical to another plant in their family with a considerably lower cost. That's because transplants grown from seed are generally less expensive than plants grown from cuttings or tissue culture (called vegetative reproduction), because the latter involve costly human handling and often a royalty of as much as $2 per plant is paid to the breeder. This is true of certain varieties of coral bells (*Heuchera*) and cone-flower, where even a slight color variation can command a higher price.

Buying Live Plants by Mail

There is a big difference between starter plants sold in a garden center or store and starter plants sold by direct mail. Generally speaking, plants you buy from a catalog or from an Internet Web site are smaller in size. They have to be shipped while young to reduce damage during transit.

Live plants purchased by mail are more perishable than seed, of course, so checking the reputation of a company via the Internet is critical. Some companies are good at shipping live plants. They ship with the plant rooted in a pot with soil, using special containers that hold the plants upright, nested in polystyrene or shredded newspaper.

Mail-order companies will ask you for a date to ship, or they may specify that they will ship at the proper planting time for your area (usually after your last frost date), using your ZIP code to determine the correct time. Direct-planting a mail-order shipment of live plants can be risky because of the stress the plant experienced during transit, so I usually transplant to a larger pot to give the plant a chance to reestablish itself before transferring to its permanent garden space.

Many companies ship "bareroot," which means the plants have been dug from the field and the roots have been washed clean of soil and inserted into a plastic pouch. Some companies ship raw bulbs, which are unsprouted bulbs in a paper or plastic bag with wood shavings to resist damage. A bareroot plant will be dormant or just breaking dormancy, with perhaps a small green shoot already sprouting from the crown. The success rate from bareroot plants is not as good as from potted plants or from bulbs because the roots can become moldy or dehydrated during transit.

Examine the bareroot carefully. If you see any broken roots, trim them away and give the root a good soaking in water for at least an hour or overnight.

Some bareroot plants like asparagus and strawberries can be transplanted directly into the garden after you receive them, but others (like bareroot perennials) will show a better survival rate if first planted in a pot and then, after 4 to 6 weeks of top growth and root development, transplanted to their permanent flowering positions. Bulbs can be planted directly into their flowering positions as soon as they arrive.

Regional Differences

North America has 11 climate zones, ranging from USDA Hardiness Zone 1 (the extreme Arctic with permanent snow cover) to frost-free Zone 11 (Key West, Florida). Although the Pacific Northwest (Oregon and Washington) has a longer growing season than New England, gardeners there do not experience the summer heat and intense light that New England and most other areas of the United States see. Therefore, gardeners in the Pacific Northwest need to grow early varieties, like 'Early Cascade' tomatoes that do not need extended hot periods to ripen, or cold-tolerant kinds, like 'Sweet Gypsy Hybrid' bell pepper. The same advice applies to flowers that require a long, hot growing season, like zinnias.

Check the Internet for regional variety recommendations if you live in a zone with special weather conditions. Gardening 101 tells us that plants grow best when they're grown in a climate suited to their needs, so it's imperative that you're aware of a plant's attributes and limitations before you buy. For example, if you want to know which tomato varieties are recommended for Florida, simply type in "Florida tomatoes" as a search, and you'll probably be directed to a site with specific recommendations. If possible, look for suggestions from a state university or Cooperative Extension office. A surprising number of varieties are widely adaptable. The All-America Selections award-winning 'Celebrity Hybrid', 'Big Boy Hybrid', and 'Better Boy' hybrid tomatoes appear on most regional lists because they're adaptable to a wide range of zones.

How to Read a Seed Packet

If you've bought seeds from a catalog or a seed rack, you've bought into a dream! Seeds as fine as dust can transform turfgrass or bare garden soil into bountiful displays of vegetables and blooms. To ensure these seeds perform as you hope, read the packet, for starters.

Some seed packets (and catalog descriptions) are good at explaining the cultural needs of a variety, but others are not, and you may have to do an Internet search to obtain sufficient information for success. How do you decide between seeds labeled open pollinated, F1 hybrid, GMO, organic, heirloom, patented, supersweet, sugar enhanced, triple-sugary, all-female, all-male, triploid, diploid, gynoecious, and parthenocarpic? I explain all of these terms beginning on page 18 because they are important to know so you can choose varieties that are right for your needs and your space.

Seed packets don't have much room to explain all you need to know, so check online when in doubt. The most important information on a seed packet is contained on the back, usually in small print. Besides a brief description, you may see different terms used to describe the plant and helpful information about sowing depth, spacing, days to maturity, and whether tender or hardy to frost. If this essential information is missing, look it up.

Instructions for seeding flowers usually will be different from seeding vegetables. For some reason, for example, seed companies will give maturity dates for vegetables but not flowers. Here are some insights into the information most seed packets will provide.

Days to maturity is especially important for vegetables because some early varieties of cabbage like 'Early Market' will mature within 65 days, while others require 100 days or more.

Spacing is important when planting seeds because space is needed between individual plants and also between rows; for example, head lettuce requires a minimum of 8 inches of space in any direction or it may not develop tight heads and instead develops just a loose arrangement of leaves. Some flowers tolerate crowding (such as poppies) and will flower dramatically if the seed is simply broadcast over bare soil.

Planting depth is critical because some seeds need light to germinate and require simply pressing sufficiently into the soil surface to anchor them. Other seeds prefer light excluded when germinating, such as tomato seeds.

Soil temperature is often the biggest reason seeds fail to germinate. Spinach prefers cool soil temperatures as low as 40°F, whereas many warm-season crops like melons, okra, and lima beans may fail to germinate unless the soil temperature is 70°F or higher.

Seed count and germination percentage are also helpful bits of information that you can compare between competing brands.

For the most part, buying seed from a catalog or seed rack and growing your own transplants is much less expensive than purchasing transplants from a nursery or garden center. A packet of tomato seed containing 20 or 30 seeds, for example, can cost $2.50, whereas you will need to pay that same amount for a single transplant.

How to Read a Catalog Description

What can be more welcome after a long, cold winter than to receive a colorful seed catalog with its promise of spring and renewal? Most catalogs try to establish a personality and use descriptions that attract you to a plant's charms (some descriptions are witty, some use a lot of superlatives, and others feature a distinctive voice intended to establish trust). Some catalogs feature color photos, others show line drawings, and some don't use illustrations at all but rely entirely on words to sell the product. I look for a hint of passion, an authoritative tone, and a careful use of superlatives. Personally, I also like it when a seed company acknowledges the breeder, because it takes a long time to breed a new variety and it helps establish credibility when a person has allowed his or her name to be associated with a variety.

Catalog descriptions and seed packets contain similar information, but some seed companies mark special varieties with a star, a bull's-eye, an All-America Selections symbol, or another icon to show they're bestsellers or recommended varieties. Some may even label a variety as "exclusive" to their seed house, but that's not necessarily a mark of a desirable variety—because if it's so wonderful, why aren't other companies offering it? In my experience, varieties listed as exclusives are not as good as varieties featured in a wide selection of catalogs.

After decades of managing and studying seed catalogs, here are a few things I've learned.

✦ Hybrids are usually worth the extra cost through improved yields, providing they receive timely feeding and watering.

✦ Heirloom vegetables usually will yield poorly compared to modern varieties, but their comparatively poor yields are significantly improved (up to 10 times in the case of 'Brandywine' tomato) by choosing "grafted" varieties (meaning the heirloom portion of the plant is grafted onto a special vigorous rootstock).

✦ Mixtures of flowers and vegetables generally offer the best value, compared to buying separate colors.

✦ Almost all seed catalogs offer certain popular varieties as plants, particularly among tomatoes, peppers, and onions. The survival rate on these through the mail is high. Live plants of cucumbers and melons are not so dependable, since the plants are more brittle and more easily dehydrated.

When you've made your catalog selections and start to fill in the order form, you will notice that some companies include shipping in the price. Other catalogs provide free shipping for orders of a certain value or by a certain date, and others require an extra amount for shipping and handling regardless of the size of your order.

Seed and Plant Terminology Explained

Here are some of the special terms you may encounter in a seed packet description, on a plant label, or in a catalog.

AAS Winner means it won an award from All-America Selections, the national seed trials.

AGM means the variety has been awarded an Award of Garden Merit from the British Royal Horticultural Society.

All-female refers to a plant that produces only female flowers, or very few males. Since only the female flowers are capable of bearing fruit, the higher the percentage of females, the higher the yield. Some all-female varieties require a male pollinator; others are self-pollinating, depending on the variety. The packet or catalog description will tell you if a pollinator is needed and whether seed of a male pollinator is included (usually dyed a special color for identification).

All-male refers to plants that possess only male pollen-bearing flowers and no females. This can result in a higher yield (especially with perennial vegetables like asparagus, where pollination is not needed to produce yields), as males don't need to expend energy on producing seeds.

Bareroot means that the plant is shipped not in a pot with soil, but with soil washed from the roots and the roots wrapped in paper or plastic wrap for shipment.

Bicolors are usually flowers with two colors in the petals.

Biennial is a plant that requires two seasons to flower, then dies. Biennials usually set prodigious quantities of seed to self-sow for a new generation; money plant is a great example of a biennial.

Corms are a type of bulb.

Cuttings are usually living stems with roots sprouted from the bottom.

Determinate and **Indeterminate** are terms used to describe the habit of a tomato. Determinate means bushy and compact; indeterminate means vining.

Cucumber 'Diva' is an all-female hybrid that won an All-America award for its high fruit yield.

Diploid is a plant in which breeders have doubled the number of chromosomes, usually resulting in larger-size fruits or larger flowers.

Double flowers have more than one row of petals. "Fully double" means the flower has so many petals it forms a ball shape.

Dwarf means bushy and compact rather than tall or vining.

Fleuroselect winner means the variety has received an award from the European seed trials, the equivalent of All-America Selections.

Foliar feeding means spraying the leaves with a liquid fertilizer so the leaves, rather than the roots, absorb the nutrients.

F1 hybrid is a first-generation cross between two plant species that do not normally mate in the wild. Like animal hybrids such as the mule (a cross between a jackass onto a mare), the first-generation cross is more vigorous than either parent, and also, like the mule, the seed from first-generation hybrids can be sterile (or inferior) to the original cross.

Free-flowering usually means abundant bloom.

Germination means the successful sprouting of a seed.

GMO stands for genetically modified organism, referring to plants that have had their genes altered artificially to create a desirable growing trait. For example, certain sweet corns have been modified to contain a built-in resistance to the corn earworm by incorporating the bacterial control BT in its genes. GMO varieties are controversial because the long-term effects on humans are not known, and GMOs are not allowed in organic production.

Gynoecious means the variety is all-female and refers mostly to varieties of cucumbers, melons, and squash. The plant either needs a male pollinator in order to set fruit or it sets fruit without pollination, depending on the variety. Check the catalog description to determine whether a pollinator is needed.

Hardiness Zone refers to one of 11 climate zones in North America.

Hardy refers to cold hardiness. Generally a plant that can survive winters in Zone 6 and colder is considered hardy, while Zone 7 and south is considered tender.

Heirloom originally referred to an open-pollinated variety that was introduced before World War II, but some seed houses consider an heirloom to be a variety that has been on the market for 50 years.

An abundant harvest of 'Trombone' zucchini squash shows the young fruit with long, curved necks. Free of seeds when young, they are as tender as a baby zucchini.

Hybrid means the plant is a man-made cross between two compatible parents, usually resulting in increased vigor and other desirable benefits. Hybrids are more expensive than open-pollinated varieties because a human workforce must be used to pollinate. Seed saved from hybrids is generally sterile or will result in an inferior crop the following season because of a drastic reduction in vigor.

Meristem is a form of vegetative propagation. Small clusters of plant tissue are placed in a growing solution to create exact replicas of the parent. It allows for a large number of plants to be grown from a single specimen—many more than regular vegetative reproduction such as cuttings. Meristem plants are generally more costly than regular cuttings because a special sterile lab is needed to grow the plants and it takes much longer to grow the meristem plant to a salable size.

Open pollinated means a variety that will breed true from seed. Open-pollinated varieties are pollinated by bees or wind and therefore generally cost less than hybrids, which must be isolated and tediously hand-pollinated.

Organic seed means seed that has been grown on land not contaminated by chemicals, fertilized only with organically approved products, and protected against pests and diseases with nonchemical products.

Organic vegetable means that the harvest has been grown on uncontaminated land using approved organic practices similar to the regulations required for growing seed. Since certification for using the term *organic* requires inspection and a fee to cover government oversight, some growers who grow organically will refer to their vegetables as "natural" instead of organic.

Parthenocarpic means the production of fruit without need for fertilization, as with some varieties of cucumber and zucchini squash.

Patented or PPAF means the variety has been granted a patent or a plant patent has been applied for. There are two kinds of plant patents—one for plants grown from seed and one for plants grown vegetatively. If you have a plant under patent or with a patent pending, other growers and gardeners are prohibited from propagating the variety for commercial purposes. That does not mean you cannot save the seed or take cuttings and use it privately for your next season's crop, since compliance among home gardeners is impossible to regulate. Patents only apply to open-pollinated varieties, since hybrids cannot be reproduced without knowing the parents used for the cross, meaning hybrids have their own built-in "patent" protection.

Propagation means increasing a plant by seed or vegetative means.

Sugar enhanced identifies a special kind of hybrid sweet corn that holds its sweetness up to 14 days after harvest, compared to regular sweet corns that convert their sugar to starch as soon as the cob is removed from the stalk.

Supersweet identifies a special kind of hybrid sweet corn that holds its sweetness for a longer period than open-pollinated varieties. Supersweets are different from sugar enhanced in that the supersweets must be isolated from other corns in order to develop their supersweetness. A wide row of tall sunflowers between varieties of supersweets can provide sufficient isolation.

Tender annual means a plant that completes its life cycle in a year and is killed by frost, such as tomatoes and petunias.

Thinning describes the act of removing crowded seedlings so the strongest survive to develop fully.

Triple-sugary identifies a special kind of sweet corn that contains both sugar-enhanced and supersweet kernels.

Triploid means a plant in which breeders have tripled the number of chromosomes. This can result in a vegetable that is seedless, like seedless watermelons. In marigolds, it prevents seed formation and so stimulates the plant to keep blooming, thus producing more flowers over a longer period than nontriploids.

Vegetative reproduction refers to any form of plant reproduction other than seeds; for example, vegetative reproduction can describe cuttings taken from roots, stems, or leaves and also meristem culture.

CHAPTER 2

WHAT EVERY GARDEN NEEDS

Wherever you garden—on fast-draining, alkaline sandy soil or sticky, acidic clay soil—you need good growing conditions for healthy plants. Every garden is a challenge in the beginning, but if you amend poor soil, maintain proper moisture levels, control weeds, and nip troublesome pests and diseases in the bud, you will be rewarded with a bountiful harvest of fresh vegetables, armloads of beautiful flowers, and a velvet green lawn suited to your region.

START WITH GOOD SOIL

The remedy for most gardening problems is improving the condition of your soil. Healthy soil is the foundation of bountiful harvests and blooms, since an impoverished soil can yield only meager results. Soil is such a complex substance that it is the cause *and* cure of many ailments involving plant growth, including moisture-holding capacity, fertility, and pests and diseases.

The first important role of soil is to provide an anchor for plant roots. A sandy soil or a shallow soil can cause plants to keel over in the wind. Similarly, a heavy clay soil can present a barrier to root development. A quick way to improve either a sandy or a clay soil is to add compost. All that fluffy, fibrous decomposed kitchen and garden waste will add body to sandy soil and soak up and hold water like a sponge while allowing excess moisture to drain freely. Compost added to a clay soil will break up the fine clay particles and allow plant roots to penetrate deeper and will provide aeration for roots. You simply cannot have enough compost when it comes to keeping your soil in good condition.

Another important role of good soil is providing nutrients to plants (even hydroponic systems need a soil substitute for roots to grow in, such as felt or vermiculite). Plants must absorb nutrients in soluble form through their roots or through pores (stomata) on their leaf surfaces. Either way, intake of nutrients is possible only by receiving regular amounts of moisture.

Homemade compost—full of nutrients and beneficial microorganisms—is easy to make. Simply pile garden and kitchen waste into a bin, let it decompose, and the pile will rot down into a fluffy, nutritious soil amendment. With the right balance of ingredients (such as shredded leaves, green leafy garden waste for nitrogen, wood ashes from a fireplace, eggshells for calcium, stable manure and fish bones for phosphorus, and fruit waste like melon rinds and banana peels), compost can provide essential plant nutrients—nitrogen for healthy leaves, phosphorus for healthy root and flower development, and potash for overall vigor and disease resistance, plus a host of micronutrients.

If you need to know the condition of your soil, visit your local garden center for a mailing pouch to send for a soil test. You'll fill the pouch with several samples of soil from different parts of the area you wish to cultivate, then mail it to a lab, usually located at your state university. You'll receive a report that will tell you what your soil lacks and how to amend it. Even if you want to grow a wide range of vegetables and flowers, the report will give you a specific recommendation to benefit a particular vegetable group (like vine crops) *and* a general recommendation to benefit all the plants you wish to grow. In my experience, it's better to have a lab give you results than trying to test your soil with a do-it-yourself test kit.

BOOST YIELDS WITH ORGANIC FERTILIZER

While many organic gardeners rely entirely on homemade compost to feed plants, others (like me) provide a fertilizer boost by using an organic fertilizer. Purchased organic fertilizers not only provide the essential plant nutrients in natural form, but the organic filler they use acts as roughage to aerate your soil and benefits microorganisms that can enrich soil from their waste. The problem with a lot of packaged fertilizers is that they are formulated from chemicals that, over time, can produce a toxic buildup in the soil that may harm plants.

The three major plant nutrients—nitrogen (N), phosphorus (P), and potassium (K)—are given as percentages on a fertilizer package, such as 10-20-10, meaning 10 percent nitrogen, 20 percent phosphorus, and 10 percent potassium. The rest is filler, which acts as a distributing agent. When you compare a commercial chemical fertilizer with an organic formulation, you will often find that the analysis of N-P-K for the organic fertilizer is lower than a similar-size chemical fertilizer package—for example, 3-6-3 instead of 10-20-10. You may think that the organic fertilizer is less nutritious, but, in fact, an organic fertilizer is more efficient at feeding plants and will feed over a longer period of time because it releases its nutrients more slowly.

Both chemical and organic fertilizers can be granular or liquid, as well as slow acting or fast acting. Most organic liquid fertilizers can be applied as a soil drench using a watering can or a backpack sprayer; just apply the liquid directly to the root zone. You can also spray on the upper and underside of leaves as a foliar feed, since plants are capable of absorbing nutrients through stomata on leaf surfaces. Phosphorus (responsible for flower and root development) and potassium (responsible for disease resistance and overall vigor) can remain in the soil for long periods, but nitrogen (responsible for healthy leaves) is notorious for leaching away quickly after a rainfall. Leafy crops like cabbage and lettuce are especially in need of nitrogen.

Generally speaking, vegetables, berry bushes, and fruit trees require more regular feeding than flowering plants like annuals and perennials. With flowering plants, one application at the start of the growing season is usually sufficient. However, vegetables can be greedy feeders, especially fruiting vegetables like tomatoes, peppers, melons, and squash. If you are relying on compost to feed these plants, be sure to make several applications around the roots during the growing season, and be sure that the compost is rich in phosphorus, since lack of phosphorus is often the cause of late ripening of tomatoes and melons or poor yields. The addition of bonemeal to compost will improve its phosphorus content and effectiveness significantly. For fruit trees and berry bushes, keep the area out to the drip line weed free, and gently rake a general-purpose fertilizer into the upper soil surface.

Plants also require a total of 16 trace elements for good growth. If any one of those elements is missing, the plants can suffer stress. That makes composting even more important, because it is only through composting a wide range of organic materials (especially plant parts) that you can be assured all those essential plant nutrients and trace elements are present.

In general, annuals and perennials do not need the heavy feeding that vegetables, berry bushes, and fruit trees need, and one application at the start of the season is usually sufficient to maintain a generous amount of bloom. Of course, there are fertilizers formulated specifically for flowers, and these generally have a high phosphorus content, but a balanced general-purpose fertilizer will work fine, especially in combination with an application of compost to start the season.

THE DYNAMICS OF LIGHT

Most vegetables require at least 6 hours of sunlight a day (warm-season vegetables like tomatoes, melons, and peppers need more than 6 hours for worthwhile yields, and they especially need noonday sun). For a vegetable garden, therefore, choose the sunniest spot on your property. If you are heavily shaded by trees, consider pruning away some overhead branches. The removal of a single branch can often mean the difference between flowers and no flowers.

Certain annuals (like impatiens) and perennials (like hostas) will tolerate fairly heavy shade since they come from forested parts of the world, but the majority of flowers come from semidesert or mountainous areas. For example, annual zinnias come from arid regions of Mexico, while perennial lavender grows wild in the mountains of Provence. Both are grown in high-intensity light, so they thrive in sun.

DRAINAGE ISSUES

Although some annuals (like forget-me-nots) and perennials (like astilbe) will thrive in moist soil, most vegetables demand good drainage (horseradish is an exception, and watercress can be grown in a clear running stream). If you have a vegetable garden site that puddles after rain or that stays soggy, you should consider laying down some crushed stones and building raised beds (see page 33 for more on raised beds). Planting in raised beds not only allows you to have excellent drainage, but your plants will also benefit from better and looser soil texture. When creating a raised bed, the soil depth should be at least 6 inches, and preferably 8 inches or more if you are growing vining crops like lima beans.

Raised beds offer good drainage, and drip irrigation hoses allow for regular watering of young cabbage during dry spells.

These raised beds use black plastic as a weed control for a cutting garden at the author's home, Cedaridge Farm.

WEED CONTROL

Weeds not only rob the soil of moisture and nutrients, they crowd out roots of beneficial plants, causing them to suffocate and die. The simplest way to control weeds is by using mulch (a covering over the soil that creates a weed barrier), such as shredded bark, shredded leaves, and grass clippings. Most cool-season crops like lettuce and peas prefer an organic mulch such as shredded leaves, as this helps keep the soil cool. Warm-season crops like melons and tomatoes perform better when planted through black plastic or a mulch fabric (which allows moisture penetration), because this keeps the soil warm.

Similar mulches can be used for flowerbeds, but since black plastic and mulch fabrics can look unsightly, these should be covered with a decorative organic mulch such as straw, shredded leaves, and licorice root.

When using an organic mulch like shredded leaves, you may find that some aggressive weeds will still come up. Be aware that weeds are generally either surface rooted (such as chickweed and henbit), which are easily removed by hand, or deep rooted (like thistle and dandelion), where the root will usually break when pulled by hand, leaving a portion of root to regenerate itself. My favorite tool for all kinds of weeding is a dandelion weeder. It has a long handle and a pronged end that is easily pushed deep into soil and levered against the root to pull it up.

WATERING WHEN IT'S NECESSARY

Adequate rainfall makes gardening easier, but even a rainy season may leave plants thirsty on occasion. Depending on the amount of space you cultivate and where your gardens are located, there are three ways to water plants—by hand with a watering can, with a sprinkler system, and with a drip line. For watering cans, choose a 2-gallon-capacity can rather than a smaller can to save frequent fill-ups, as long as you can safely carry 16 pounds of water. There are many styles of cans available, with different designs for balance and water delivery. You might need to try a few designs to find the one that feels right in your hand. Sprinklers, such as oscillating, rotating, and even traveling sprinklers, can be set to deliver water over a prescribed area. There are two types of drip line you may find helpful in a home garden—soaker hoses and irrigation lines with emitters. The most efficient drip systems can be placed on top of the soil or hidden beneath an organic or a plastic mulch right at a plant's base. Attached to a spigot, soaker hoses and drip lines will "sweat" moisture at a slow-and-steady rate directly at the root zone. Most can be attached to timers that will turn on the water at prescribed intervals and durations (such as for 30 minutes at 8:00 each morning or once or twice a week). Drip lines with emitters are best used for raised beds and container gardeners; avoid drip lines with emitters for a regular flowerbed or vegetable plot, since mulches can easily clog the emitters and it can be tedious work to peg or place emitters at every plant station.

PEST AND DISEASE CONTROL

I've gardened on two continents: in England since the age of 6; in Pennsylvania (a USDA Hardiness Zone 6 garden) since 1964, and additionally on Sanibel Island, Florida (a Zone 10 frost-free garden), since 2008. I vividly recall eagerly awaiting my first sweet corn harvest in the United States, only to discover it infected with sooty mold or corn smut disease. It looked horrible—big blue-black blisters emanating from the ears of corn, making them misshapen and inedible. (However, I later discovered that corn smut is a type of edible fungus with a mushroom flavor for adding to egg dishes and meat. In Mexican grocery stores, it is even sold in cans!) The corn smut fungus enters the corn during wet weather through any kind of wound on the stem. My crop—and my appetite for sweet corn—was ruined that season.

Over the years, I've encountered just about every pest problem a gardener can experience, including slugs eating my lettuce, green caterpillars eating my cabbage, aphids on my Brussels sprouts, flea beetles on my eggplant, powdery mildew disease on my cucumber vines, borers in my peach trees, and a host of other spoilers. Common problems in the flower garden have included mildew on zinnias, Japanese beetles eating roses, and yellows disease wilting my asters. What's a person to do?

The first rule in fighting pests and disease is to ensure your soil is in good condition and your plants are well fed. Like people, plants under stress fall victims to disease more readily than those that are not stressed. For me, the foundation of a good soil is good compost applied twice a year—in spring before planting and again in fall after frost. It's true that I still must stay diligent for signs of trouble, but the damage to my vegetables when they're planted in healthy soil is manageable.

I remember reading an analysis of the nutrient value of various vegetables and found it puzzling that broccoli had a measurable amount of protein. When I asked a broccoli breeder why, he laughed and pointed out that the protein comes from cabbage worms that lay hidden under the head and get analyzed with it when the lab runs tests. Now I always separate my broccoli heads carefully and expel any worms hiding among the stalks. (Soaking the heads briefly in salt water also drives out the caterpillars.)

In a vegetable garden, due diligence is key to keeping plants healthy. Cut-worms that lie hidden in the soil during daytime can be a big problem at planting time; when the seeds come up or the transplants are set out, a grub emerges from the soil during the night and eats the tops. To prevent this, I fit transplants and young seedlings with a cutworm collar—usually a cardboard paper cup with a slit for the stem to slide into. I then bury the upturned rim in the soil to create an effective barrier against the pest reaching the tender—and tasty—plant top.

There is also a soilborne disease that will often attack susceptible seedlings like spinach. Called damping-off, it is a fungal disease that attacks plants at the soil line, making them keel over. It is particularly troublesome when using last year's pots to grow transplants, as the spores lay hidden in the old soil. When using old pots, be sure to wash them in hot water with a 10 percent bleach solution, and rinse thoroughly before filling with potting mix.

Japanese beetles can be a huge problem in summer when the grubs turn into voracious beetles. They are especially fond of eating rose petals and skeletonizing leaves like grapevines and pole beans. Commercial traps can lure the beetles into disposable bags, but sometimes all you succeed in doing is luring your neighbor's beetles to your garden. When my children were young, I showed them how collecting the beetles and throwing them onto our pond would cause the sunfish in the pond to start a feeding frenzy. My youngest son and daughter often would race out into the garden in the early morning to find as many beetles as possible to feed the fish. These days, I turn to a product called milky spore that's suitable for controlling Japanese beetles. A white powder, milky spore is a bacterial control that attacks the beetle larvae (called grubs) in the soil. Apply milky spore according to package directions, and your lawn and garden will get long-lasting protection from Japanese beetles.

I am not a believer in home remedies, like using beer to drown slugs, because I found many of them to be ineffective. The beer will attract a few of the slimy creatures and drown them, but it won't attract enough to be an effective control over a large garden. Instead, I simply go out in the mornings before they hide and, with a gloved hand, pick them off and feed them to my fish. I also have found many so-called deer repellents ineffective, especially for protecting vegetables. What the labels don't tell you is that deer are neophobic, meaning they have a natural fear of anything new. So when they see home remedies like bar soap or bags of human hair hanging from bamboo canes or tree branches, deer will naturally avoid them; eventually—through familiarity—they will overcome their fear and ignore the soap or bags. Fencing out deer is really the only good remedy. Most of the fencing around my vegetable garden is 4 feet high, and it keeps them out. (You may find that an 8-foot fence works better for large spaces.) I've found that deer are generally lazy and will walk around an obstruction rather than jump over it, especially in spring and summer when there are plenty of other things to forage just a few feet away.

The one home remedy I have found effective is a garlic-pepper spray using 1 cup each of chopped hot peppers and chopped garlic, liquefied in a blender, and mixed with a gallon of water. It has a repellent effect on soft pests like aphids, flea beetles, spider mites, and bean beetle larvae. I apply it preventively with a backpack sprayer, although a handheld bottle sprayer can suffice for a small area. I reapply it after rainfall and usually once every 2 weeks.

A very effective all-purpose protection for vegetables is horticultural fleece, a lightweight fabric that covers plants like a spiderweb. It is light enough to rise as plants push up from beneath it, yet highly effective for blocking all kinds of entry from insects, disease organisms, and even foraging animals like rabbits, groundhogs, and deer. (If you are growing fruiting crops like zucchini and cucumbers, open up the fleece when flowering begins, or plant self-pollinating types.)

I'm also a big believer in attracting predatory insects to a garden by planting flowering annuals. Ladybugs, for example, eat aphids, and praying mantises eat lots of beetles. A toad can eat a lot of slugs, of course, while songbirds eat lots of grubs, caterpillars, and harmful beetles.

Frogs and toads are a gardener's friend, eating many harmful insect pests such as slugs and snails.

You may never eliminate every pest and problem from your garden, but if you maintain healthy garden conditions, deal with trouble as soon as you notice it, and clean up garden debris so pests and diseases can't multiply unnoticed, you'll be rewarded with a healthier garden.

CHAPTER 3

SPACE-SAVING IDEAS

The less space you need to cultivate, the less time and labor you will need to be successful. There are three ways to garden efficiently: growing in raised beds, growing vertically, and growing in containers.

GROWING IN RAISED BEDS

Over the years, many passionate gardeners have promoted special ways to grow plants. Ruth Stout advocated making beds from compost in situ and planting directly into the compost, gardeners-turned-authors have described various container-growing techniques, and there are books on block planting (planting in squares) and vertical gardening (using various structures to grow up). But all things considered when you compare all the methods, the one growing technique that promotes superior growth is using raised beds for both vegetables and flowers.

Raised beds have many benefits and advantages: Raised beds offer greater control over the quality of your soil, allowing a person to improve drainage, improve soil depth for stronger and deeper plant roots, and improve soil quality by allowing compost and other soil amendments to be concentrated in the main growing area. Raised beds also dry out quicker in spring and warm up sooner for early yields. Once the soil has warmed, it's easy to apply a mulch to retain soil moisture.

It's easier to irrigate a raised bed, whether by the use of a watering can, a long-handled watering wand, a sprinkler, or a drip hose. It can be easier to set up horticultural fleece for insect control or to place plastic hoop covers for frost protection.

Raised beds allow you to plant more in less space. You can use traditional horizontal row or block planting methods in conjunction with vertical gardening techniques. For example, you can attach upright posts to the sides of your raised beds, add a horizontal bar, and hang nylon garden netting from the bar to create a trellising support for growing vegetable vines (such as beans or cucumbers); you can then plant low-growing plants like peppers and cabbage in the soil around the netting. Flower gardeners can grow morning glories, climbing nasturtiums, and sweet peas on the trellis and plant a multitude of bushy annuals such as French marigolds and 'Profusion' zinnias as low growers to fill the bed.

Although the initial expense of installing raised beds can be costly for lumber bought from a lumberyard, many kinds of discarded materials can be used, such as stones, old bricks, and spare wooden boards from do-it-yourself projects or from discarded wooden pallets. But even lumberyard boards will pay for themselves the first year; in Pennsylvania, a local gardener just built five 4-foot-square raised beds using 2 x 12 pine and 3-inch decking screws at a cost of $110. That's 80 square feet of growing space for less than one trip to the

Young Brussels sprouts grow in a raised bed, with several drip lines providing moisture at the root zone.

grocery store. Even though pine is a soft wood, this gardener's previous pine beds lasted for 5 years before they rotted and needed to be rebuilt.

With raised beds, it's easy and practical to vary soil texture from one bed to another; for example, a sandy, organically rich soil can be used for melons; a heavier clay soil for cabbages; a deep soil screened of stones and garden debris for picture-perfect carrots; a gravel soil for foxtail lilies; an acid soil for 'Million Bells' mini-petunias; an alkaline soil for cottage pinks; and a sterile soil for sweet peas susceptible to root rot diseases.

In my experience, many aspects of companion planting have been overstated, since most vegetables, annuals, and perennials get along fine together. Rather than wonder whether garlic near carrots will deter carrot flies (it doesn't), take a creative approach to companion planting. Plant a row of cabbage beneath a planting of pole beans to make maximum use of a narrow plot. Consider the "three sisters" companion planting practiced by native Lenape Indian tribes (and more recently by the Amish), which has three crops sharing one space: tall sweet corn, pole beans to grow up the corn stalks, and vining winter squash to grow on the ground between the corn rows. Of course, it's both beautiful and practical to mix flowers with vegetables.

If you live in an area with drenching rainfall or you garden on a slope subject to washouts, a raised bed prevents good topsoil from spilling into pathways or washing away.

VERTICAL GARDENING

Less space is needed to grow plants up in the air instead of across the ground. A planting width of just 1 to 2 feet is all you'll need to grow productive vegetables such as pole beans, 'Sugar Snap' peas, and climbing cucumbers among vegetables and climbing sweet peas, morning glories, and nasturtiums among bedding annuals. There's even a heat-resistant, everbearing climbing spinach (called Malabar) and many kinds of single-serving-size melons (such as 'Minnesota Midget' cantaloupe). 'Ha-Ogen' (from Israel) and 'Charentais' (from the south of France) are other excellent single-serving melons that will climb easily. Also consider 'Trombone' zucchini (also known as 'Tromboncino'), vegetable spaghetti, and 'Delicata' squash, which will all grow on trellis or garden netting.

Moreover, a trellis or garden netting can be mounted against a sunny wall, such as along the house foundation, or it can be mounted between

A lean-to trellis is perfect for growing climbing cucumbers because it keeps the fruit free of soil and blemishes.

posts to create a freestanding unit. Vines growing against a wall will not only benefit from the house heat that staves off late frost, but the reflected heat and light from the wall will help generate high yields. This type of foundation bed needs only a small footprint (4 feet long by 1 foot wide by 8 inches deep), so it's easy to improve the soil by adding compost, and only a small amount of mulch is required to keep down weeds. It's often used to stellar effect at botanical gardens around the world to showcase specimen plants or mass plantings.

Even a short 4-foot-wide trellis or netting on a foundation wall can grow four kinds of vining vegetables or ornamental plants, such as a vining tomato, a vining squash, a climbing cucumber, and a pole snap bean. Watering is easy with a watering can. If the foundation bed extends along the entire structure, it's easy to install a drip line that waters the length of the trellised section at the turn of a faucet. And think of the increased production you can achieve—up to a tenfold increase, based on my observations, when you grow vertically! Bush snap beans, for example, might bear for 3 weeks, while a pole snap bean grown vertically will bear generously all season.

I think that one of the most beautiful floral effects is a curtain of flowering annuals knitting their vines together to create a colorful mosaic of flowers. My favorite flower curtain combination is using 'Heavenly Blue' morning glory with a mix of 'Galaxy' sweet peas and a mix of climbing nasturtiums.

CONTAINER GARDENING

Even a person without garden soil—with just a paved area or a balcony—can enjoy homegrown vegetables and flowers by growing in containers. Consider whiskey half barrels for a planting of lettuce, window-box planters for a dozen strawberry plants, and hanging baskets dripping with 'Tumbling Tom' tomatoes. Avoid plastic and metal containers wherever possible, as I've found that these heat up quickly and burn tender root tips. Wood and terra-cotta containers are the best because they have good insulation qualities and look attractive to boot.

When container gardening, use containers that are large yet manageable—because the bigger the container, the less likely it is to dry out quickly. Always ensure there is a drainage hole for excess water to escape, and use a watering wand (a long-handled watering hose) so you can poke the nozzle end in between foliage and apply water directly to the root zone.

Although potting soils can be purchased from garden centers to fill containers, these can be too light in texture and without the moisture-holding capacity a container garden needs. In my containers, I prefer to mix a commercial potting soil (or well-decomposed compost) with the same amount of garden topsoil. This helps anchor plants and produce a vigorous root system.

Hanging baskets in particular are prone to rapid dehydration, so consider adding a hydrogel to the soil to resist rapid moisture loss. If you do use a hydrogel, you should not empty this soil mix into your garden.

Made from sections of old ladders, this arbor is used to grow pole beans in a backyard vegetable garden.

CHAPTER 4

ENJOY THE HARVEST

A fter much tender loving care, the time comes when you reap your reward and harvest what you have sown. With vegetables, you hope for a worthwhile yield, good flavor, and the ability to store or preserve the harvest over a long period if you have grown too much to eat fresh.

FACTORS THAT INFLUENCE FLAVOR

The vegetable we value most for good flavor is the tomato. For a thorough review of commercial tomato growing in America, I recommend the book *Tomatoland*, in which the author, food writer Barry Estabrook, reveals that a third of supermarket tomatoes are grown in Florida in areas where the impoverished sandy soil, aggressive weed growth, and high prevalence of insect pests and plant diseases require the application of more chemicals than any other tomato-growing area in the country, including California. During winter, the percentage of Florida-grown tomatoes rises to 90 percent, and as a consequence, the Florida growers use five times more fungicide and six times more herbicides in their quest for a blemish-free product. The author claims that Florida farmers can choose among 100 chemicals, including 54 that are considered potential risks to human health. "Today's industrial tomatoes are as bereft of nutrition as they are of flavor," he writes. "According to analysis by the US Department of Agriculture, 100 grams of fresh tomato today has 30 percent less vitamin C, 30 percent less thiamin, 19 percent less niacin, and 62 percent less calcium than it did in the 1960s."

The answer to this dilemma is to grow one's own or buy from an organic grower and to select varieties noted for good flavor or high nutritional value. 'Sun Gold' tomato, for example, is famous for its exceedingly sweet flavor compared to other tomatoes; 'Health Kick' has above-average nutritional value.

Welcome to the headquarters of Earthbound Farms, organic vegetable growers, along Carmel Valley Road in Carmel, California.

There is much confusion over whether hybrids or nonhybrids are best for home gardeners and whether you should grow certain heirlooms or an improved modern equivalent. For example, 'Silver Queen' sweet corn is a nonhybrid and as sweet as most hybrids but a fraction of the cost to produce. Also, it completely outclasses the white heirlooms 'Country Gentleman' and 'Stowell's Evergreen' for flavor. Of course, the perception of good flavor varies among individuals. With melons, for example, there is a notion that heirlooms like 'Rocky Ford' (an orange-fleshed cantaloupe) and 'Emerald Gem' (a green-skinned, orange-fleshed cantaloupe) are as sweet as modern hybrids. While it is true they are sweet, no nonhybrid melon can compare with the sweetness of the hybrid cantaloupe 'Ambrosia' in my experience and in the opinions of many other melon growers I have interviewed. Developed by the late Ted Torrey at Burpee Seeds, 'Ambrosia' is a poor shipper and may never make an appearance at local supermarkets. But farm stand growers love it and sell it at premium prices because it is so sweet and has such a strong following. Many farm stand and farmers' market growers even keep its name a secret or call it something fictitious to prevent customers from growing their own and to keep them coming back each year.

A similar situation exists with watermelons. For the sweetest watermelon, choose a seedless variety like the 4- to 6-pound small-size 'Solitaire' or a nearly seedless kind like the yellow-fleshed 'Yellow Baby'; the lack of seeds or just a few seeds in a watermelon not only enhances sweetness but also improves a person's enjoyment by not having to spit out a mouthful of seeds, as you do with a variety like 'Sugar Baby'.

After variety selection, time of harvest is often critical for great-tasting produce. This is especially true of snap beans that are generally at their best when the pods are slim and before the beans swell the pod; left to become overmature, the pods can become fibrous. Timing for a watermelon is critical, since an underripe fruit can be tasteless and an overripe fruit will taste fermented. Your best clue to watermelon ripeness? Look at the tendril closest to the fruit and if it is shriveled, give the fruit a rap with your knuckle. If it sounds like tapping your forehead (a dull sound), it is probably underripe; if it is like tapping your stomach (a soft sound), it is undoubtedly overripe. But if it has a sharp, clear sound like tapping your knuckles together, it is most likely just right.

Many vegetables are most flavorful when they are small, like baby carrots, baby beets, baby turnips, and baby zucchini, even though they can be delicious when mature. For the most flavorful sweet corn, adequate watering at time of tasseling will help fill out the kernels to the tip, since sugars move into them in liquid form. Radishes must not experience a check in growth (meaning a slowing) through irregular watering, or they can taste pithy. In Chapter 5, I describe various vegetable varieties to grow, and I give tips for knowing when to pick vegetables for peak flavor.

In terms of nutrition, be aware that pale, off-colored vegetables—such as yellow carrots, 'Iceberg' type lettuces, white cucumbers, and self-blanching celery—do not have the nutritional value of green or dark red–colored vegetables like cabbage 'Ruby Ball', and that special high-nutritional vegetables like 'Health Kick' tomato and 'Fiskeby' edible soybean are available to the health-conscious gardener.

FACTORS AFFECTING YIELDS AND SIZE

Adequate light and moisture are important factors governing yields and size of any vegetable (or ornamental plant), but variety selection is also crucial. In Alaska, they can grow monstrous cabbages weighing more than 100 pounds because of the long daylight hours during summer and the discovery that the hybrid cabbage variety 'O-S Cross' thrives in those conditions.

Large size is not always desirable. Small size in cucumbers, for example, often translates to tenderness. All-female cucumbers like 'Diva' will always outperform regular cucumbers because every flower can set fruit. The same holds true for asparagus. The Dutch pioneered all-male hybrid asparagus because males grow higher yields and thicker edible stalks than females; that's because females need to expend a lot of energy on seed production. Rutgers University was the first to introduce the first US-bred all-male asparagus; their popular 'Jersey Giant' hybrid will produce tender stalks as thick as a man's thumb, but the best is yet to come in the contest for best asparagus. 'Purple Passion', a nonhybrid variety from northern Italy, grows stalks just as thick as 'Jersey Giant'. Moreover, it is earlier by 2 weeks over any green asparagus, and the stalks are more tender. The Rutgers University plant breeders are currently using 'Purple Passion' as a parent to develop a new race of superhybrids. The quest for improvement continues—to the benefit of gardeners everywhere.

All-female cucumber 'Sweet Success' won an All-America award for its high yields of tasty fruit.

Soil fertility is another important factor

DEREK'S COMPOST TEA

Crushed eggshells

Fish bones (very important)

Kitchen waste

Stable manure

Wood ashes

Combine eggshells, bones, kitchen waste, manure, and ashes in a compost bin and allow to rot down until dark and fluffy with a yeasty aroma. From the bottom of the bin, extract three bucketsful of finished or partially finished compost and empty it into a trash barrel. Fill the barrel with warm water and allow it to steep for 3 days. Stir and pour the brown, soupy liquid into a 2-gallon watering can and apply it directly to the root zone of plants. Stir the liquid before each application. When you reach the bottom of the barrel, empty the slurry onto your compost pile or use it as a mulch around plants.

NOTE: I obtain the fish bones for this recipe from fishmongers or from walking the shorelines of rivers, lakes, and the sea. You can also save fish bones from seafood meals and the peelings from shrimp.

affecting crop yield and size, and most champion vegetable growers have a special formula—usually a compost tea—that they use to feed their plants regularly. I've had good results using compost tea in my own vegetable garden. I revealed my secret recipe in my last book, *Vertical Gardening*, and I'm happy to share it again here.

Adequate moisture is also critical for successful yields. A giant pumpkin will need 3 gallons of water a day to grow to a world-record size. Mulching the soil not only helps conserve moisture, it keeps the soil warm for vigorous vine growth. However, adequate or regular watering does not mean overwatering, which can induce rot. Good soil drainage helps avoid an overwatering situation.

FACTORS AFFECTING STORAGE

The older I get, the more particular I am about what I eat, and I'm always looking for ways to enjoy fresh fruits and vegetables. If I don't grow them in my own garden, then I patronize farmers' markets, choosing vendors who grow organically as much as possible.

Of course, growing your own often means a long delay between the first frost of autumn and the last frost of spring, unless you have taken precautions to preserve surplus vegetables. Actually, it's amazing what you can still grow outdoors during winter. Collards, kale, Brussels sprouts, and chard remain healthy until heavy frosts or heavy snowfalls. Turnips and carrots can remain in the ground until the soil actually freezes. I even have a watercress bed in a clear running stream that does not freeze. The watercress is so hardy I can pick it all winter.

Onions are notable because they store well after they've been dug, cleaned, and dried, but sweet onions like 'Candy' won't keep as long as traditional varieties like rock-hard but pungent 'Copra'. Most seed packet or catalog descriptions will tell you what onions are recommended for long-term storage.

There are several ways to store vegetables—dry storage, freezing, dehydrating, and canning. Regardless of the method you choose, you want to select blemish-free vegetables for preservation. Any tomatoes with soft parts, beans with worm holes, peppers with sunscald (a pale patch on the side of the fruit), or potatoes with signs of rot should be discarded. These blemishes will simply create conditions for spoilage during storage, so enjoy the imperfect vegetables immediately and save the best for storing.

Dry storage means everything from glass jars with lids to carrots or beets nested in sand or peat moss. Shell beans and shelled peas are easily stored in glass jars with airtight lids; simply shell the pods after they have turned brittle and place the beans in the jar. Store in a dry, dark place such as a frost-free basement or pantry. Another form of dry storage—your refrigerator—is suitable for vegetables like winter squash and many root crops like potatoes, carrots, and beets that naturally store a long time if kept cool (but above freezing). These long-storage vegetables will keep for a month or more in the crisper section of your refrigerator. You can also dry-store root crops by nesting the roots (with tops cut off) in layers inside a crate of peat moss or sand. Be sure to leave a length of dry stem intact on squash such as vegetable spaghetti, acorn, and butternut, because a bare stem area can serve as an entry for rot.

Freezing is a good way to preserve many vegetables and fruit, such as strawberries, zucchini squash, and 'Sugar Snap' peas. This usually requires thoroughly washing the product free of soil particles and drying prior to freezing in transparent freezer bags. With some produce such as broccoli and carrots, blanching is necessary to destroy potentially harmful bacteria and enzymes that cause a decline in texture, color, and flavor.

Dehydrating, whether in an oven, solar dryer, or commercial dehydrator, is a great way to preserve harvested vegetables, fruits, and herbs. The biggest

FLOWER POWER

Factors affecting yields for vegetables are also true for flowers. Much of the breeding work on flowers has been concentrated on creating dwarf varieties because they look good in public places for mass bedding displays. The extra-dwarf varieties often flower earlier in six-packs and look good on the sale bench at garden centers. Most home gardeners, however, would prefer an intermediate-height plant—not too squat and not too tall, like the 'Lady' and 'Perfection' series of marigolds, each capable of 50 large blooms all open on one plant at one time and with stems long enough for cutting. Breeders realize that spectacular bloom is always a desired trait.

In the future, look for new introductions with mildew resistance among flower families that are notoriously susceptible to the disease. 'Benary's Giant' zinnias are an example of a new breeding achievement that makes these a must for the cutting garden on account of their extraordinary vigor and disease resistance. Similarly, breeders are now frantically trying to breed mildew resistance into impatiens. Although some varieties are resistant, the main varieties of bedding impatiens are suffering from a new strain of mildew disease that has sharply curtailed sales of impatiens in Europe and now is spreading fast throughout the United States. I remain hopeful that plant science will prevail and that new plant choices with many improved characteristics will please millions of home gardeners.

American marigolds are evaluated in test plots at Syngenta Flowers in California. Side-by-side comparisons allow breeders to judge the best for flowering performance and other desirable traits.

This harvest of the original 'Sugar Snap' pea shows large edible pod size, thick crunchy walls, and sweet green peas.

benefit of dehydrating is that you can dry small batches as produce matures all through the season, rather than face a large preservation project on a single day. There are many online sources of information about the process of dehydration and storage of the dried harvest.

Canning allows you to preserve and store vegetables and fruit in special glass jars, sealed using either a water bath or pressure canner. As with freezing, careful inspection of the produce is necessary to ensure that it is free of blemishes and bacteria. When canning, you usually blanch or boil the vegetables and fruits first or you prepare and fully cook a recipe featuring the produce (such as jellies or sweet-and-sour pickles). There are guidelines you'll need to follow in order to ensure food safety when canning, but canning is definitely the most attractive method of food storage.

For more complete information about canning, freezing, dehydrating, and dry storage of vegetables, the following USDA publications are available either online (www.gpo.gov) or through your local library or Cooperative Extension Service: *USDA Complete Guide to Home Canning; Home Freezing of Fruits and Vegetables; Making Pickles and Relishes at Home*; and *Storing Vegetables and Fruits in Basements, Cellars, Outbuildings, and Pits*. There are also many detailed books on food storage and preserving harvests, which recommend different methods and benefits.

While all of these preservation methods are worth your time and effort, I actually prefer something even easier! I deal with surplus vegetables by making a hearty soup that I freeze for consumption during winter months. I vary the ingredients based on whatever is mature, although tomatoes, onions, diced potatoes, and beans generally feature in every combination for consistently good flavor.

Another way I enjoy surplus fresh vegetables is to make bruschetta. I finely chop an onion, a green or red bell pepper, a zucchini or crookneck squash, a small cucumber, a red tomato, and cooked sweet corn kernels. I usually add some finely chopped parsley, chives, and chervil for extra flavoring; the juice of half a lemon or lime; and salt and pepper to taste. This delicious mix can be spooned onto crisp green lettuce leaves for a delicious instant salad, used as a pizza topping, and spooned atop toasted bread.

GROW THE BEST

PART 2

How do you make the best plant choice every time? Read on! In this section, you'll find my personal recommendations for more than 600 plant varieties, including the reasons why I've included them in this collection. From tasty to tender, from spring to fall, my suggestions for the must-have vegetables and herbs promise a flavorful and nutritious harvest, whether you grow from seed or from starter plants you discover in nurseries, garden centers, or catalogs. You'll also learn about annuals and perennials with stellar blooms, seasonlong good looks, and excellent disease and pest resistance. And to round out your landscape, try my picks for dependable lawn grasses and a few lawn alternatives!

CHAPTER 5

BEST CHOICE VEGETABLES

A s gardeners, we all have our favorite vegetables, and during a lifetime our preferences often change as some milestone in breeding achievement makes its presence known—either by word-of-mouth recommendation or gourmet chefs extolling the virtues of a particular vegetable, or by special praise from the media, seed and nursery catalogs, and the Internet. That happened with the introduction of the first red cabbage, the first golden beet, the first seedless watermelon, the first supersweet sweet corn (that kept its sugary sweetness for a week), the first vegetable spaghetti squash, and the first yellow zucchini squash, as well as the introduction of arugula as a salad green.

While we may know our tastes, we aren't as familiar with specific variety names for these everyday vegetables. New introductions can come so quickly, or represent such inconsequential improvements, it is difficult to keep up with the names and name changes, not to mention variety quality.

The fact is that variety selection can make a huge difference in your satisfaction as a vegetable gardener. Among hundreds of varieties to choose from, there still is no better-tasting lettuce than 'Buttercrunch', first introduced by Cornell University plant scientists in the 1950s. Among at least five varieties of snap peas, there is still none better than the original 'Sugar Snap' developed by Idaho pea breeder Calvin Lamborn; and for all the hoopla over sugar-sweet and supersweet sweet corn, the one that satisfies for sweetness is 'Silver Queen', a nonhybrid developed by Rogers Brothers Seed Company (who, to this day, have no idea why it still beats many of the best hybrids for sweetness). Furthermore, for those of you who haven't had the pleasure of tasting a 'Burpee's Ambrosia Hybrid' cantaloupe, introduced by Burpee Seeds in 1970, I can confidently say you have not yet tasted the sweetest melon you are ever likely to savor. Varieties and variety selection do matter!

You may wonder why I'm so confident of my recommendations in this chapter about vegetable varieties. To be truthful, there aren't many people in the garden industry who are qualified to make such impartial, objective, and accurate evaluations concerning variety selections. I believe I am one of the few because I maintain two test gardens—one at a farm in Pennsylvania (Zone 6) and another on Sanibel Island, Florida (Zone 10)—for evaluating vegetables year-round. I also travel widely to visit breeders worldwide, and I frequently visit test plots at various institutions, such as the Rodale Experimental Farm (Pennsylvania), the Penn State University Trials, Syngenta Flowers (California), Johnny's Selected Seeds (Maine), and Burpee's Fordhook Farms (Pennsylvania), among others.

I learned to judge quality in vegetable selections at an early age, first in England with Europe's biggest and oldest-established seed house, Hurst Seeds Ltd.; then as catalog manager for America's largest mail-order seed house, Burpee Seeds; and later as executive director of All-America Selections, the national seed trials, and the National Garden Bureau, an information office sponsored by the American seed industry. During my 45 years of evaluating and writing about vegetable varieties, I have also authored several books about vegetable gardening and worked as a consultant to the White House on vegetable gardening during the Ford administration. My full-color book *Vegetables: How to Select, Grow, and Enjoy* sold more than 100,000 copies and won a best book award from the Garden Writers Association.

During my association with All-America Selections, I helped to introduce some outstanding new varieties among vegetables, including 'Premium Crop' giant broccoli and 'Snow Crown' giant cauliflower, as well as 'Celebrity' tomato, judged to be the best-tasting large-fruited tomato, and 'Yellow Baby', a cold-tolerant watermelon with 50 percent fewer seeds than other similar-size, ice-box-type watermelons. Through All-America Selections, I also introduced to the world the award-winning 'Sugar Snap' edible-podded pea, and independently introduced the 'Tomato-Potato' (a graft I perfected so that tomatoes ripen on the vine and potatoes mature among the roots).

At my Cedaridge Farm test garden, I was the first to recognize the value of all-male asparagus pioneered by Dutch breeders. I was the first to grow the award-winning 'Bright Lights' chard ahead of its All-America introduction and the highly productive, smooth, round, beefsteak-size tomato 'Super-steak' while I was manager for the Burpee Seeds catalog. I popularized the chocolate-flavored peppermint variety 'Chocolate Mint' (*Mentha* × *piperita* 'Chocolate Mint') and the first day-neutral strawberries, such as 'Tristar', that can crop several times a season.

All of this experience, I believe, qualifies me to pass judgment on the vege-tables you are likely to see offered at garden centers as seed or transplants and from mail-order catalogs and Internet sources.

Naturally, all the claims I make in the following pages are based on ideal growing conditions. These include a fertile soil that drains well, at least 6 hours of sun each day, adequate irrigation during dry spells, pest and disease controls, mulching to control weeds, and harvesting at the peak of ripeness.

Artichokes, Globe

You'll find green or purple and thorny or thorn-free globe artichokes. The 'Imperial Star' hybrid makes other globe artichokes obsolete and yields reliably the first season.

GROW THIS! 'Imperial Star' hybrid

The globe artichoke is a type of perennial thistle native to coastal meadows around the Mediterranean. It's grown for its ball-shaped edible flower buds that contain succulent green or purple scales, depending on the variety. In the

Globe artichoke 'Imperial Star' reliably produces edible globes the first season from seed.

United States, 95 percent of globe artichokes are grown along a narrow strip of shoreline around Monterey Bay, California, where cool coastal mists, fertile soil, and a relatively frost-free climate ensure high yields. For the rest of the country, growing artichokes is a challenge, especially in northern gardens, where 10-week-old transplants usually require 500 hours in a coldframe before being set out into the garden after frost danger has passed.

In 1991, Wayne Schrader and Keith Mayberry, working with the California Cooperative Extension Service, introduced a new hybrid artichoke called 'Imperial Star' that is earlier than previous varieties, fruits the first season, and requires as little as 200 hours of cold (called vernalization) before transplanting. These globes are green and thornless, and seed production and distribution is controlled by the University of California.

Artichokes prefer a deep, fertile, sandy soil and regular watering, planted 3 feet apart in rows also spaced 3 feet apart. They will tolerate mild frosts, but they will not survive winters where the ground freezes. In areas where they can be left in the ground, plants should be examined in spring and all but four shoots pruned away so the plant's energy is concentrated on producing the largest possible globes.

BE AWARE! The variety 'Green Globe' has been made obsolete by 'Imperial Star'. Seed of 'Green Globe' is not always true to type, and fewer than 70 percent of the seed will produce plants capable of yields the first season.

And don't confuse globe artichokes with Jerusalem artichokes, which are a type of perennial sunflower that produces tubers. Although edible, Jerusalem artichokes are not worth the trouble, and eating too many will cause diarrhea. Also, the Jerusalem artichoke is extremely aggressive, producing underground runners that can spread into areas where it is unwanted.

Globe artichokes can resemble another thistle—cardoon. At the transplant stage, they can look alike, but cardoon is grown for its edible stalks when young, rather than its edible flower buds. Cardoon can grow to 10 feet high in a season compared to 3 to 4 feet high for globe artichokes.

PLANT PROFILE

ZONES: 7–9 as a perennial without protection; 5–6 grown as an annual

PROPAGATION: Start seed 10 weeks before outdoor planting. In northern gardens, provide 200 hours in a coldframe before outdoor planting.

PLANTING: 3 feet apart in rows spaced 3–4 feet apart in full sun

PESTS AND DISEASES: Mostly chewing insects such as slugs

PERFECT PARTNERS: Other perennial vegetables such as asparagus, horseradish, and rhubarb, because it is best to concentrate your perennial vegetable plantings in an area that is not tilled each season.

Asparagus

Choose between green or purple asparagus and all-male or mixed-sex (male and female) plants. 'Purple Passion' is noted for extra-earliness and tenderness.

GROW THIS! 'Purple Passion' and 'Jersey Giant'

Discovered in northern Italy, 'Purple Passion' asparagus is a remarkable vegetable that's as easy to grow as green asparagus, with spears as thick as a man's thumb. But its big benefits over green asparagus are its early harvest time (by up to 2 weeks) and its spears that are more tender than green varieties. It is such a superior asparagus that plant scientists at Rutgers University in New Jersey are using it as a parent to introduce its superior flavor and earliness into green varieties. Eat the tips raw in salads and as a crisp, nutty snack, or steam them for just a few minutes to make a delicious side dish. As the plants mature, they produce both thin and thick spears.

Traditionally, the main asparagus varieties to grow have been nonhybrids that produce both male and female parts on separate plants. You can tell the females by the red berries that form among the foliage after pollination by a male. It is the males that produce thicker, more succulent spears and more of them, compared to the females that must expend a lot of energy producing seed.

Dutch growers discovered how to create a hybrid asparagus that produces only male plants. The variety 'Franklym' (named for the Franklym Institute in Holland that first released an all-male asparagus) was renamed 'Ben Franklin' for release in the United States, and it was quickly followed by another all-male variety called 'Jersey Giant' bred at Rutgers by Dr. Howard Ellison. Unfortunately, the first year's release of seed from 'Jersey Giant' was contaminated, resulting in 20 percent females. Since then, the strain has been cleaned up, and so 'Jersey Giant' asparagus today should produce 100 percent males.

Although 'Purple Passion' asparagus is not an all-male, it is earlier and more tender and produces thicker spears than any all-male hybrid I have tried. The purple coloring turns green after steaming. You can freeze any surplus spears.

Asparagus is native to the salt marshes of Europe, including the United Kingdom and France, where locals still gather its slender stems from the wild. Cultivated kinds can be grown from seed or from year-old roots. From seed, it normally takes 3 years for a harvestable crop; from year-old roots, a light harvest can be made the next season after planting. Also, seed from all-male hybrids can produce a light crop the second season. The roots are fleshy and resemble the outstretched arms of an octopus. Experiments in England have shown that shallow planting—allowing 4 inches of soil above the root crown—will produce a heavier crop than deeper planting. Seed and nursery companies used to recommend digging a trench 8 inches deep and setting the roots in the bottom, but I prefer to fill those 8-inch-deep trenches with 4 inches of screened topsoil and compost. Mulch around the plants to deter weeds because asparagus cannot compete with aggressive weed growth, and space plants at least 12 inches apart in rows 24 inches apart.

At Cedaridge Farm, the first spears of 'Purple Passion' are harvested as early as mid-March and until the middle of June. After that, the stems are allowed to reach maturity and develop a cloud of billowing fernlike leaves so the roots are not drained of energy. After the foliage turns yellow in fall, it can be cut down to the ground to allow the next season's spears unrestricted emergence.

In fall, after frost, add a high-phosphorus, general-purpose granular fertilizer to asparagus beds, and add more in spring as soon as the soil starts to warm up. Intermittently during the summer, spray the foliage with an organic foliar feed for thickest spears.

Asparagus beetles can be a nuisance, living among the green foliage and eating it. Several kinds of organic remedies can be used if beetles prove troublesome, including insecticidal soap, neem, and pyrethrum sprays.

Incidentally, 'Purple Passion' asparagus can be blanched to make it white in the same way that green asparagus can be made white—by heaping a 6- to

8-inch layer of shredded leaves over the bed to exclude light as the spears emerge from the soil, and then harvesting the spears the moment they peak through the leaf layer.

BE AWARE! The heirloom varieties 'Martha Washington' and 'Mary Washington' are identical in appearance to one another except that the latter is slightly earlier than the former. They are not as early or heavily yielding as new all-male asparagus, and the berries from the females can fall to the ground and root around the mother plant, competing for nutrients like weeds.

 PLANT PROFILE

ZONES: 4–8 as a hardy perennial

PROPAGATION: By 1-year-old dormant roots or seed started 10 weeks before outdoor planting

PLANTING: 12 inches apart and 4–6 inches deep in rows at least 2 feet apart in full sun

PESTS AND DISEASES: Mostly asparagus beetles

PERFECT PARTNERS: Horseradish, rhubarb, and strawberries, all perennial vegetables best planted in a part of the vegetable garden that is not tilled each season

Beans, Snap

Pole bean varieties like 'Blue Lake' and 'Lazy Wife' deliver superior flavor and heaviest yields.

GROW THIS! Bush beans 'Blue Lake', 'Tavera', 'Goldcrop', and 'Roma II', and pole beans 'Lazy Wife' or 'Musica'

Bush snap beans are mutations from pole snap beans (for example, bush 'Blue Lake' is a dwarf version of pole 'Blue Lake'). These compact, bushy, low-growing versions became popular because the beans mature earlier than their pole parents that require staking. Now pole snap beans are making a strong comeback for several good reasons—they crop longer than bush beans (from early summer to fall frost, compared to only several weeks for a bush snap bean), and they save space (a single plant of a pole snap bean will produce 10 times the yield in the same space as a bush snap bean). Most importantly, pole snap beans produce the best flavor.

For early crops of bush snaps (58 days from seed to harvest), choose 'Bush Blue Lake 274', a version of the famous flavorful pole 'Blue Lake'. It will crop for a week or two longer than other bush varieties, yielding 6-inch-long dark green pods resistant to mosaic virus. The white seeds are slow to mature, and thus that 'snap' flavor lasts longer on the vine than comparable bush snaps. For extraslender, dark green, melt-in-the-mouth French filet–type beans, consider 'Tavera' (54 days). Yellow snap beans are not nearly as popular as green snap beans, but 'Goldcrop' won an All-America Selections award for its crispy yellow pods that can grow straight as a pencil.

High-yield bush snap bean 'Romano II' features flat, long, tender pods with quality comparable to a pole Romano.

Another bush bean, Romano, has a strong following for flavor and is easily distinguished from regular snap beans by its flat pods and a more buttery, melt-in-the-mouth flavor after light cooking or steaming. The 'Roma II' Romano bean is from the same breeding establishment as the famous 'Sugar Snap' pea—Gallatin Valley Seed Company of Idaho, a company that specializes in pea and bean breeding. Maturing in 59 days from direct seeding, the wide, smooth green pods measure a hearty 5½ inches long. Like 'Blue Lake', the seeds are slow to develop, so the good eating quality lasts longer than other comparable bush Romanos.

Among heirloom pole beans, none can compare in flavor with the 'Lazy Wife' bean. Before too much excitement builds for this variety, though, I must state in earnest that the true 'Lazy Wife' bean is not available commercially at this time. I hope that my continued quest to raise awareness about this phenomenal bean will result in it being introduced in the spring of 2014 through reputable seedsmen so everyone can grow and enjoy it.

Named for the fact that it was the first-ever

stringless pole snap bean (hence a boon to the "lazy" housewife who traditionally did the destringing in Colonial times), the 'Lazy Wife' (aka 'Lazy Housewife') was introduced by Burpee Seeds in 1888, discovered among a German immigrant farming family in Bucks County, Pennsylvania. After World War II, the bean suffered a series of crop failures and was dropped from the catalog.

The 'Lazy Wife' bean made a brief appearance in the 1980s through a seed company that quickly ran out of seed and substituted another variety when fulfilling orders. The incorrectly identified variety was propagated and offered to other seed sources, unfortunately, so most (if not all) of the 'Lazy Wife' seed sold today is not the historical variety known for such wonderful flavor.

Seed of the true 'Lazy Wife' is not kidney shaped like most other beans, but almost round and shiny white like polished marble. Another way to distinguish the true 'Lazy Wife' pole bean is the shape of the pod. It is not long and round like a 'Kentucky Wonder' or long and flat like a pole Romano, but rather it is knuckle shaped and up to 5½ inches long. In other words, the pods are flat but the seeds swell up to stretch the skin out like the knuckle of a clenched fist.

Regardless of its appearance, what sets the 'Lazy Wife' pole bean apart from other snap beans is its flavor. Just a few minutes of cooking (or steaming) renders the pods buttery flavored, meaty, and delicious. Moreover, the white, marblelike beans make the best baked beans after the pods turn brittle.

Perhaps there are seed savers in the United States who are still propagating the 'Lazy Wife' bean in their home gardens without realizing the treasure they have. I was able to secure a shoebox full of seed from a Bucks County farmer, Bill Byrd, who saved his own seed to ensure a continuous supply.

In the meantime, if you would like a sample packet of 15 seeds to start your own production, write to me at derekfell@verizon.net. Plant 'Lazy Wife' beans after the last spring frost when the soil has been allowed to warm; cold, wet soil will rot the seed. Give the plants full sun and good drainage and strong poles up to 12 feet high for support. And be sure to share seed with other gardeners!

BE AWARE! Unless you live where summers are cool (such as the Pacific Northwest and coastal Maine), do not grow bush runner beans like 'Early Half Runner' or pole runner beans like 'Excalibur'. They are British varieties that relish a maritime climate; the long, wide, flat pods may look appealing, but the pods turn stringy and bitter over most areas of the United States where summers get hot and humid. A far more reliable long, flat, wide bean is the Spanish 'Musica' pole bean, also popular in France as a substitute for runner beans.

Another pole bean I shy away from is the asparagus bean or winged bean, similar in appearance to the asparagus pea, with membranes extending out from the green pods. Although all parts of the vine are edible—leaves, stems, roots, and pods—the pods are mostly sliced thinly in cross section and used in stir-fries. They're a novelty bean for Asian dishes but are not worth the garden space, in my experience.

Although hyacinth beans make beautiful ornamentals with their shiny purple pods, some seed catalogs actually offer them as an edible bean. I wouldn't eat it, not after reading one catalog description, which warns: "Old pods and seeds can be poisonous." Beware!

I love fava beans (also called broad beans), but they are challenging to grow in the United States. UK gardeners are luckier because they are one of the easiest vegetables to grow there due to their mild winters and long, cool spring season. Winters in the United States are generally too cold to get an early start to the season, and the beans stop producing as soon as days turn hot. Also, fava beans are a magnet for aphids. Consider yourself lucky if you get one decent picking. Again, they are just not worth the trouble, in my experience.

PLANT PROFILE

ZONES: All zones as an annual; winter planting preferred in Zones 9–11

PROPAGATION: By seed direct-sown after frost danger

PLANTING: 6 inches apart in rows at least 2 feet apart in full sun

PESTS AND DISEASES: Mostly bean beetles and cutworms

PERFECT PARTNERS: Bush cucumbers, bush lima beans, and New Zealand spinach

Beans, Lima

Also called butterbeans, grow 'King of the Garden' and 'Dr. Martin's' pole limas for large size, superior flavor, and heavy yields.

GROW THIS! 'Dr. Martin's' pole lima, 'Fordhook 242' bush lima, and 'King of the Garden' pole lima

I once sat down to a meal with the late Lyddon Pennock, the famous Philadelphia florist and a founder of the Philadelphia Flower Show, to be served a dish of 'Dr. Martin's' lima beans. He considered these beans special because, at the time, the beans were in short supply, and the seed cost $1 per seed. Today, 'Dr. Martin's' lima beans are still a prized heirloom variety because the pods measure up to 5 inches long and the individual beans within the pod can be up to 1½ inches across. Bred by a Pennsylvania dentist, Dr. Harold E. Martin (1888–1959), in 1920, he also bred and introduced the 'True Black Brandywine' heirloom tomato. The pale green delicious beans need at least 90 days to mature, and the vines will grow as high as 15 feet, so start seed 2 weeks before the last frost date, one to a transplant pot. Moreover, the price has come down considerably from $1 per seed. Landis Valley Museum in Pennsylvania currently offers a packet of 10 seeds for $3.99 from its Web site—quite a bargain!

'Fordhook 242' bush lima bean grows large seeds, three to a pod, on bushy plants. The seeds are almost as big as pole limas.

When growing lima beans, gardeners have a choice between bush limas and pole limas. Without a doubt, the best bush lima bean is 'Fordhook 242', a disease-resistant version of the famous 'Fordhook' lima bean that Burpee Seeds unveiled in 1907 after bidding $1,000 for the privilege of introducing to the world the first large-seeded bush lima bean. Burpee had been willing to bid $5,000 for the stock seed put up for auction by a California farmer!

Indeed, Burpee's first catalog offering was limited to five beans per customer, with a word of advice that customers might not wish to eat the beans but save them as stock seed for the following season, as the company did not expect to be able to bring the price down for several years.

Another superior lima bean is the pole lima 'King of the Garden'; it will produce 10 times the yield of a 'Fordhook 242' lima bean because it will grow to 15 feet high, given support. The pods form in generous clusters of up to 12 pods with up to four large pale green beans per pod. These change color from pale green to ivory white after the pod turns brittle and the beans are shelled. Allow 90 days from direct seeding to harvest, and be sure the pods are mature before picking. Do this by squeezing the pod between your fingers to feel the plump seeds. Often, the pod will look mature, but the seed has not properly filled out.

Do not plant seeds before the last frost date in spring, and provide good drainage in full sun for all lima beans. A cold, wet spell can rot the seed, so start the packet indoors on a moist paper napkin to pregerminate the seeds. Store the dried seeds in a glass jar and they'll keep for years; the shelled beans also freeze well. Add them to soups or use them as a side dish.

BE AWARE! Before Burpee Seeds introduced the famous 'Fordhook' bush lima, the bush lima to grow was 'Henderson Bush' lima. The individual seeds of 'Henderson Bush' are pathetically small, and it takes a lot of time to shell enough for even a single serving. Save yourself some shelling time and grow the larger-seeded 'Fordhook 242'.

 ## PLANT PROFILE

ZONES: 5–9 as a summer crop; 10 and 11 as a winter crop

PROPAGATION: By seed direct-sown after frost danger

PLANTING: 6 inches apart in rows 3 feet apart in full sun

PESTS AND DISEASES: Groundhogs, deer, rabbits, bean beetles, and cutworms

PERFECT PARTNERS: Peppers, sweet corn, and tomatoes (for a succotash bean-and-corn medley)

Beans, Edible Soy

Also called edamame, soybeans are bred for their high
levels of vegetable protein, and 'Fiskeby' is one of the best.

GROW THIS! 'Fiskeby', 'Envy', and 'Butterbeans'

Edible soybeans are different from agricultural soybeans. Although the beans
are emerald green at maturity with three or four seeds to a pod, they do not
have an oily flavor like agricultural soybeans. They are a prime source of vegetable protein, as well as vitamins A and B and calcium. In Japanese restaurants,
a side dish of cooked pods for shelling and eating (called edamame) can cost up
to $10. A 10- to 15-foot row of the bushy plants can yield more than 1,000 pods,
making them one of the most productive vegetables to grow. Harvesting and
eating the beans is easy. The entire plant will usually
mature all its pods at one time, allowing you to
uproot the plant and strip it clean of its harvest.
Place the pods in a pot with boiling water, or in a
steamer, and cook for 10 minutes. The pods will
become soft and the beans will slip from the skins if
you apply gentle pressure at the stem end. You can
squirt the beans directly into your mouth, just like
eating popcorn. You can intensify the flavor by boiling them in salted water or by sprinkling the beans
with salt after cooking.

The edible soy bean 'Butterbeans'
was introduced by Johnny's
Selected Seeds of Maine.

'Fiskeby' is a small-seeded high-protein variety
developed in Sweden by Sven Holmberg and introduced to the world by British seedsmen Thompson &
Morgan. Before 'Fiskeby', there had been little demand
for edible soybeans among US gardeners. Since
'Fiskeby's' introduction, Dr. Elwyn Meader at the
University of New Hampshire produced 'Envy', a
larger-seeded variety specifically bred for the
American home gardener. Johnny's Selected Seeds
has introduced an even larger-seeded variety called
'Butterbeans'.

Soybeans demand full sun and good drainage. Space plants at least 12 inches apart. From a direct seeding, expect to harvest within 70 days. Beware: Soybeans are a favorite food of groundhogs, rabbits, and deer.

BE AWARE! Avoid edible soybeans with Japanese names, indicating that the beans were bred in Japan and thus usually perform poorly in North American climate conditions. Also, avoid agricultural soybeans, as these have a strong oily flavor. Due to my preference for larger beans, I avoid the smaller 'Fiskeby' soybeans, but you may find them to your liking.

 PLANT PROFILE

ZONES: 5–8 as a summer crop; 9–11 as a winter crop

PROPAGATION: By seed direct-sown after frost danger

PLANTING: 12 inches in rows at least 2 feet apart in full sun

PESTS AND DISEASES: Rabbits, groundhogs, deer, and cutworms

PERFECT PARTNERS: Cucumbers, peppers, and tomatoes

Beets

This delicious root vegetable has tops as tasty as spinach. 'Red Ace' hybrid is my pick for earliness, rich color, and uniform round roots.

GROW THIS! 'Burpee's Golden', 'Red Ace', and 'Cylindra'

In the 1960s, when I was catalog manager for Burpee Seeds, I was responsible for introducing 'Burpee's Golden' beet to the gardening public. Sometimes, it takes a long time for a new vegetable to gain acceptance, but this was an immediate hit. We tried to gain a patent on it, but it was rejected on a technicality since a small release of seed had been made prior to the patent application. Today, there are many golden beets under a variety of names, some claiming better germination than the original.

What has made the golden beet so popular is not only its appetizing golden yellow color but the fact that it doesn't bleed like a red beet and the tops are delicious when cooked like spinach—they're far more tender and tasty than regular red beet tops. Anything you can do with a red beet, you can do with a golden beet. Cook them whole when they're the size of golf balls, or slice and dice them when they grow larger. Golden beet pickles are also delicious, especially with red beet chips (a tastier snack than potato chips). Use hot, whole beets as a side dish, cube or slice them cold for salads, and consider making one of the most famous of all Russian dishes—borscht soup, garnished with grated orange peel. From a health perspective, beets purify the blood and are high in nutritional fiber.

Habits among gardeners are hard to break, and it's understandable that traditional beets like 'Detroit Dark Red' are still popular. The newer 'Red Ace' hybrid is earlier and its round roots more uniform. Even so, I think it makes more sense to grow a torpedo-shaped red beet like 'Cylindra', since it will provide twice as many slices per root as a regular red beet.

Beet seed generally is made up of corky clusters, usually in threes, so even when you provide careful spacing of 2 inches between seeds, several seedlings will come up and require thinning. This thinning is essential since beets do not like to be crowded when swelling out, and adequate spacing means perfectly round (or cylindrical) roots. Give them full sun and good drainage. Baby beets can be harvested in as few as 45 days from direct seeding (beets dislike transplanting).

BE AWARE! Don't waste your money on the heirloom variety 'MacGregor's Favorite'. It doesn't produce a globe-shaped edible root, and the purple leaves are not as appealing or as tender as golden beet leaves. If you do want to grow edible purple beet leaves, choose 'Bull's Blood' instead. It requires 35 days from

'Chioggia' Beets: Bull's-Eye!

This novelty beet with its beautiful scarlet red skin is well worth growing. Slice through it and the interior color is white with concentric magenta-colored circles, and it's extremely attractive on a luncheon plate. It's often a component of beet seed mixtures that include purple red and golden round beets.

seed to harvest edible leaves, and 55 days for sweet, juicy edible roots. Another heirloom to avoid is 'Albino' beet. Resembling a white turnip, it is insipid looking compared to the deeply colored golden or red beets, and it has poor nutritional value.

 ## PLANT PROFILE

ZONES: All zones, though best grown as a winter crop in Zones 9–11

PROPAGATION: By seed direct-sown to mature during cool spring weather

PLANTING: 2 inches apart in rows 6 inches apart in full sun

PESTS AND DISEASES: Groundhogs, rabbits, and deer

PERFECT PARTNERS: Carrots, radishes, turnips

Broccoli

Easier to grow than cauliflower, 'Premium Crop' broccoli grows large premium-quality heads.

GROW THIS! 'Arcadia', 'Green Comet', 'Premium Crop', and 'Marathon'

It is estimated that 70 percent of the world's broccoli production is from breeding work conducted by Sakata Seeds. Their 'Arcadia' hybrid is a favorite with US commercial growers and home gardeners alike for its tight bud clusters and earliness (63 days), but it is their competitor, Takii Seeds, that has garnered two All-America Selections awards for superior home garden performance. They are 'Green Comet' hybrid, an early-maturing 55-day variety that has small, rounded heads of tightly packed buds and then multiple side shoots when the main head is cut; and 'Premium Crop', a 65-day variety that produces a single large head measuring up to 9 inches across. Sakata's equivalent of 'Premium Crop' would be 'Marathon' (67 days), especially popular in the Northeast for late summer and fall crops because of its exceptional cold tolerance.

Broccoli relishes cool weather to maintain tight bud clusters and good eating quality. Seed should be started 6 weeks before outdoor planting after frost danger in spring, which allows plants to grow quickly once transplanted and develop heads before the hot days of summer arrive. For a fall harvest, start seeds by the middle of August and transplant after the Labor Day weekend. Cut 5 inches below the main head to encourage side branches of smaller heads from both spring and fall plantings.

Plants require full sun and good drainage. Space at least 18 inches apart, and wash the head thoroughly to dislodge those small worms that often hide beneath the bud clusters. Eat raw in salads or steam for a delicious side dish.

BE AWARE! There are white forms of broccoli, resembling cauliflower, but they do not have a broccoli flavor. Their flavor is bland, and the nutritional value is poor compared to green broccoli. Older varieties of broccoli like the heirloom 'De Cicco' (also known as 'Greenbud') have been superseded by earlier-maturing hybrids with tighter, tastier heads, like 'Green Comet'.

Broccoli 'Green Comet' won an All-America award for extra-earliness, the tight heads maturing within 55 days of transplanting.

 ## PLANT PROFILE

ZONES: All zones, though best grown only as a winter crop in Zones 9–11

PROPAGATION: By seed sown 6 weeks before outdoor planting

PLANTING: 18 inches apart in rows at least 2 feet apart in full sun

PESTS AND DISEASES: Cabbage worms, cutworms, rabbits, groundhogs, and deer

PERFECT PARTNERS: Cabbage, cauliflower, collards, kale, and Romanesco

Romanesco: Is It a Broccoli or a Cauliflower?

Romanesco is one of the most bizarre and most beautiful and best tasting of all cool-season vegetables. The head is lime green and pyramid shaped, composed of intricate pointed, spiraling bud clusters that resemble an exotic form of sea coral. Eaten raw or steamed, it tastes more like a cauliflower than a broccoli.

First cultivated in Europe in the 16th century, it was rediscovered by the Scottish Horticultural Research Institute and then introduced to North American gardeners by seedsmen Thompson & Morgan. Timing can be tricky: Plants must be grown to full maturity during cool weather, and since spring can turn hot quickly before the heads can mature, Romanesco is often more successfully grown as a fall crop. Start seed indoors 4 to 6 weeks before outdoor planting just before the Labor Day weekend. Mature heads will be ready to harvest within 70 days. 'Victoria' Romanesco grows the largest heads.

Brussels Sprouts

Hardy into the winter months, Brussels sprouts' flavor is improved by frost.

GROW THIS! 'Jade Cross'

The problem with growing Brussels sprouts is that they require a longer growing season than their cousins in the cabbage family, and they resent high summer temperatures. Therefore, over most areas of the United States, they are best grown so they mature in fall and continue to remain productive even into December, surviving frozen soil and snow cover. The only Brussels sprouts variety to win an All-America Selections award for home garden performance is 'Jade Cross', developed by Takii Seeds. It is an extra-early (90 days from transplanting, compared to 110 with many other varieties), vigorous hybrid that produces sprouts of uniform size all the way to the top of the stalk. The flavor improves after frost because Brussels sprouts react to cold weather by producing sugars.

Although plants can be direct-seeded, it is best to start the seed 6 weeks before outdoor planting, transplanting in the garden by mid-August to allow time for a fall crop. As plants mature, the lower leaves will turn yellow. Remove these and, after the first frost, pick sprouts in batches from the bottom up. Then remove the top whirl of leaves so the topmost sprouts develop to full size.

Brussels sprouts require full sun and good drainage. Space plants at least 18 inches apart and cover the soil with shredded leaves or similar organic mulch to keep the soil cool.

BE AWARE! Avoid the Brussels sprout novelty known as 'Cabbage-Sprout'. It claims to grow sprouts along the stalk and a full head of cabbage on top—in other words, a two-in-one vegetable—but the cabbage is extremely poor quality and the sprouts are sparse.

Long Island, New York, used to be a major source of commercial farm-raised Brussels sprouts, and so the major variety to grow among home gardeners was 'Long Island', later changed to 'Long Island Improved' after the original got a bad name for uniformity and late maturity (110 days). There's also a purple Brussels sprout oddity named 'Rubine' available, whose only benefit seems to be its color. There's an advantage to growing purple asparagus (it's extra-early and extra-tender), but I don't see those same claims mentioned with oddly colored 'Rubine'.

 PLANT PROFILE

ZONES: 4–8 as a fall crop; 9–11 as a winter and spring crop

PROPAGATION: By seed, started 6–8 weeks before outdoor planting

PLANTING: At least 18 inches apart in rows 2 feet apart in full sun

PESTS AND DISEASES: Cabbage worms, aphids, and cutworms

PERFECT PARTNERS: Broccoli, cabbage, cauliflower, collards, kale, and Romanesco

Cabbages

Choose 'Stonehead' cabbage for resistance to bolting
and 'O-S Cross' for mammoth heads.

GROW THIS! 'Stonehead', 'O-S Cross', 'Savoy King', 'Ruby Ball', 'Tatsoi', and 'Jade Pagoda'

European cabbages are all heading types, classified as green, red, and savoy. Chinese cabbages are mostly classified as rosette types and heading. European cabbages are believed to have been bred from wild cabbage that grows along the beaches in the south of England and in Brittany, France. The wild kinds are nonheading, but the cultivated varieties form round, firm heads. 'Stonehead'—bred by Sakata Seeds—won an All-America Selections award for its earliness and rock-hard heads that are slow to bolt to seed. The heads hold together for a long time, and you can split them open to eat the crunchy white heart raw, since it is sweet and delicious.

'O-S Cross', bred by Takii Seeds, won an All-America award for its huge size. Though commonly reaching a weight of 22 pounds, it is the variety most often used to win giant cabbage contests at the Alaska State Fair, where the summer daylength is so long it encourages extralarge sizes. A 127-pound monster (nicknamed "the Beast") established a world record in 2009. 'Savoy King' won an All-America award for its blistered leaves and tight, buttery yellow heart, while 'Ruby Ball' won for its dark red, solid heads. All are hybrids.

Chinese bok choi rosette-forming cabbages mature quickly—within 45 days. They have crystal white ribs and dark green leaves that fan out and are delicious when chopped like celery and mixed into stir-fries. 'Tatsoi' produces tasty spoon-shaped greens and crisp white ribs in a glossy rosette within 35 days. Among the heading types of Chinese cabbage, 'Jade Pagoda' is a pillar of crisp white outer leaves and buttery yellow central leaves, best grown as a fall crop to mature during cool weather.

When choosing cabbages, check the number of days to maturity. Early varieties like 'Stonehead' will mature in 65 days, while others require up to 100 days to form edible heads.

All these cabbages require full sun and good drainage. They respond well to high-nitrogen fertilizer.

BE AWARE! When you consider that a cabbage variety like 'Early Market' will be ready to harvest in 45 days from transplanting, and even larger-headed hybrids like 'Stonehead' require just 65 days, why would you want a cabbage that takes 100 days to reach maturity? Some heirloom varieties like 'Premium Flat Dutch' and 'Mammoth Red Rock' require a long season to mature; grow them only if you can spare the garden space all season.

Since the introduction of 'Ruby Ball', Takii's 'Ruby Perfection' (80 to 85 days) has gained some popularity due to its deeper red color, but 'Ruby Ball' matures earlier by 20 days! So my allegiance is still with 'Ruby Ball'.

 ## PLANT PROFILE

ZONES: 3–8 as a spring or fall crop; 9–11 as a winter crop

PROPAGATION: By seed sown 6–8 weeks before outdoor planting

PLANTING: Minimum of 18 inches apart in rows at least 2 feet apart in full sun

PESTS AND DISEASES: Cabbage worms, cutworms, club root, and rot

PERFECT PARTNERS: Broccoli, cauliflower, Chinese cabbage, collards, kale, and Romanesco

Carrots

One of the healthiest root crops to grow, 'Kaleidoscope Mix' carrots yield many colors.

GROW THIS! 'Kaleidoscope Mix', 'Scarlet Wonder', and 'Short 'n Sweet'

It's amazing to think that carrots are derived from a wild biennial wayside weed similar to Queen Anne's lace. Most garden-worthy carrots are colored orange, but red, maroon, yellow, and white are available both as individual varieties and in a mixture, such as 'Kaleidoscope Mix'. This is a formula mixture, meaning that the different colors have been grown separately and blended in equal amounts to ensure a balanced mix. Nonformula mixtures may predominate in one color.

The shape of a carrot can vary from round like a radish to long like an icicle, and the choice is generally determined by the nature of your soil—select long, tapering, straight carrots if you have deep sandy soil and stump-rooted or short cone-shaped roots if your soil is shallow clay. As far as nutrition goes, the deeper the skin color, the healthier the carrot, which is why 'Scarlet Wonder'—a deep red carrot developed by Takii Seeds—is such a good choice.

It's worth preparing a special bed for carrots, one raised 8 inches above the indigenous soil and screened of all stones, weed roots, broken glass, and other debris that can distort roots. In general, the tasty quality of a carrot can be determined by the size of its core—a hard, woody, round center section that runs the length of the root. Carrots with small cores like 'Short 'n Sweet' (developed by the late Ted Torrey at Burpee Seeds) are preferred to older varieties like 'Royal Chantenay'. Indeed, I rate 'Short 'n Sweet' the best of all carrot varieties for its broad shoulders, tapered short root, and sweet flavor.

Burpee's 'Short 'n Sweet' carrot has a small core, making it more flavorful than similar-size carrots like the 'Chantenay' series from France.

Carrot seed is tiny and will blow away if you even breathe on it. Sow thinly in a broad swath and cover the seed with a thin layer of fine soil, just enough to anchor it. Once germination has occurred, carrots like regular amounts of water so there is no arrest in their root development. Choose a sunny location and good drainage. Thin to 1 inch apart because carrots do not like to be crowded. Begin to harvest baby carrots in 45 to 55 days. Mature carrots take 75 to 80 days. Carrots can tolerate light frost and can remain in the ground well into fall and winter months, until the ground freezes. When you have an excess of carrots, consider using a juicer to turn them into carrot juice. Just scrape the roots clean before juicing. No sugar is needed when juicing because carrot juice is naturally sweet.

BE AWARE! In general, all round carrots like 'Parmex' and 'Thumbelina' are a waste of space even though they may have small cores, making them quite tasty. Shaped like a round radish, the root has a very small edible section compared to a broad-shouldered, tapered carrot, and it is tedious to clean or peel. Described as "gourmet" quality in some catalogs, they have no special flavor quality to justify this claim when compared to a small-cored, cone-shaped carrot like 'Short 'n Sweet'. Occasionally, you will see yellow carrots like 'Yellowstone' and white carrots like 'White Satin' offered in seed catalogs, but these have poor flavor and poor nutritional value. Also be aware that not all carrots live up to their colorful names: 'Scarlet Nantes' is a misnomer, as it is deep orange, but not scarlet. 'Scarlet Wonder' (see above), 'Atomic Red', and 'Nutri-Red' are true red carrots.

 PLANT PROFILE

ZONES: 4–8 as a spring and fall crop; 8–11 as a winter crop

PROPAGATION: By seed direct-sown

PLANTING: Thin to 1 inch apart in wide blocks in full sun.

PESTS AND DISEASES: Carrot fly and wireworms

PERFECT PARTNERS: Beets, celery, hamburg parsley (*Petroselinum crispum* var. *tuberosum*), and turnips

Cauliflower

You'll find white-, purple-, and orange-headed cauliflower varieties, but 'Snow Crown' reigns supreme.

GROW THIS! 'Snow Crown', 'Cheddar', and 'Violet Queen'

The edible part of a cauliflower—the head, or curd—is composed of tightly packed bud clusters, similar to broccoli, but it is not as easy to grow as broccoli and requires a longer period to mature. Under stress—such as lack of moisture and too many frosty nights—the beautiful snow white head can become blemished and unappetizing. The trick to growing beautiful, firm cauliflower heads is to plant it 2 to 3 weeks before the last expected frost date in spring so it has a chance to mature during cool weather yet avoid severe frosts. When the curds are about 3 inches wide, tie the flag leaves (the large leaves surrounding the head) up over the developing curd to exclude all light, and secure them with a twist tie or rubber band. 'Self-Blanche', developed by Michigan State University, automatically wraps its flag leaves over the developing curd, but the heads tend to be small.

'Snow Crown', developed by Takii Seeds, won an All-America Selections award for its earliness (60 days), large size, and tight heads that can measure up to 8 inches across. More recently, some colorful versions have been introduced, namely 'Cheddar' (an orange that retains its color after cooking) and 'Violet Queen' (a purple that loses its color and turns green after cooking). These oddities are useful to add color to fresh salads.

Cauliflower heads can weigh up to 2 pounds. Pull or cut apart the heads into smaller bud clusters for dipping, or enhance the flavor by steaming clusters for a few minutes—just enough to make them tender.

Cauliflower requires full sun and good drainage. Space plants at least 18 inches apart. Downy mildew, a fungal disease that can occur through overcrowding, can cause browning of the curd, but growing plants in a raised bed can deter the disease.

BE AWARE! Most people prefer a white cauliflower over some of the newer colors, such as orange, purple, and lime green, although the colored cauliflowers do have better nutritional value than the white. However, avoid the heirloom purple-headed cauliflower 'Purple Cape'. While its provenance is impressive (introduced from South Africa in 1808), this heirloom variety requires 200 days from transplanting to maturity, compared to modern varieties that can mature in 60 days.

 ## PLANT PROFILE

ZONES: 4–8 for spring and fall crops; 9–11 for winter crops

PROPAGATION: By seed started 6–8 weeks before outdoor planting

PLANTING: At least 18 inches apart in full sun

PESTS AND DISEASES: Cabbage worms, cutworms, rabbits, groundhogs, and deer

PERFECT PARTNERS: Broccoli, cabbage, collards, kale, and Romanesco

Celery

To blanch or not to blanch for the sweetest celery stalks?
No worries—'Golden Self-Blanching' blanches itself.

GROW THIS! 'Utah 52-70R' and 'Golden Self-Blanching'

The stalks of celery are delicious to eat raw as a snack, steamed to make a side dish, and added to soups as a flavor enhancer. While green celery has the highest nutritional value, blanched celery (to make the stalks white) is more sweetly flavored. Tall 'Utah 52-70R' produces erect, crisp dark green stalks up to 24 inches high. It requires 90 days to reach maturity and prefers cool nights, so plant in late summer for a fall harvest. The stalks of 'Utah 52-70R' can be blanched by wrapping the stalks with newspaper to exclude light at least 10 days before harvest.

'Golden Self-Blanching' produces a tight cluster of stalks that naturally blanches to a creamy yellow on the outside and white on the inside.

Seed should be started indoors 8 weeks before outdoor planting into a fertile, organic-rich, well-drained soil. Regular watering at all stages of growth is essential to develop a strong cluster of crisp, erect stalks.

Note that a relative of celery, celeriac, is a hardy, easy-to-grow root vegetable for fall harvest. Its round, warty, baseball-size roots are peeled, diced, and cooked like mashed potatoes to make a celery-flavored substitute for mashed potatoes. 'Giant Prague' produces the largest roots.

BE AWARE! Occasionally you will find 'Pink Celery' and 'Red Celery' offered in seed catalogs (these two look identical in appearance). They tend to be more fibrous than the green or white, so I don't recommend them.

 ## PLANT PROFILE

ZONES: 4–8 as a late summer/fall crop; 9–11 as a winter crop

PROPAGATION: By seed started 8–10 weeks before outdoor planting

PLANTING: 12 inches apart in rows spaced at least 2 feet apart in full sun

PESTS AND DISEASES: Celery fly, rabbits, groundhogs, and deer

PERFECT PARTNERS: Cabbage, carrots, and chard

Corn, Sweet

The debate rages—white, yellow, or bicolored? In my book, the nonhybrid 'Silver Queen' still satisfies home gardeners for sweetness.

GROW THIS! 'Silver Queen', 'Jubilee', 'How Sweet It Is', 'Honey Select', 'Early Xtra Sweet', and 'Mister Mirai'

In Colonial times, white sweet corn was for eating and yellow sweet corn was for feeding to livestock. That changed with the introduction by Burpee Seeds in 1902 of 'Golden Bantam', a short, stocky golden yellow sweet corn that set a new standard for sweetness—provided you had the water boiling when it was picked, as the ears soon converted their sugar to starch. A nonhybrid heirloom that matures in 75 to 85 days, 'Golden Bantam' seed can be saved, and you'd be assured of the same quality the following year, a benefit that does not extend to hybrids.

Then along came 'Silver Queen', a white variety introduced by Rogers Bros. of Caldwell, Idaho, in 1958. Its large size and sweetness turned home gardeners on to white sweet corn again. Sales of yellow sweet corn took a nosedive. The ears of 'Silver Queen' are up to 8 inches long and loaded with 16 rows of pearly white kernels. It has a sweet, milky flavor, maturing after 90 days. 'Silver Queen' is also the most earworm-resistant corn you can grow, because the wrap leaves cover the tips so tightly the larvae have difficulty penetrating the husk. Because 'Silver Queen' is a late corn, Rogers Bros. actually sells more seed of 'Jubilee' because it *almost* matches 'Silver Queen' for sweetness but matures 2 weeks earlier.

To understand the reason for so many sweet corn selections today, it is useful to know that varieties fall into five main groups. The first, and original, sweet corn is standard open-pollinated (OP). Open-pollinated sweet corn and the next three groups are better suited for home gardeners: Sugary (SU) are the normal hybrids. Supersweets (SH2) are sweeter and hold their sweetness for up to 5 days in the crisper section of your refrigerator. A supersweet hybrid equivalent of 'Silver Queen' is the All-America Selections award–winning hybrid 'How Sweet It Is' (85 days), holding its supersweetness for up to 10 days after harvest. These need to be isolated in the field from other corns to develop their supersweetness. A sugar-enhanced sweet corn (SE) has all the characteristics of a supersweet but does not require isolation. Yellow 'Honey Treat' (76 days) is probably the best example of a sugar-enhanced sweet corn that fills to the tip with plump kernels, a shortcoming of many other SE varieties. The fifth class of sweet corn is triple-sugary (SY) hybrids with characteristics of both SH2 and SE. Rogers is a company founded in 1876 that has pioneered the introduction of these sweet corns. They are sold under their brand name 'TripleSweet', the best of which is the All-America Selections award winner 'Honey Select'.

Among bicolored supersweet corns (those with a balance of white and yellow kernels), 'Honey 'n Pearl' (76 days) has the distinction of an All-America award. For earliness, grow yellow 'Early Xtra Sweet', a supersweet hybrid. An improvement of the All-America winner 'Illini Xtra Sweet', its 9-inch-long ears mature in just 76 days.

Sweet corn requires a fertile, well-drained soil in full sun. Direct-sow seed after frost danger in spring, and do not grow in single straight rows if you're a home gardener. Rather, plant in blocks of at least four rows, since pollen from the tassel on top of the stalk must fall on the silks halfway down. Each silk connects to a kernel, and the kernels will not form uniformly unless all are pollinated. If suckers (young corn sprouts) appear at the base of your corn plants, remove them and leave only two ears per plant to mature; otherwise, the kernels may not fill right to the tip.

Sweet corn needs adequate water at all stages of development, but especially when the silks appear and the kernels inside the ear are forming. A serious pest of sweet corn is the earworm, the larvae of a moth that lays its eggs on the silks. The emerging worms burrow into the ear and begin eating the kernels from the top down. Since the earworm mostly damages the tip, simply remove it with a toothpick and cut off the eaten portion. Sweet corn varieties that are designated "insect guard" are resistant to diseases, such as Stewart's wilt, that are spread by insects.

BE AWARE! With a growing interest in open-pollinated heirloom vegetables, you will find some old sweet corns offered by seedsmen, but be warned the older kinds turn their sugars into starch as soon as the cob leaves the stalk, and the sweetness cannot compare with more modern hybrids like the supersweets and sugar-enhanced kinds, which will hold their sweetness for longer periods. In my opinion (and in that of friends whom I have included in taste tests), there are two white heirloom varieties that are unacceptable by modern standards—'Stowell's Evergreen', which has been superseded by 'Silver Queen' as the sweetest nonhybrid variety, and 'Country Gentleman', which even looks inferior as its kernels are always arranged irregularly on the cob.

While 'Golden Bantam' is still an heirloom sweet corn treasured by many, I recommend 'Mister Mirai' instead; it's a similar-size supersweet that holds its flavor much longer.

 ## PLANT PROFILE

ZONES: 4–8 for summer and fall harvest; 9–11 for winter and spring harvest

PROPAGATION: By seed direct-sown after frost danger

PLANTING: 6 inches apart in rows spaced 3 feet apart in full sun

PESTS AND DISEASES: Corn earworm and sooty mold disease

PERFECT PARTNERS: Pole snap beans and winter squash, to make a three sisters planting (see page 35)

Cucumbers

Cucumber types are endless, with the 'Orient Express' hybrid satisfying most tastes for tenderness and crispness.

GROW THIS! 'Marketmore 76', 'Orient Express', 'Sweet Success', and 'Diva'

Cucumbers are classified as slicers and pickle types. The pickle types are smaller than the slicers, although pickle cucumbers can be used as slicing cucumbers and vice versa. American slicing cucumbers are straight, smooth skinned, and fat, up to 14 inches long, and they weigh up to 4 pounds each. Most have dark green skins that are best peeled to eliminate any signs of bitterness. The skins have tiny spines that can be black or white and easily removed by rubbing. All cucumbers are an efficient diuretic; the moisture in cucumber is rich in ions and enzymes that clean the blood. The minerals and vitamins are mostly in the skin, so it pays to grow the tender-skinned "burpless" kinds.

Japanese cucumbers are long, dark green, and slender. They are mostly burpless, the bitterness removed from the skin by breeding. These cucumbers are warted and grow to 14 inches long. They can be eaten like a candy stick, skin and all. The Armenian cucumber is light skinned and not really a cucumber but an edible gourd, while European cucumbers tend to resemble Japanese cucumbers in that they are long but more smooth and are best grown up trellises so the fruits mature straight instead of curled.

Cucumbers are a warm-season vegetable that will benefit from growing through black plastic. They can be direct-seeded after frost danger in spring. Sow seed in groups of three and thin to one strong seedling, spaced at least 12 inches apart so the vines knit together. To save space, grow cucumbers up a trellis, spacing plants 6 inches apart. Growing up a trellis also encourages the fruit to hang straight and not curl like those grown across the ground. Provide full sun and good drainage and keep the fruit picked to keep the vine productive.

'Marketmore 76' (68 days) is an American-type slicing cucumber developed by Cornell University for resistance to the most common cucumber diseases: powdery mildew, scab, and cucumber mosaic virus.

'Orient Express' (55 days) is an extra-early Japanese-type bitter-free cucumber with a tender skin developed by Petoseed in California. It is especially recommended for growing up a trellis so that the slender, 10- to 14-inch-long cucumbers hang straight.

'Sweet Success' (55 days) won an All-America Selections award for its higher yields as compared to other slicing-type cucumbers—because it is all-female and also self-pollinating.

'Diva' (58 days) won an All-America award for its remarkable high yields. It grows bright green fruits with extremely tender, smooth skins that require no peeling. The shorter length of 'Diva' is preferred by many gardeners, who

All-Female Cucumbers

Some cucumbers are described as all-female, meaning they set only female flowers or a higher percentage of females than males. This increases yields dramatically. However, a cucumber that sets only female flowers generally needs a regular cucumber vine nearby to provide male pollen; others set a small number of male flowers, just sufficient to ensure pollination of the females, and other all-females are self-pollinating (called parthenocarpic). Read the catalog or seed packet description carefully to determine what kind of all-female you might want to purchase. The All-America Selections award winner 'Sweet Success' (54 days) is an all-female that is self-fertile. Expect 50 percent higher yields than from regular cucumbers.

consider it ideal for serving two to four people as a side dish without having to store any surplus length.

BE AWARE! There are many oddity cucumbers out there that cannot compare in flavor to an American or Japanese cucumber. For example, Snake (an Armenian cucumber) is excessively seedy, with just a small ring of moist cucumber flavor under the pale green skin. Then there is 'Crystal Apple', a pale version of the more attractive 'Lemon' cucumber. Avoid all cucumbers with a pale skin, like 'Miniature White' and 'White Slicer', as the nutritional value in cucumbers is mostly contained in the skin, and the darker the green, the better. Avoid Jelly Melon cucumber, also known as Horned Cucumber. The oblong yellow fruits have a tough, spiny skin and a mass of seeds set in a green jellylike interior. It's mostly used for squeezing over salads to add a citruslike dressing. Since it requires 120 days to reach maturity, I recommend you skip this one.

 PLANT PROFILE

ZONES: 4–8 for summer harvest; 9–11 for winter and spring harvest

PROPAGATION: By seed direct-sown after frost danger

PLANTING: At least 12 inches apart in rows spaced 3 feet apart in full sun, or grown up a trellis

PESTS AND DISEASES: Cucumber beetles and mosaic and wilt diseases

PERFECT PARTNERS: Melons, summer and winter squashes, and watermelons

Eggplants

Eggplants are also called aubergines; the 'Nadia' hybrid grows to a generous size, has glossy purple black skin, and is cold tolerant.

GROW THIS! 'Nadia', 'Neon', and 'Purple Rain'

Native to India, eggplants can take the heat better than most other vegetables. Related to tomatoes and peppers, they require a warm, sunny growing season and like to be grown through black plastic for earliest yields. The most popular are known as Italian types. They have black or dark purple glossy pear-shaped fruits and a white interior and are used for slicing and grilling. 'Nadia' hybrid is my eggplant of choice because of its ability to set fruit during cold weather, for its earliness (67 days from transplanting), and for its high yield of large-size (and small-seeded) delicious fruit.

In addition to black and purple, there are white, bicolored white and purple, a blush pink large-fruited eggplant, and even red (though the reds are not tasty, quite bitter, and should be avoided). The one that outshines them all is 'Neon', about half the size of 'Nadia' (but still a useful size) and with an incredibly bright shiny purple color that I like to see used as an ornamental in container plantings. Also for containers, try the variety 'Purple Rain'. It's a 2-foot-high plant that loads itself with 5-inch-long pear-shaped marbled white-and-purple eggplant. It looks attractive when mixed with 'Sweet Banana' pepper in a pot.

The biggest problem when growing eggplant is flea beetles. They are attracted to eggplant more than any other vegetable, colonizing an entire plant and causing the leaves to appear as if riddled with buckshot. Leaves that have been colonized quickly turn brown and the entire plant defoliates, with no energy left to set fruit. Control plants with floating row covers or an organic spray regimen, such as garlic-pepper spray or insecticidal soap.

BE AWARE! There is a special class of eggplant called Asian, and these are mostly small and slender, usually black (but can also be all green and all white when ripe). 'Millionaire' and 'Slim Jim' are tiny-fruit varieties, but I feel that most gardeners prefer Italian-type eggplant that produces big, meaty, round slices for frying, grilling with barbecued ribs, or layering in a lasagna. You can't do that with any of the red eggplants (they are all bitter) or the golf ball–size green-and-white heirloom 'Kermit'. For culinary use, I recommend Italian over Asian every time.

 ## PLANT PROFILE

ZONES: 5–8 for summer harvest; 8–11 for winter and spring harvest

PROPAGATION: By seed started indoors 8 weeks before outdoor planting after frost danger

PLANTING: At least 18 inches apart in rows 3 feet apart in full sun

PESTS AND DISEASES: Flea beetles primarily

PERFECT PARTNERS: Peppers and tomatoes

Herbs

One of the top 10 flavor enhancers, basil 'Siam Queen' is flavorful *and* decorative.

GROW THIS! Arugula 'Adagio'; basil 'Green Ruffles' and 'Siam Queen'; dill 'Fernleaf'; and 'Chocolate Mint'

My father was one of the great chefs of Europe, and I learned a lot about cooking just by watching him prepare meals. I enjoy cooking with herbs. In my experience, the 11 most useful culinary herbs, in order of importance, are arugula, parsley, chives, basil, cilantro (also called coriander), dill, mint, sage, oregano, rosemary, and thyme.

Arugula enhances the flavor of any salad, and there are many kinds available, some with slender, smooth leaves and others with broad, indented leaves. My preference is for the broad-leafed 'Adagio', as it produces a generous yield of leaves per plant.

It was Ted Torrey, at Burpee Seeds, who introduced the basils 'Green Ruffles' and 'Purple Ruffles' that have ornamental value as well as good flavor, as well as the highly ornamental and flavorful 'Fernleaf' dill, an All-America Selections award winner on account of its generous edible leaf production on short (3-foot-high) plants. 'Siam Queen' basil won an All-America award not only for its rich herbal aroma but for the ornamental value of its deep pink flower clusters.

Gourmet chefs tend to favor Italian flat-leaf parsleys over curly-leaf kinds, although the curly kind is easier to chop into fine pieces as a garnish. Chefs also prefer broadleaf cilantro like 'Santo'; spearmint over peppermint because of its broader, greener leaf; gray leaf sage like common sage (*Salvia officinalis*) to the golden 'Aurea' or purple kinds like 'Purpurascens'; regular onion chives to garlic chives; and regular green oregano over the golden oreganos.

Among mints, my preference is for 'Chocolate Mint', a variety of peppermint. Chop it fine and sprinkle over fruit salad or ice cream to see what a delightful chocolate-mint flavor it can impart. Grow some in a pot and discover what an uplifting aroma it can provide by picking a sprig and inhaling its mint-chocolate aroma. However, be aware that all mints are invasive and

Italian flat-leaf parsley is favored by gourmet chefs.

Broad leaf arugula enhances the flavor of fresh salads and can be cooked as a spinach substitute.

'Green Mound' basil forms a mounded plant similar in appearance to a clipped dwarf boxwood.

'Lettuce-leaf' basil is typical of most basils sold as transplants, but its small white flowers are not as ornamental as 'Siam Queen'.

are best grown in confined spaces like a sunken section of chimney flue or a whiskey half barrel.

Give all these herbs full sun and good drainage. Herbs are required only in small amounts because of their pungency, so they are perfect candidates for containers or simply tucking into odd corners of the vegetable garden. Many come from arid areas of the world and survive long periods of neglect. If you're interested in making potpourri, you'll find that drying often increases the fragrance of most herbs.

BE AWARE! Although it's not on my list of preferred herbs, when buying tarragon be sure it is *French* tarragon that can be propagated only from cuttings, and not the vastly inferior Russian tarragon grown from seeds. Also, not on my herb list is lavender, of which there are many tender varieties (such as Spanish lavender *Lavandula spicata*). Stay with varieties of English lavender (*L. angustifolia*) like 'Munstead' and 'Phenomenal' for best aroma and hardiness.

 ## PLANT PROFILE

ZONES: Varies according to variety. Most are heat tolerant and suitable for all zones, whether for summer harvest or winter and spring harvest in frost-free areas.

PROPAGATION: Annual kinds like parsley and basil are grown from seed; perennial kinds like lavender and chives are grown from seed and by root division.

PLANTING: Minimum of 12 inches apart in full sun

PESTS AND DISEASES: Mostly carefree. Deer and groundhogs love parsley.

PERFECT PARTNERS: Chard and lettuce when paired with herbs in containers

Leeks

For meaty stems as thick as a man's arm, choose 'Robinson's Mammoth Blanch'.

GROW THIS! 'Robinson's Mammoth Blanch', 'Giant Musselburgh', and 'Titan'

A member of the onion family, the leek grows a thick, succulent white stalk and a tuft of blue green straplike leaves. It is the national emblem of Wales, and Welsh coal miners are famous for competing in local county fairs for the heaviest leek; prize specimens often measure 4 inches in diameter—as thick as a man's arm. Wales has perfect weather for growing prizewinning leeks: regular watering from frequent rainfall and cool growing conditions, along with the well-decomposed manure from coal-mine (or pit) ponies when they did the hauling before machines.

If you want to win a leek-growing contest or just impress your family or fellow gardeners, send away to England for a special leek that consistently wins at county fairs. Called 'Robinson's Mammoth Blanch', it's from W. Robinson & Son, a firm that specializes in breeding giant-size vegetables. Their 'Mammoth Blanch' leek received an Award of Garden Merit from the Royal Horticultural Society, and examples of its huge size are often displayed in the horticulture tent at the Chelsea Flower Show. Plants can grow to 3 feet high.

Leek stalks are tender when cooked and have a mild onion flavor. They are slow growing, and seed is best started indoors 6 to 8 weeks before outdoor planting. The seedlings will tolerate mild frosts and mature 100 days from seeding. Give them a sunny position and good drainage, and heap shredded leaves up against the elongated stalk to help whiten it. 'Giant Musselburgh' and 'Titan' (with extra-thick stalks) are flavorful varieties suitable for cock-a-leekie soup (which features leeks and potatoes as its main ingredients).

BE AWARE! Unless a leek can grow big, I don't consider it worth space in my garden because there is no difference between small leeks and big leeks in flavor. Therefore, I consider varieties like 'King Richard', 'Blue Solaise', and 'Prizetaker' inferior.

 PLANT PROFILE

ZONES: 3–8 for late summer and fall harvest; 9–11 for winter and early spring harvest

PROPAGATION: By seed direct-sown and by planting 8-week-old starter plants

PLANTING: At least 4 inches apart in rows spaced 18 inches apart in full sun

PESTS AND DISEASES: Onion fly and thrips

PERFECT PARTNERS: Chives, garlic, onions, potatoes, and shallots

Lettuces

'Buttercrunch' is the gourmand's favorite for crispness and sweetness.

GROW THIS! 'Buttercrunch', 'Marvel of Four Seasons', 'Simpson Elite', and 'Little Gem'

Lettuce is a fast-growing cool-season vegetable with hundreds of varieties from loose leaf, heading, and romaine (or cos) available to home gardeners. But the head lettuce 'Buttercrunch' is still the leader. Winner of an All-America Selections award, it was developed by Cornell University plant scientists. The outer leaves are succulent and tender and wrap tightly around a crisp, golden heart. It is so flavorful and crunchy you can eat it fresh from the garden like an apple. Fancy gourmet restaurants often serve a salad called 'Kentucky Limestone', which is a made-up name for 'Buttercrunch' and other head lettuces like 'Boston Bibb' or 'Burpee's Bibb'.

A good slow-to-bolt American crisphead lettuce is 'Nevada' (48 days). Crispheads start off with a loose-leaf arrangement but then form a firm head—not as tightly packed as 'Buttercrunch', but still crisp and delicious. Loose-leaf lettuces can be direct-sown into the garden since they tolerate crowding, but head lettuce needs to be carefully spaced apart in order to develop crisp heads. They are best transplanted 4 weeks after sowing seed indoors and spaced at least 8 inches apart. Plants mature in 64 days.

Another excellent-quality head lettuce is the French heirloom variety 'Marvel of Four Seasons', introduced about 1885. It is identical in outward appearance to 'Buttercrunch', except it has a red tint to the wrap leaves and a shiny green head that is buttery yellow inside.

Because loose-leaf lettuces tolerate crowding, they can be direct-sown into a wide seed bed to create a block planting. Loose-leaf lettuce is also a prime ingredient in mesclun, or "mini-greens mixes," because of its early maturity (40 days) and the fact that the outer leaves can be harvested without killing the plant. 'Simpson Elite' forms a beautiful wide rosette of crisp, bright green ruffled leaves similar to (but larger than) the famous 'Black-Seeded Simpson'.

Romaine (cos) lettuces have leaves that stand erect like a column. They have a prominent crunchy midrib and are the favored lettuce for making a Caesar salad.

The heirloom variety 'Little Gem' (60 days) is especially good for home gardens, as it grows just 5 to 7 inches high and can be planted shoulder to shoulder 5 inches apart in a block planting. The light green succulent leaves surround a buttery yellow heart. Indeed, a favorite way to enjoy it is to slice a head lengthwise, each half sufficient for a single salad serving, drizzled with hot bacon dressing.

Give lettuce full sun and good drainage. All types are suitable for growing in containers.

BE AWARE! The most maligned of lettuces is 'Iceberg'. The variety most commonly sold at the supermarket, it has bland flavor and poor nutritional value. Even though the first 'Iceberg' lettuce was introduced in 1894 by Burpee Seeds, it has become a generic name for many lettuce varieties that produce a crisp, pale green head and ship well.

Occasionally, you will see offered seed of miner's lettuce (also called claytonia) and corn salad (also known as mache), two lettuce substitutes. They mature about the same time as regular loose-leaf lettuce, and, to my taste, they pale in comparison to regular lettuce.

In general, the darker the leaf color, the better the flavor and nutritional value, which is why I don't choose to grow yellow-leaved 'Australian Yellow' (also called 'Australian Yellowleaf') or 'Gold Rush'. Avoid lettuce varieties that are notoriously quick to bolt to seed; these are mostly heirloom lettuces and include the English variety 'Webb's Wonderful'.

The speckled cos variety 'Freckles' is the same as 'Speckled Trout' and similar in appearance to 'Sanguine Ameliore'. While there's nothing wrong with them as plants or nutritionally, I find that the brown spots on the pale green leaves are reminiscent of a plant disease, making it hard to serve to guests; for everyday meals, you may not find it's an issue.

 PLANT PROFILE

ZONES: 3–8 for a spring and fall harvest; 9–11 for a winter and spring harvest

PROPAGATION: By seed either direct-sown or started indoors 4 weeks before outdoor planting

PLANTING: Loose-leaf types can tolerate crowding; space heading types 8 inches apart in full sun.

PESTS AND DISEASES: Mostly aphids, slugs, and foraging animals like rabbits

PERFECT PARTNERS: Arugula, peas, radishes, and spinach

Melons

Cantaloupe, honeydew, or Crenshaw? Of all the melons, 'Ambrosia' cantaloupe wins my vote for sweetest flavor.

GROW THIS! 'Ambrosia', 'Tigger', 'Ha-Ogen', and 'Sugarshaw'

How is it possible to single out one melon variety among the hundreds that profess to be the sweetest? And who can say whether a cantaloupe is sweeter tasting than a honeydew or a Crenshaw or a casaba? While it's true that each type has a distinctive flavor and that personal tastes can vary considerably, there is one melon that stands out as supreme. Moreover, you are not likely to find it at the supermarket produce counter because it doesn't ship well once it has been picked at its peak ripeness. Its name is 'Ambrosia', and it is such a delicious, sugar-sweet, and juicy cantaloupe that some growers at farm stands and farmers' markets keep its name a secret or else they use a fictitious name to deter home gardeners from growing their own. Many melons are noted for good flavor—especially the Charentais melons of France, but these are small, single-serving melons not much more than 2 pounds in weight. 'Ambrosia' is not only as sweet—or sweeter—it is larger, up to 4 pounds. It's also better than similar-size melons for another reason: It has an unusually small seed cavity and thick, delicious orange flesh that seems to melt in your mouth, all the way to the rind. Its uplifting perfume will waft through your garden.

Bred by the late Ted Torrey at Burpee Seeds while I was catalog manager, 'Ambrosia' melons are slightly oval with attractive rind netting. Fruits bear a striking resemblance to the famous heirloom variety 'Rocky Ford' but are sweeter and more productive. The fruits turn beige when fully ripe and slip easily from the vine. Fruits mature 86 days from direct seeding. Plant through plastic for highest yields and extra-earliness.

A new variety of small melon from Armenia is named 'Tigger' and has both a wonderful scent and a pleasant flavor. A single-serving-size melon, it is almost perfectly round like an orange with red zigzag stripes on a yellow background. Cut it open and the interior flesh is white like a coconut. It forms beads of moisture like an Asian pear, and it even tastes like an Asian pear—crisp and delicious. Because the fruits weigh no more than 1 pound, this variety is easily trained to grow up a trellis, producing up to 30 fruits on a single vine in a season. Moreover, the fruits require no support or slings to stay on the vine.

The green-fleshed 'Jenny Lind' is a favorite among heirloom growers, introduced before 1840, but I feel that its large seed cavity yields only a thin section of sweet, juicy flesh. Instead, if you want sweet green flesh, grow 'Ha-Ogen', a green-fleshed single-serving-size melon that originated in Hungary but found its way into US seed catalogs due to its popularity in Israeli markets. After orange-fleshed 'Ambrosia', it is my favorite melon for chin-dripping sweetness.

BE AWARE! Not many people see the point in growing a melon whose only attribute is an attractive skin color and a pleasant perfume, which is what you will get when you grow the flavorless heirloom melon named 'Queen Anne's Pocket' melon, so named because Victorian ladies used to carry it in their pockets to perfume carriages and musty rooms. Despite its aroma, 'Queen Anne's Pocket' melon is flavorless. Choose 'Tigger' instead.

When choosing any melon, first check the days to maturity, as some will yield within 75 days and others require 100 days and longer. Moreover, that's 100 days of soil temperatures above 70°F—so in northern gardens, a 100-day melon may never have time to ripen. Be aware also that soil fertility and adequate moisture once the vine has started to set fruit are essential requirements for sweet flavor. Here is a list of poor performers: 'Crane' is the name for the first Crenshaw-type melon, bred by a farmer in Santa Rosa, California. A cross between a casaba and a cantaloupe, it's late and ugly and has a huge seed cavity with just a thin juicy rind. Stick with a modern Crenshaw variety such as 'Sugarshaw'. Another ugly, late-maturing heirloom melon is 'Bidwell Casaba' (95 days). The French heirloom 'Boule d'Or' is too late for most northern gardens (up to 110 days).

 ## PLANT PROFILE

ZONES: 5–11 as a summer crop; 9–11 also as a winter and early spring crop

PROPAGATION: By seed direct-sown after frost danger or started 6 weeks before outdoor planting to produce transplants

PLANTING: At least 12 inches apart in rows spaced 3 feet apart when grown in rows in full sun; space 6 inches apart for growing up a trellis to save space

PESTS AND DISEASES: Mice and crows eating the maturing fruits

PERFECT PARTNERS: Cucumbers, summer and winter squash, and watermelons

Okra

Okra is sometimes called gumbo or lady's fingers, and 'Clemson Spineless' is the top choice among home gardeners.

GROW THIS! 'Clemson Spineless' and 'Annie Oakley'

Okra is a type of hibiscus from India, and, like tropical hibiscus, it relishes the heat of summer. The seed is bullet hard and needs soaking in lukewarm water overnight to aid germination. Plants grow quickly, producing long, strong stems studded with self-pollinating flowers that last a day. As the flower fades, a green, pointed pod starts to enlarge, growing to 12 inches long and turning brown. The pods are best picked when they're 2 to 3 inches long for steaming as a side dish or for adding to soups and stews. Okra pods also make delicious pickles. 'Clemson Spineless' is the most popular variety. An All-America winner, the plant will grow to 6 feet high. 'Annie Oakley' grows shorter stems (3 to 4 feet high) with multiple side branches. It's best grown in containers and bears earlier than regular okra by 5 days with only slightly lower yields than 'Clemson Spineless'.

Delay direct seeding until after the last frost date of spring and after the soil has had time to warm up. Growing through black plastic promotes earliness.

Plants are drought resistant and everbearing until fall frosts.

BE AWARE! Avoid any okra with spines (which includes most heirlooms), as the spines can occur on the fruits as well as the stems and can puncture skin when you handle the pods. 'Red Burgundy' is a dull red-podded okra. It's a novelty bred at Clemson University, but, in my opinion, green-podded okra is the best for eye appeal and flavor.

 PLANT PROFILE

ZONES: 6–11 for summer and fall harvest; 9–11 for winter and spring harvest

PROPAGATION: By seed direct-sown after frost danger

PLANTING: At least 6 inches apart in rows 2 feet apart in full sun

PESTS AND DISEASES: None serious

PERFECT PARTNERS: Sunflowers and sweet corn. Pole snap beans can be interplanted among okra, sunflowers, and sweet corn so they can use the tall stems for support.

Onions

Choose 'Robinson's Mammoth Improved' for its large size and 'Candy' for sweetest onion flavor.

GROW THIS! 'Red Torpedo', 'Walla Walla Sweet', 'Candy', 'Super Star', and 'Robinson's Mammoth Improved'

Onions are grown from seed and from "sets," which are 1-year-old bulbs. Since onions are biennials, they make a bulb and leaves the first year and then flower the second. You'll get the largest onions when you grow from seed, since all the energy will be directed into growing a big bulb, while a 1-year bulb from an onion set will direct its energy into growing a seed stalk at the expense of bulb size.

Onions can be red, yellow, and white, and most are globe shaped or slightly flattened, but 'Red Torpedo' is zeppelin shaped, producing more slices per bulb than a round variety.

The most famous onion in the United States is the Vidalia, which is a trademark name for large, sweet, short-day onions that can be used only on onions from two counties in Georgia. Their superb crisp, sweet flavor is derived from special minerals in the soil in that area. Look for Vidalia onions named 'Yellow Granax' and 'Texas Granax', which are the best offerings, in my opinion.

Egyptian Walking Onions

Since regular onions are biennial, you might want to grow a useful perennial in your garden: the hardy Egyptian walking onion that can be used many ways. The leaves can be substituted for chives when chopped into a salad or as a garnish in soup; the underground bulbs can be used as a substitute for shallots when chopped fine and mixed with vinegar to use as a flavoring for salads and meat dishes; and the small, round onions that form on the top of the flowering stems are a means of propagating more plants.

The term *walking onion* is derived from the fact that the flower stems, when mature, form miniature onions that bend the stem over and plant themselves next to the mother plant. This continual formation of a topknot of small onions bending the stalk to self-plant can be seen as a slow-motion walk.

Gather the bulbs in fall (usually with roots and a green sprout already formed) and replant wherever you want to create a colony, choosing a location in full sun with good drainage. Cover the bulb with just enough soil to anchor it.

For northern areas of the States, the best onion for sweet flavor is the 'Walla Walla Sweet', while yellow-skinned 'Candy' and white-skinned 'Super Star' are suitable for growing in all areas. Both have brown skins and grow to 6 inches across. 'Walla Walla Sweet' originated in Italy and was brought to the United States by a French soldier who settled near the town of Walla Walla, Washington, and grew it as a commercial crop. Its fame spread, and Washington eventually adopted it as the state vegetable. A Walla Walla Sweet Onion Festival is held each year in Walla Walla, and taste contests are held to determine whether the Vidalia or 'Walla Walla Sweet' is the best flavored.

The biggest onion you can grow is called 'Robinson's Mammoth Improved', and it's not available from any US seed house but only from W. Robinson & Son of Preston, England. It's the one to grow if you desire an onion as big as a soccer ball. And I can assure you they are definitely as big as soccer balls, because I visited the company's farm in Lancashire and saw them at peak maturity.

When buying onion seed and sets, be aware that some are bred for the South, some are bred for the North, and others (like 'Walla Walla Sweet' and 'Candy') are suitable for growing in all areas. Read signage and descriptions carefully, and be sure the onions you're buying are suitable for your growing conditions and weather.

To grow big, onions like a phosphorus-rich soil, so add this mineral in the form of bonemeal if phosphorus is deficient. Also provide regular watering. When transplanting seedlings, do not set the roots too deep, as onions like their shoulders exposed to the sun. Similarly, when planting sets, ensure that the top of the bulb is clear of the soil. Direct-seeded onions will find their own equilibrium. Give them full sun and good drainage and harvest after the green tops have bent over. Once the neck is bent and the leaves have started to turn brown, the onion bulb stops growing. To prepare onions for storage, brush off all soil, dry on tables or racks in full sun for a day, and then store in a dark, cool place, or braid the dried leaves and hang as "onion ropes."

BE AWARE! Almost all gardeners can have success with onions—if you grow what's suited to your climate. When choosing onions from a seed list, check to determine the regionality of the variety, whether it's for the South, the Midwest, or the Northeast. For example, the 'Yellow Sweet Spanish' and 'White Sweet Spanish' are suitable for northern gardens but not for the South. However, there are also onions suitable for growing in all areas, like 'Candy', which is a 'Yellow Sweet Spanish'–type suitable for all regions. The All-America

Selections award-winning 'Super Star' is a 'White Sweet Spanish' type suitable for all areas. Your local USDA Cooperative Extension Service will provide a list of onions suited to your location.

 PLANT PROFILE

ZONES: 3–8 for summer harvest; 9–11 for winter and spring harvest. Some varieties are zone specific.

PROPAGATION: By seed started indoors 6–8 weeks before outdoor planting; also from "sets"—year-old small onion bulbs

PLANTING: 4 inches apart in rows spaced at least 12 inches apart in full sun

PESTS AND DISEASES: Onion fly; rot from poor drainage

PERFECT PARTNERS: Chives, leeks, potatoes, and shallots

Peas, English and Chinese

'Sugar Snap' is America's favorite home garden variety for snacking off the vine, pod and all.

GROW THIS! 'Green Arrow', 'Sugar Snap', Sugar Ann', 'Oregon Sugar Pod II', and 'Knight'

Peas are popular garden vegetables, but gardeners are often confused by the different types—shell peas, snap peas, and edible podded (also called snow peas). Shell peas have tough, fibrous pods that must be shelled to release the sweet, green peas; snap peas look like shell peas but the pods are crispy and edible raw; snow peas also have edible pods, but they must be picked when the pods are flat and before the peas swell the pod, or the pods will turn bitter and fibrous. English peas are distinctly different from Southern crowder peas, which claim the California black-eyed pea as its most familiar pea. English peas come from Europe and North Africa, while black-eyed peas are a type of small bean from South America. English shell peas have fibrous pods yielding up to 11 round, sweetly flavored green peas. 'Green Arrow' (70 days) is a favorite English pea and grows vines up to 6 feet high, loaded with 5-inch-long, dark green straight pods.

Snap peas are now the most widely grown type of pea. This popularity began when 'Sugar Snap' (70 days) won an All-America Selections award (a gold medal) in 1979. Introduced by pea breeder Calvin Lamborn, never before had there been such a plump-podded pea that stayed crisp and crunchy when the pea pods were fully mature. Not only is it a top-selling variety among home gardeners, but it has also become a staple in frozen food mixes. Nearly every snap pea consumed in the United States comes from his company's genetic material. At maturity, 'Sugar Snap' has a pod similar in size and shape to a shell pea, but the pod is edible rather than fibrous. Simply remove a suture (or string) along the topside of the pod by pinching the stem and peeling away the suture; the pod and its plump peas are delicious to eat fresh off the vine or lightly steamed. Shortly after the introduction of 'Sugar Snap', Lamborn introduced 'Sugar Ann' that grows a shorter vine and just slightly smaller pods *and* is 18 days earlier. It requires no staking and also won an All-America award, but home gardeners seem to stay loyal to the original 'Sugar Snap' (as I do) for its higher yield potential.

Another type of edible-podded pea, the Chinese snow pea, is a favorite of Asian chefs. The pods start off flat and are best eaten before the peas have a chance to swell up inside. After they swell the pod, the peas inside are still edible as shelled peas, but the pod wall turns bitter and fibrous. 'Oregon Sugar Pod II' (65 days) grows large, flat pods that are best steamed until tender or added to stir-fries. The 3-foot-high vines are resistant to several pea diseases (including powdery mildew) and therefore can be grown as a fall crop as well as a spring crop.

Peas are a cool-season crop tolerant of light frosts. Cold, wet soil can rot the seed, so it is best to pregerminate the seed indoors in a moist paper towel and plant 4 inches apart in rows at least 2 feet apart. Provide full sun and good drainage. Highest yields are possible by treating seed with an inoculant. Inoculants, in a black powder form, introduce soil bacteria that form nodules among the roots and draw extra nitrogen from the atmosphere to stimulate the roots and help the plants grow more vigorously.

BE AWARE! Many gardeners fail with peas as a fall crop because of mildew disease, which kills the vines before the pods ripen. The only variety I have found to be reliable as a fall crop is 'Knight', developed by Dr. Jerry Marx at the New York State Agricultural Experiment Station.

I do not care for many of the other snap peas that followed the original 'Sugar Snap', because none has improved on its thick, crunchy pod walls and delicious sweet flavor. There is an heirloom variety that also falls short of the original 'Sugar Snap' on quality. Called the 'Amish' sugar snap, it is half the size of 'Sugar Snap', with thin walls and tiny peas that are not so sweetly flavored.

Another heirloom vegetable I will not grow again is called the asparagus pea. It is an odd-looking legume that must be steamed or stir-fried when the pods are only 1 inch long in order to taste pleasant.

 PLANT PROFILE

ZONES: 3–8 for spring and fall harvest; 9–11 for winter harvest

PROPAGATION: By seed direct-sown

PLANTING: 4–6 inches apart in rows spaced at least 2 feet apart in full sun

PESTS AND DISEASES: Powdery mildew, especially plants for a fall harvest

PERFECT PARTNERS: Beets, lettuce, mint, radish, and turnips

Peppers, Sweet

There are green, red, yellow, orange, and black sweet peppers, but the multicolored 'Sweet Gypsy Hybrid' beats them cold.

GROW THIS! 'New Ace', 'Sweet Gypsy Hybrid', 'Big Bertha', 'Golden Goliath', and 'Carmen'

Most home gardeners want a blocky sweet bell pepper with three to four lobes, and one that changes from green to red when ripe. That's what 'New Ace' hybrid provides, with the added advantage of earliness (65 days from transplanting 6-week-old seedlings after frost danger). It is the earliest traditional "blocky" bell pepper. However, there is a slightly earlier kind that produces cone-shaped fruit. Called 'Sweet Gypsy Hybrid', it is the most cold-tolerant sweet pepper you can grow, maturing in 60 days. Another advantage of 'Sweet Gypsy' is its multicolored fruit—starting green, then changing to yellow and orange, then red when fully ripe so that four colors can occur on one plant at the same time.

There are several huge bell peppers, and the one I favor for early maturity and giant size is 'Big Bertha' (70 days). Individual fruits can measure up to 10 inches long and 5 inches across. The skin is thick and crisp when green and holds its crispness when turning red. Another advantage: The seeds are clustered at the stem end, so they are easily removed simply by encircling the stem with a sharp, pointed knife and pulling the seed cluster out in one swift motion. If it's a giant yellow you desire, then choose 'Golden Goliath', which isn't as long as 'Big Bertha' but has a blockier shape.

A special series of sweet peppers known as Italian 'Bull's Horn' for their broad top and pointed end are popular for stuffing and roasting. My favorite is 'Carmen' (60 days to green; 80 to red), winner of an All-America Selections award for its tasty 6-inch-long fruits; it's a perfect candidate for container growing.

Pepper 'Big Bertha' is valued for its extra-large size and crunchy, thick walls compared to regular-size peppers.

BE AWARE! Since most people want their bell peppers to be green or red, it's a wonder there are so many novelty colors available, such as 'Sweet Chocolate' (despite its name it doesn't taste like chocolate, it's just a chocolate brown color). There are also black sweet peppers ('Blackbird'), purple ('Purple Beauty'), and an anemic-looking creamy white, but other than their strange looks, they are not an improvement over a traditional sweet bell pepper that turns bright red when ripe, like 'New Ace' hybrid.

If you want to grow a range of colors, instead of buying them individually, look for sweet bell pepper mixes that include three or more colors in a packet.

 PLANT PROFILE

ZONES: 5–8 for summer and fall harvest; 9–11 for winter and spring harvest

PROPAGATION: By seed started indoors 8 weeks before outdoor planting after frost danger

PLANTING: At least 18 inches apart in rows spaced 3 feet apart in full sun

PESTS AND DISEASES: Sunscald and blossom-end rot

PERFECT PARTNERS: Eggplant, hot peppers, and tomatoes

Peppers, Hot

Grow ancho hot peppers, stuff with Monterey Jack cheese, and bake for a delicious flavor experience.

GROW THIS! 'Anaheim', 'Tiburon', 'Hungarian Yellow Wax', and 'Monster Jalapeno'

Hot peppers vary in their degree of hotness, from mild and medium to hot and hotter. They are ranked on a scale of 1 to 25, with 1 being the hottest and 25 the mildest. 'Anaheim' (70 days) is a mildly hot pepper shaped like a knife sheath—wide at the top and pointed at the bottom and up to 8 inches long. It is the favored kind for chile rellenos, stuffed with cheese, chopped onions, and chopped meat and served with salsa in Mexican cooking. Plants are bushy and everbearing until fall frost. The green fruits turn red at maturity. The poblano series of hot peppers are a dark glossy green (almost black) and a favorite in southwestern cooking, especially for making mole sauce. When they turn red, they are called anchos, and they are just the right degree of mild hotness for stuffing and eating. The hybrid 'Tiburon' turns ripe green in 65 days, red in 85 days. These sturdy plants can hold loads of fruit.

'Hungarian Yellow Wax' (70 days) is a medium-hot pepper that is shaped like a curved horn, changing color from yellow to orange to red. The shiny fruits grow to 6 inches long, and a single plant can have a dozen or more peppers in various stages of ripeness, making it an excellent choice for container growing.

'Monster Jalapeno' (75 days) is as hot as most people ever want a pepper to be, although there are hotter varieties. Its cone-shaped fruits grow

'Anaheim' is a mild hot pepper perfect for stuffing with chopped meat, Monterey Jack cheese, and chopped onion, making it a favorite Mexican dish.

to 4½ inches long and ripen from glossy dark green to red. Use the whole fruit as pickles, slice them thinly to spice up a bland meal, chop finely to sprinkle over pizza, grate into guacamole, or use cubed as a salsa ingredient.

Hot peppers should be transplanted to the garden after all danger of frost into a sunny, well-drained soil. Space plants at least 18 inches apart. For extra-early yields and highest production, grow through black plastic mulch.

BE AWARE! Most home gardeners do not want fiery hot peppers like 'Thai Hot', 'Habanero', 'Scotch Bonnet', and some of the ornamental peppers like 'McMahon's Texas Bird Pepper' (with tiny oval red fruit) and 'Candlelight' (with small, cone-shaped fruit). Some gardeners may relish the hottest varieties, but they are often difficult to incorporate into most dishes without overpowering them and can actually cause your skin to burn if you handle them without gloves (and can be excruciatingly painful if they get near your eyes). If you want heirloom varieties, choose carefully, as many are fiery hot—and dangerous for children to try to eat or handle, since rubbing the eyes after touching the peppers can cause painful eyesores and even eye damage.

 PLANT PROFILE

ZONES: 5–9 for summer and fall harvest; 9–11 for winter and spring harvest

PROPAGATION: By seed started indoors 8 weeks before outdoor planting after frost danger

PLANTING: At least 18 inches apart in rows spaced 3 feet apart in full sun

PESTS AND DISEASES: None serious. The large-fruited kinds are susceptible to blossom-end rot and sunscald.

PERFECT PARTNERS: Cilantro, eggplant, sweet bell peppers, tomatoes

Potatoes, Irish

'Yukon Gold' wins most flavor tests for a creamy flavor.

GROW THIS! 'Yukon Gold', 'Red Pontiac', 'All Blue', and 'La Ratte' fingerling

Sir Walter Raleigh, the British explorer, is credited with introducing the potato to England from travels to Virginia in the 16th century. The Spanish conquistadors had already brought the potato to Spain from Chile, where it grew high in the Andes, but it was treated with suspicion in a land where more exotic fare like citrus, bananas, and pomegranate were available for consumption. The British, and especially the Irish, relished potatoes as a food staple. In their cooler climate, it proved easy to grow, was high yielding in limited space, and provided most of the vitamins needed for sustenance. Most importantly, during harsh winters, it stored for long periods in a cool, dark place. Irish peasants became so dependent on the potato for survival that when a blight disease ruined crops from 1845 to 1849, it caused a famine that led to the death of more than one million people from starvation and a mass exodus of Irish families to North America and other British colonies.

Many gardeners today avoid growing potatoes because store-bought potatoes are inexpensive to buy and keep relatively easily (because most are sprayed with a sprout inhibitor). However, you'll discover that new potatoes harvested fresh from the garden are far superior to anything you will find in a store, and they are extremely easy to grow, even in poor soil. The range of colors, from white to blue and pink to red, has become a novelty as well.

It was the famous plant breeder Luther Burbank who developed the world's most widely grown potato—the 'Russet Burbank', also known as the Idaho. It grows a large tan brown oblong tuber with a rough skin, and it is still the best variety for french fries. However, there are many more varieties to choose from, including my favorite, 'Yukon Gold', which has a thin yellow skin. A 1987 release from Canada, it has become more popular than the 'Russet Burbank' among home gardeners. 'Red Pontiac' is a large white with bright red skin that is easy to grow and widely adaptable. 'All Blue' has blue skin and blue flesh, making it a popular novelty as a potato chip. These varieties are mostly known as Irish potatoes, although they originate from the Andes mountains of Peru.

The 'Yukon Gold' potato has a tender yellow skin and creamy texture when cooked.

A special group of potatoes grows mostly small, elongated tubers known as fingerlings. A particularly tasty variety, 'La Ratte', was discovered by a French farmer in the Swiss Alps. Smooth and creamy with a rich chestnut flavor, it is the preferred choice among French chefs, especially for potato salad.

Most potato crops are grown from seed potatoes—small tubers that can be sliced so each section contains a minimum of two eyes (immature sprouts). These are best planted 2 inches deep, with eyes facing up, after frost danger in spring into a slightly acid, well-drained soil in full sun, spaced at least 12 inches apart in rows 2 feet apart. To make a soil more acidic, add compost or feed with an organic fertilizer that's recommended for acid-loving plants.

A curious fact about wild potatoes is that many of them are poisonous to eat, and it was probably Inca farmers who developed the first edible kinds. With modern home garden varieties, all parts of a potato plant are poisonous except the tuber.

Blight is evident when purple spots and blotches infect the leaves and defoliate the plant. Good drainage reduces the chance of infection. Scab is a series of corky blemishes on the tubers; it can be avoided by choosing disease-resistant varieties and maintaining a slightly acid soil.

Harvest potatoes when the stems have died down by gripping the cluster of stems at the base and teasing the roots out of the soil, aided by a garden fork. Brush off the soil and store the harvest in a cool, dark, frost-free place.

BE AWARE! There are varieties of potatoes that can be grown from seed to produce edible tubers the first season. However, starting from tubers is easier and faster and usually produces the largest size of potatoes. When growing from tubers (rather than from seed), you can harvest within 40 days of planting to yield "new potatoes" (small golf ball–sized, tender-skinned tubers); scrape the topsoil away with your hand and select the largest tubers, leaving smaller tubers to grow to full maturity.

PLANT PROFILE

ZONES: 3–8 for summer harvest; 9–11 for winter and spring harvest

PROPAGATION: By seed and tubers, but more commonly tubers as they assure earliness and the largest crops

PLANTING: 12 inches apart in rows spaced 2 feet apart in full sun

PESTS AND DISEASES: Blight and scab disease

PERFECT PARTNERS: Eggplant, peppers, sweet potatoes (where zones overlap), and tomatoes

Potatoes, Sweet

'Beauregard' supersedes 'Centennial' as the favorite home garden variety.

GROW THIS! 'Beauregard' and 'Porto Rico'

The sweet potato, also called a yam in the United States, is closely related to morning glories. It comes from Asia and migrated to Polynesia when seafaring tribes began colonizing islands of the Pacific. On many islands, the survival of a tribe often depended on two plants—the coconut palm, which produces nutritious nuts year-round, and the sweet potato (known as *kumara*) that could produce a crop year-round in frost-free locations. The sweet potato was so highly regarded by the Polynesians that Captain Cook had two sailors flogged when they stole tubers from a chief's garden in Hawaii because he needed to maintain friendly relations with the natives.

The sweet potato is a warm-season vining vegetable that is grown from offsets called slips. These sprout all around the tuber when it is planted below the soil surface, in moist peat, or when half-submerged in plain water. Each slip can be detached from the tuber to create a new plant. The slips must be planted outdoors after frost danger, the root of the slip buried in an organically rich, well-drained, sandy soil in full sun. Earliest yields are possible by growing through black plastic.

The variety 'Beauregard' was developed by the late Larry Rolston of Louisiana State University and released in 1987. It immediately became the preferred variety to grow commercially and in home gardens, not only for its earliness (90 days, which is 10 days ahead of other comparable sweet potatoes) but also for its improved disease resistance. The big, zeppelin-shaped tubers have a red skin and deep orange flesh.

'Porto Rico', a red-skinned tuber with yellow interior, is a space-saving bush type, suitable for growing in containers and limited spaces.

BE AWARE! 'Beauregard' replaces 'Centennial'. It was previously the most popular sweet potato grown in the States, but it is later maturing and more susceptible to disease than 'Beauregard'. There are sweet potatoes more suitable for window-box decoration, mostly with golden, silver, and bronze leaves. Although they do make edible tubers, they are not the same quality as 'Beauregard'.

PLANT PROFILE

ZONES: 6–11; can be grown as a winter and spring crop in Zones 9–11

PROPAGATION: Offsets called slips that appear all around the tuber when submerged to half its height in soil, moist peat, or plain water

PLANTING: At least 18 inches apart in rows spaced 3 feet apart in full sun

PESTS AND DISEASES: Rot during cold, wet weather and from poor drainage

PERFECT PARTNERS: Eggplant, Irish potatoes, peppers, and tomatoes

Pumpkins

'Prizewinner' replaces 'Big Max' as the favorite for giant size, attractive shape, and deep orange color.

GROW THIS! 'Prizewinner', 'Amish Pie', 'Baby Pam', 'Pennsylvania Neck Pumpkin', 'Sorcerer', 'Magic Lantern', 'Howden', 'Jack Be Little', and 'Rouge vif d'Etamps'

From contest winners to pie pumpkins to minis, you may be surprised to learn that pumpkins are a type of gourd related to cucumbers. The fruits are mostly orange skinned, round, and ribbed, but pumpkins can also be white, dark green, tan, and almost red. In years past, if you wanted to grow a giant pumpkin, you probably grew Burpee's 'Big Max', but today the preferred variety is 'Prizewinner' because of its deeper color and more uniform shape, and because it always looks attractive no matter how large it grows. Although these two varieties are considered giants—often exceeding 100 pounds—they are unlikely to win at state fairs and other pumpkin-growing contests since the world record is now more than 1,500 pounds. To set a new world record, you'll need to obtain seed from the world record holders; they are obligated to share their seed with other contestants so everyone has an opportunity to create a new record.

Pie pumpkins tend to be smaller than the heavyweights, and a good heirloom pie pumpkin is 'Amish Pie' (100 days). A more modern introduction, 'Baby Pam' (100 days) grows deep orange fruits and deep orange flesh. A larger pie pumpkin favored by Amish farmers is the 'Pennsylvania Neck Pumpkin', a tan variety with a long, curved neck and a bulbous base. The inside flesh is orange, and each fruit has several times more meat than a regular pie pumpkin.

The best jack-o'-lantern pumpkins are medium size and are also good for pie filling and pumpkin soup. Look for the All-America Selections award-winning 'Sorcerer' (115 days) with deep orange

'Jack Be Little' is a mini pumpkin prized as a Halloween decoration.

skin, 'Magic Lantern' (115 days) with good mildew resistance, and 'Howden' (115 days) that stays firm a long time after carving. Mini-pumpkins, such as 'Jack Be Little', are too small to carve but are suitable for painting. For sheer good looks when decorating at Halloween, consider the French pumpkin known as 'Rouge vif d'Etamps'. Its shape—slightly flattened, perfectly circular, and deeply ribbed— inspired the illustration for Cinderella's pumpkin coach; in real gardens, it's large enough for carving, and the flesh is tasty.

Pumpkins can be direct-seeded 3 feet apart in rows 5 to 6 feet apart, which allows the vines to knit together. It's often best to put pumpkins at the back of the garden where the vines can sprawl over soil or grass and be left undisturbed until harvest. They require a fertile, well-drained, sunny soil and frequent watering during dry spells. What makes a pumpkin grow large is high nitrogen fertilizer and constant moisture, because it is moisture that contributes most of the weight in a prizewinner. As soon as the flowers appear, examine them to determine which are male (the male flowers have powdery centers and slender stalks) and female (females have a flower with a shiny center and a bulbous shape underneath). Take one of the male flowers and dab the pollen on as many females as possible to ensure an early fruit set. After about six females have set fruit, examine them for the thickest stem and shapeliest fruit, and eliminate all but the best one so the vine's energy goes into growing a supersize specimen.

BE AWARE! Although 'Dill's Atlantic Giant' will beat 'Prizewinner' for size, it has more squash genes than pumpkin. This gives it an anemic, pale coloring that is less appealing for decoration or beauty contests. You should also avoid most miniature pumpkins in favor of tastier varieties if you're baking a pie. The miniatures are suitable for Thanksgiving decoration but are poor quality for eating. These would include 'Baby Boo', 'Lil Pump-ke-mon', and 'Munchkin'.

 ## PLANT PROFILE

ZONES: 5–11 for summer and fall harvest; 9–11 for winter and spring harvest

PROPAGATION: By seed direct-sown after frost danger in spring

PLANTING: At least 3 feet apart in rows 5 feet apart in full sun

PESTS AND DISEASE: Squash vine borers and mice chewing into the fruit and inducing rot

PERFECT PARTNERS: Melons, summer and winter squash, and sweet potatoes

Radishes

'Cherry Belle'—just 20 days from seed to harvest—is the earliest red radish.

GROW THIS! 'Cherry Belle', 'French Breakfast', and 'Easter Egg'

Radishes are considered a beauty food because they are high in vitamin C (which promotes healthy skin) and silicon (which makes nails strong and hair lustrous). Radishes are available in a variety of skin colors, even though they're mostly all white on the inside, and you'll find round, oblong, and icicle-shaped radishes. The most popular color is red, of course, and the variety 'Cherry Belle' is a notable All-America Selections award winner. It's ready to harvest just 20 days from sowing seed directly into the garden, and it is perfectly round and the size of a 'Bing' cherry. For eye appeal, the bicolor variety 'French Breakfast' is popular because its torpedo shape requires three bites to eat it instead of the one-bite 'Cherry Belle' *and* the flavor is crispy. It is attractive, with red shoulders and white tips, and it holds its crispness longer than round red radishes, in my experience. White radishes can be small and round, such as 'Burpee White', or icicle shaped, such as 'White Icicle'. If you'd like a colorful assortment of radishes, choose a radish mixture like 'Easter Egg'; you'll be able to harvest a beautiful bunch of red, purple, and white round radishes. The black radish (with white interior) can grow to the size of a baseball; its flavor is powerful and bitter at harvest but mellows with storage; it's an heirloom (reportedly from Spain) and was stored successfully in root cellars during long, harsh winters.

The radish is a cool-season crop that tolerates mild frosts. The seed germinates almost the instant you add water to it. Sow thinly in wide rows, then thin seedlings to 1 inch apart, as crowding will inhibit root development. Provide full sun and good drainage and water regularly; any arrest in root development can cause misshapen roots, poor flavor, and pithy texture.

There is a separate class of large-rooted radish known as Chinese radish or Daikon that grows much larger, up to 10 inches long and 4 inches thick. The Daikon radish is most demanding of cool conditions in order to form firm roots, and so it is best to plant it as a fall crop, sowing seed in late August over most of the country, for harvesting in late September, October, and November.

BE AWARE! Although red radishes are the most popular (and the best nutritionally), seedsmen offer white, pink, and even yellow varieties. Heirloom varieties like 'Philadelphia White Box' (30 days) and yellow 'Helios' (30 to 35 days) are oddities dating back to the 1800s, but they don't have a crisp, clean flavor and often tend to be a little too pungent.

 PLANT PROFILE

ZONES: 3–8 for spring and fall harvest; 9–11 for winter and spring harvest

PROPAGATION: By seed direct-sown

PLANTING: 1 inch apart in blocks or wide rows in full sun

PESTS AND DISEASES: Wireworms and flea beetles

PERFECT PARTNERS: Beets, lettuce, spinach, and turnips

Spinach

Grow climbing Malabar for heat resistance and a never-ending supply of healthy greens all season.

GROW THIS! 'Bloomsdale Long Standing', Malabar, New Zealand, and 'Tyee'

Spinach is a cool-season vegetable that forms a rosette of broad, dark green leaves rich in iron, which promotes a healthy bloodstream. It can be eaten raw in salads or cooked—lightly steamed or boiled—as a nutritious side dish. It is one of the hardiest vegetables you can grow. It can be direct-seeded when the soil is a little above 40°F and will germinate quickly. Sown after Labor Day in Zones 7 and colder, it will produce a healthy crown of leaves, remain dormant after frost, and produce an extra-early spring crop, even before asparagus starts to strike through the soil.

For years, 'Bloomsdale Long Standing' was the preferred variety on account of its extra-hardiness and usefulness in overwintering, even when covered with snow. It is still a popular, reliable variety, although several hybrids have been introduced with a higher leaf count and good uniformity.

A drawback of spinach is its tendency to bolt to seed as soon as the weather turns hot, so seed companies offer several heat-tolerant substitutes, the most useful of which is Malabar spinach. Malabar grows as a vine and needs support to climb up to 10 feet, creating a curtain of glossy dark green leaves and flowers. The more you pick the succulent heart-shaped leaves, the more the plant is stimulated into growing additional leaves. They are sweeter than regular spinach and can be eaten fresh off the vine. Moreover, there are two varieties—one with green stems and another with purple stems. Both kinds flower soon after sprouting and continue to flower all season. The flowers are pink, formed in clusters, and decorative.

New Zealand spinach is also a vine, but it spreads over the soil to form a groundcover 3 to 4 feet wide. Discovered by Captain Cook during his circumnavigation of the world in the 1700s, the leaves are a lighter green than regular spinach and are delicious. Both Malabar and New Zealand spinach can be direct-seeded, but be careful—they are sensitive to frost.

Spinach 'Tyee' is now favored by cooks as the most succulent, tender spinach for spring or fall harvests.

The finest spinach the world has ever seen was an All-America Selections winner called 'Melody Hybrid'. It formed perfectly symmetrical rosettes with succulent, lightly blistered dark green leaves and an incomparable tenderness. However, when Monsanto bought out the breeder Seminis Seeds and incorporated Seminis breeding lines into their own, they decided to take 'Melody' off the market. They also declined to release the parents, so other growers are unable to perpetuate the variety. The nearest comparison to 'Melody' would be 'Tyee'—so look for that variety.

Give all spinach varieties full sun and good drainage.

BE AWARE! There are a number of so-called spinach substitutes that I would not consider worthy of the name spinach. One is strawberry spinach (*Chenopodium capitatum*). The leaves, though edible, are small, triangular, and toothed and tedious to gather enough for a serving. I find that Malabar is much tastier and more productive and can save space by growing up a trellis. Mountain spinach (also commonly called red orach and green orach, depending on the variety) is not my idea of a good spinach substitute, and neither is tampala spinach. I find that they both lack the substance and succulence that regular spring spinach provides.

 ## PLANT PROFILE

ZONES: 3–8 for regular spring spinach; 9–11 as a winter crop. Zones 5–10 for Malabar and New Zealand spinach.

PROPAGATION: By seed direct-sown. Spring spinach tolerates frost; summer spinach does not.

PLANTING: 6 inches apart, shoulder to shoulder for all varieties, in full sun

PESTS AND DISEASES: Damping-off disease, slugs, and foraging animals like rabbits

PERFECT PARTNERS: Beets, carrots, peas, and radishes

Squashes, Summer

Climbing green 'Trombone' zucchini never quits bearing until fall frost.

GROW THIS! 'Burpee Golden Zucchini', 'Richgreen Hybrid', 'Elite', 'Sunburst', 'Trombone' (also called 'Tromboncino'), and 'Early Prolific Crookneck'

The most popular summer squash by far is the green zucchini; in its juvenile stage (up to 5 inches long), it's so tender it slices like butter. The zucchini (also known as courgette) owes its popularity not only to its easy culture but also its fast maturity (as little as 45 days from direct seeding) and high productivity. If a zucchini squash vine is kept picked so the fruit do not swell up to the size of a baseball bat, it can remain productive for several months. Zucchini squashes can also be yellow ('Burpee Golden Zucchini' is highly productive), gray, dark green, and almost black. The skin is soft and sweet when young, and the entire fruit can be sliced and eaten raw like a cucumber. Steamed for just a few minutes, the fruit is delicious sliced crosswise or lengthwise, and it can be julienned for stir-fries. It's also wonderful when batter-dipped and fried.

Zucchini squash. Most zucchini squashes have male and female flowers on the same plant. You can tell the females because they have an immature zucchini directly underneath the flower, which has a shiny center; the male flowers have a bare stem beneath the flower and a powdery center. Bees generally transfer pollen from the male flowers to the females for the fruit to develop. Without successful pollination, the fruit will stay small and quickly turn black. To increase yields, you can take a male flower, peel away the yellow petals, and rub the powdery center onto the shiny part of the female flower.

Usually the male flowers appear first, and it can take a week for the first female flowers to appear. However, the variety 'Richgreen Hybrid' (40 days) is an almost all-female zucchini that sets more female flowers than males for a high yield. A similar handsome hybrid dark green zucchini is 'Elite'. The fruits are uniformly straight and slender, best harvested when 6 to 8 inches long.

Seed can be direct-sown after frost danger. Thin the seedlings to 2 to 3 feet apart. Provide full sun and a well-drained fertile soil. Mulching with black plastic will promote earliness and increase yields. Keep the fruit picked for continuous production.

There are round varieties such as light green 'Ronde de Nice' (45 days) and dark green 'Eight-Ball' (55 days), but these are novelties and not as popular as the slender, bright green courgette-type varieties. A novelty summer squash I can recommend is an All-America Selections winner: 'Sunburst' (52 days) is a scallop or pattypan squash that produces generously on bushy plants.

'Trombone' zucchini. Also known as 'Zucchino Rampicante' and 'Tromboncino', it's hard to decide whether to call this Italian heirloom squash a winter squash or a summer squash, but I

Although zucchini squashes are edible when large, most people prefer them as "courgettes"—when they are no more than 5 inches long. This variety is 'Richgreen', an all-female variety that is high yielding.

would classify it as a summer squash because it is the soft-skinned immature fruit that is the most delicious, tasting exactly like a regular courgette-type zucchini squash. Left on the vine, these will mature into large beige-colored curled fruit with a bulbous base, somewhat resembling a crookneck pumpkin, crookneck golden cushaw squash, or long-necked butternut squash. At this stage, they can be baked and eaten like a butternut squash or stored in a frost-free area for several months like a butternut squash.

'Trombone' zucchini is a gorilla in the garden, since the aggressive vines will cover a large space like a pumpkin vine would, unless you train the vines to climb. The fruit begin to appear within 60 days and at first are a light green, with a long, curled neck and a swollen end where the seeds are concentrated. I have cut 300 slices from a single immature fruit and sautéed them with onions for a delicious side dish.

'Early Prolific' crookneck squash. I have harvested as many as 50 fruits from a single bushy vine before the plant exhausted itself. Within 40 days of direct seeding after frost danger, the plant begins a parade of fruit that is truly remarkable. Shaped like a swan's neck, the glossy golden yellow fruits have a bulbous base and a narrow, curved neck. The sliced fruits are delicious raw or lightly steamed, especially served with fried onions or a parsley-butter sauce. The more you pick, the more the plant is stimulated into bearing more fruit. Culture is the same as zucchini squash.

BE AWARE! Zucchini squash fruits used to be all green, but in recent years plant breeders have made them yellow, gray, striped green and white, and almost black. Most of a zucchini's nutrition is in the skin (because the interior flesh has a high water content), so choosing a rich green zucchini packs a more powerful nutritional punch than the other colors.

It's hard to fault any zucchini squash on flavor as they are so similar, but I can fault them for color. People expect their zucchini squash to be a medium green or dark green, not gray (as with the variety 'Greyzini'). If you want an assortment of colors for novelty value, you can purchase zucchini mixtures with seeds stained different colors to indicate green, yellow, and gray varieties. Offer the three colors to guests, and I guarantee the green will be selected over the other two every time.

Look in *Bailey's Cyclopedia of American Horticulture* and you will find under *Cucuma pepo* an intriguing squash vine called "the vine peach." Occasionally you will see this vine peach advertised as though it were a genuine peach, but it's actually an inedible gourd with a yellow skin that's related to summer squashes. Don't buy it or try to eat it.

 ## PLANT PROFILE

ZONES: 5–8 for summer and fall harvest; 9–11 for winter and spring harvest

PROPAGATION: By seeds direct-sown

PLANTING: At least 2 feet apart in rows spaced 3 feet apart in full sun

PESTS AND DISEASES: Squash vine borer and powdery mildew

PERFECT PARTNERS: Eggplant, peppers, sweet potatoes, tomatoes, and winter squash

Squashes, Winter

The most useful long-storage squash is low-calorie vegetable spaghetti, and it can be trained to climb!

GROW THIS! Vegetable spaghetti, 'Burpee's Bush Table Queen', and 'Waltham Butternut'

Winter squashes mature later than summer squash, and their hard-shelled fruits are perfectly suitable for winter storage. There are dozens of different shapes and sizes. Some are shaped like a flattened pumpkin with prominent ribs; others resemble a large acorn shape. There are pear-shaped kinds and huge oval, warted types called Hubbards. Colors range from yellow, orange, and red to beige, blue, and almost black, with bicolors such as green and white striped. All have a hard orange interior that turns to the texture and flavor of a sweet potato when cooked. The flavor is improved with a pat of butter or a spoonful of maple syrup.

Winter squashes are best direct-seeded after frost danger. The largest fruits grow on sprawling vines, but some varieties have been bred to grow short, bushy vines. Give them full sun and a fertile, well-drained soil. Mulching with black plastic will promote earliness and increase yields.

Vegetable spaghetti. Although classified as a winter squash because it will store for months over winter, vegetable spaghetti is the earliest-maturing winter squash, ready to harvest first fruits within 65 days of sowing seed directly into the garden after frost danger in spring. Allow it to sprawl across the ground or train it up a trellis to save space, since it has tendrils that enable it to climb. One vine can produce up to a dozen fruits weighing 4 to 5 pounds each.

Vegetable spaghetti was introduced to the world by the great Japanese seedsman Takeo Sakata. He trained in the United States at seed and nursery firms in California before founding Sakata Seeds in Yokohama, Japan. In 1974, a few years before his death, I interviewed him at his company's headquarters, and in the evening we enjoyed dinner at his home in the hills above Tokyo Bay. As a snack, his wife served edible soybeans that had been cooked in boiling salt water. Just a few minutes of cooking loosened the skins, and we watched sumo wrestling on television before dinner, picking up pods with our fingers and squirting the tender beans directly into our mouths.

Also on the menu was one of his proudest introductions, vegetable spaghetti. He discovered it in a part of China known as Manchuria and introduced it as spaghetti squash, but it was slow to gain public acceptance. Only when he changed the name to vegetable spaghetti and described it as a low-calorie substitute for pasta spaghetti did the sales increase. Today, there is an entire industry based in Oxnard, California, devoted to supplying grocery stores and supermarkets with vegetable spaghetti fruits, often selling at $2.50 per pound. When you consider that a single vine will grow up to 12 fruits weighing 4 to 5 pounds each, that's a lot of money you can save by growing your own.

Most vegetable spaghetti fruits are cream colored or yellow when ripe, but some newer varieties are a glowing orange or speckled yellow and orange on the outside. Irrespective of the variety, vegetable spaghetti is one of the easiest plants to grow. When the vine is allowed to climb, the fruits do not need support. They have a strong stem, so they can hang securely from any height until the foliage is discolored by frost. Harvest with a section of stem attached. If grown on the ground, harvest before mice feast on the interior.

In appearance, the seed looks like a pumpkin seed—oblong, white, and flat, and they're easy to plant. Germination is generally high, up to 90 percent, and rapid—6 to 7 days at a soil temperature of 70°F or more. I sow the seed 1 inch deep in groups of three or four, each group spaced 3 feet apart, and later I thin to one strong seedling per group. The vigorous vines need full sun and a fertile, well-drained soil. I dig in plenty of compost and a sprinkling of organic general-purpose fertilizer (5-10-5) at the start of the season. Growing the plants through black plastic will promote earliness and suffocate weeds. Powdery mildew can discolor the vines after a wet season, but usually the damage is not enough to prevent your harvesting a good crop. Squash vine bugs and cucumber beetles can also infest vines, but an organic garlic-pepper spray can deter them; even left alone, I find that the vines are tough enough to withstand insect depredations.

The fruits appear on female flowers (you can tell the females because they have a small, immature oblong oval fruit beneath the flower ready to be fertilized by a male). When the flowers appear, I generally pick a male flower and rub its powdery middle onto the shiny part of a female flower to ensure pollination, although insects are also efficient pollinators. The vines are male-dominant, meaning they produce more male flowers than females, so hand-pollination will ensure a 100 percent fruit set. The plants like plenty of water at all stages of growth and will show their need for water by wilting. The fruits are ripe for picking when they turn from white to yellow or orange, depending on the variety.

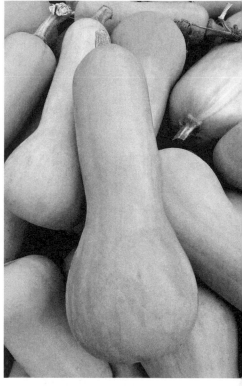

Butternut squash 'Waltham' is the standard for high yields and excellent flavor among winter squashes; it's also an All-America award winner.

Like other winter squashes, vegetable spaghetti stores for long periods if kept in a cool, dark, frost-free location. The 6- to 8-inch-long fruits will keep for up to 6 months if you leave a length of dried stem attached.

Cooking is also easy. Simply pierce the skin with a fork to allow steam to escape while cooking, and set the oven at 450°F for 40 minutes. Place the fruit on a metal cooking tray in ½ inch of water and turn over once during the baking process so it cooks evenly. Remove from the oven, slice the fruit in half lengthwise, and spoon out the seeds. Then take a fork and scrape the cooked spaghetti out from the bottom and sides. It fluffs out to fill a large bowl, and a single fruit easily serves four people. Simply spoon your favorite sauce or toppings over the cooked "spaghetti": marinara, parsley and butter, clams, even meatballs, and you will experience a satisfying, delicious, low-calorie meal.

Acorn and butternut squashes. You'll get good production and save space by growing a bush variety like 'Burpee's Bush Table Queen' and the semibush powdery mildew–resistant variety 'Royal Ace'. Also consider the All-America Selections winner 'Honey Bear'. Developed by the University of New Hampshire, it produces an average of four fruits per plant on a compact plant.

In my opinion, butternut squash is even more appealing than acorn squash; shaped like an enormous pear, butternut squash has a thick neck and beige skin color. Even though I generally like to recommend space-saving bush varieties of squash, I recommend the vining 'Waltham Butternut' in order to get worthwhile yields and full-size, delicious fruit that is orange on the inside. It won an All-America award for its large size, substantial yield, and fine flavor. For a space-saving alternative, try 'Harris Betternut' (88 days), growing medium-size fruit on short vines.

BE AWARE! While acorn squash can be a wonderful addition to a garden, avoid the vining types like 'Royal Acorn' because their vines sprawl and can overtake other garden plants.

If you're interested in edible winter squashes, read seed packet labels before you buy. Winter squashes are closely related to gourds, and while most gourds are edible when young and delicious in stir-fries, you wouldn't want to eat them when they mature. When you purchase a seed packet of large, mixed colors ornamental gourds, it will likely contain both edible winter squashes and nonedible gourds, such as the bicolored green and red 'Turk's Turban', which has poor flavor, and the dipper-type gourds that are mostly hollow (and make great nesting boxes for purple martins and wrens).

 ## PLANT PROFILE

ZONES: 5–8 for summer and fall harvest; 9–11 for winter and spring harvest

PROPAGATION: By seed direct-sown after frost danger

PLANTING: Vining kinds at least 3 feet apart in rows spaced 3 feet apart in full sun

PESTS AND DISEASES: Squash vine borer and powdery mildew

PERFECT PARTNERS: Eggplant, peppers, pumpkins, summer squash, sweet potatoes, and tomatoes

Strawberries

June bearer, everbearing, or day neutral? The day-neutral, all-seasons variety 'Tristar' yields several flushes of fruit spring, summer, and fall.

GROW THIS! 'Earliglow' June bearer and 'Tristar' day neutral

To shop intelligently for strawberry plants, you'll need to be aware that there are basically three classes of strawberry: June bearers, which fruit during the month of June in most areas of the United States; everbearers, which will fruit in June and again in September, since their fruiting capability is controlled by the length of daylight hours; and day neutrals, which are unaffected by day-length and fruit in several flushes during the spring, summer, and autumn growing seasons, provided they receive sufficient nutrients and water.

Since everbearers and day neutrals crop more than once a season, it begs the question: "Why bother with a June bearer?" The answer is that June bearers crop more heavily during a 3-week period; their potential fruit size can be much bigger than an everbearer or a day neutral; and the flavor can be superior. 'Earliglow' is a delicious large-fruited June bearer that crops heavily and produces fruit the size of a small peach. The "king berry"—the first one to ripen on a fruit cluster—is usually the biggest and the shape of a cockscomb, while other berries on the cluster may be large and cone shaped.

Dr. Gene Galetta, strawberry breeder for the USDA, produced 'Tristar' from wild day-neutral genetic material collected in Brighton Canyon, Utah. Although he released three for home gardeners, including 'Tribute' and 'Tribune', his 'Tristar' is the most widely available. The mostly cone-shaped fruits are bright red, sweet, and juicy and mostly a medium size.

If you live in the South or California and want to grow large-fruited or day-neutral strawberries, check with the local USDA Extension Service or Internet for specific regionalized recommendations.

Generally, strawberries are best planted in the fall, as soon after Labor Day as possible, so that during cool fall days and winter they have a chance to develop a vigorous root system before going dormant. Then, in spring, the plants will become bushy, flower profusely, and set a good harvest of large fruit.

Spring planting is also suitable, but it is best to remove any flowers and runners that develop so the plant's energy goes into developing a healthy root system. You can stop removing flowers by the middle of July.

Strawberries cannot tolerate weed competition, so you should mulch around the roots with straw or grow the plants through black plastic. The black plastic will promote earliness. For even earlier crops, cover the plants with horticultural fleece, which covers plants like a spiderweb and generates heat. This helps ward off frosts and maintains a stable soil temperature so the fruit ripen up to 2 weeks earlier than normal. The fleece even protects against birds raiding the patch.

Give the plants full sun and good drainage. Fertilize with a high-phosphorus fertilizer. Strawberry plants respond well to foliar feeding, especially when the nutrient content is in a 1-2-1 ratio, such as 5-10-5 or 10-20-10.

When buying strawberry plants, you have a choice of "bareroot" or the more expensive "potted" plants, which are rooted in soil. Bareroot strawberries are dug from the nursery fields, and the sandy soil is washed off. They are then bundled together with an elastic band and placed in a plastic bag, nested in peat. Examine the roots carefully and cut away any that are broken or show signs of rot. The roots are fibrous and can become tangled, so tease the roots apart, spread them wide, and cover with soil up to the crown (the thick section, usually with a green bud showing).

Potted strawberry plants need to be removed from the pot and planted so the crown of leaves is clear of the soil. Strawberries grow best in sandy soil and do well in raised beds.

BE AWARE! Avoid white strawberries, as they are pathetically small and look anemic; and don't waste your energy on any strawberry advertised as a climbing variety, such as 'Everest'. Strawberries cannot climb, and even if the runners are trained up a trellis and attached with twist ties, the runners have difficulty bearing fruit. Technically, yes, you can train strawberries to grow vertically, since newer strawberry varieties bred for sale as hanging baskets will fruit on the runners; I have seen runners grow to 4 feet in length, but "a pillar of fruit"—as advertised—is an exaggeration. The tedious task of tying the runners up is not worth the result.

Beware of a wild strawberry sold under various names as a patio or ground-cover strawberry, botanically known as *Fragraria vesca*. Its common name is sow's teat strawberry because of the small red, cone-shaped fruit. Although edible, the fruits are exceedingly seedy and not nearly as productive as the alpine kind Fraises des Bois, whose fruits are small but pleasant to eat.

You sometimes see a groundcover strawberry advertised called a mock strawberry (*Duchesnia indica*). It is a lawn weed that looks like a strawberry, with small strawberry-shaped fruit and vigorous runners. However, the strawberries are tasteless and the runners will become invasive.

PLANT PROFILE

ZONES: 4–8 as a spring, summer, and fall crop using day-neutral varieties. Zone 9 can produce winter harvests.

PROPAGATION: Mostly from year-old dormant roots, but also from seed, requiring 16 weeks from seed to fruiting

PLANTING: Plant at least 12 inches apart in blocks with at least 12 inches between rows in full sun.

PESTS AND DISEASES: Birds and rodents will eat the berries at the point of ripening. Avoid red stele disease by purchasing certified virus-free plants.

PERFECT PARTNERS: Other perennial edible crops such as asparagus and rhubarb

Swiss Chard

For 11 vibrant stalk colors ranging from yellow and orange to purple, red, and bicolors (and the most tender leaves), choose 'Bright Lights'.

GROW THIS! 'Bright Lights'

Swiss chard is also known as perpetual spinach and silverbeet. It's grown for its crisp stalks that resemble blanched celery when cooked and for its nutritious, dark green leaves that make an excellent warm-season substitute for spinach when eaten cooked or raw. The erect plants are everbearing until hard freezing weather, and the stalks can be so decorative that they are used in ornamental containers and mixed into flower borders.

A New Zealand amateur gardener, the late John Eaton, is the person responsible for 'Bright Lights' chard. Before Eaton began working on extending the color range of this easy-to-grow, nutritious vegetable, there were basically two stalk colors available to US gardeners—white, such as 'Lucullus' and its look-alike 'Fordhook Giant', and the crimson-stalked 'Ruby Red' (also called 'Rhubarb' chard). In Australia, there was a mix called 'Five-Color' chard (also called 'Rainbow'), but these mixtures are unstable, often producing only three colors with a lot of red and white and a little golden yellow. Working in his backyard near Wellington, Eaton separated out nine distinct colors in addition to the white and crimson, making a total of 11 bright colors. By careful selection among crosses over many generations, his new mixture, called 'Bright Lights', includes white, lemon yellow, canary yellow, gold, rose pink, red, apricot, orange, purple, and bicolors. The leaves are dark green or bronze depending on the stalk color (the reds tend to show bronze leaves). Moreover, the color of the leaves and stalks remains during cooking. The glossy, ruffled leaves are more tender than any other chard variety, and for its superior performance 'Bright Lights' won an All-America Selections award. Today, it is one of the most popular vegetable varieties in the world.

The more you harvest the outer leaves of 'Bright Lights', the more the plant is stimulated to produce new leaves at its core, even after fall frost. Only a hard freeze will end its productivity. Seed can be direct-sown, and even in the seedling stage the colors are evident. This allows you to select the most desirable colors when thinning and transplant the thinnings to containers for nonstop, all-season ornamental effect. Plants tolerate heat and drought and poor soil. You never want to be without 'Bright Lights' in your garden.

BE AWARE! 'Bright Lights' has made all other chard varieties obsolete, including 'Ruby', 'Rhubarb', 'Fordhook Giant', 'Lucullus', 'Rainbow', and 'Five-Color'. In the years ahead, you will find many more multicolored mixtures of Swiss chard introduced, but, in my opinion, it will be a long time before 'Bright Lights' is improved upon. It is simply that good.

 ## PLANT PROFILE

ZONES: 3–8 as a summer and fall crop; 9–11 as a winter and spring crop

PROPAGATION: By seed direct-sown in early spring

PLANTING: At least 12 inches apart in rows spaced 2 feet apart in full sun

PESTS AND DISEASES: None serious except for rabbits, groundhogs, and deer

PERFECT PARTNERS: Beets, cabbage, carrots, and snap beans

Tomatoes

Most gardeners have a favorite, but cherry-size 'Sun Gold' is extra early and extra sweet. 'Better Boy' holds the record for most large-fruited tomatoes per plant—more than 300 pounds on vines 25 feet tall.

GROW THIS! 'Big Rainbow', 'Delicious', 'Better Boy', 'Celebrity', 'Sun Gold', 'Early Cascade', 'Paul Robeson', and 'Health Kick'

One of the delights of midsummer is picking your first homegrown tomato, slicing it into sections, and sprinkling it with salt, a dash of balsamic vinegar, and a little chopped basil; it's one of nature's most satisfying taste treats. People everywhere appear to be more passionate about the flavor of tomatoes than anything else in the garden. The tomato is variable in shape (from small pear to large pincushion types), size (from cherry to grapefruit size), and color (from red, pink, maroon, and purple to yellow, orange, white, and lime green), but it is the scarlet red medium- to large-fruited tomato that is most desirable for use in many culinary ways—eaten fresh off the vine, sliced into salads or as a pizza topping, and made into sauce, bruschetta, salsa, chili, soups, and stews.

There are more than 5,000 varieties of tomatoes, though many heirloom varieties are known by several names (like 'Big Rainbow', which is also called 'Striped German', 'Flame', and 'Pineapple'). The world record for a single tomato is 7½ pounds using seed from a large-fruited variety called 'Delicious' (which was bred from a variety named 'Ponderosa'), while the record for highest yield is held by 'Better Boy', at 342 pounds of fruit from a single plant that grew more than 25 feet tall in Arkansas. 'Ponderosa', by the way, is a popular heirloom beefsteak tomato with a pink skin, but I rate it poor for flavor; its improved selection, 'Delicious', however, has excellent flavor and is well deserving of its name.

Tomato popularity is often based on opinions about flavor and texture. Some people prefer a tomato that is sweet; others like a sweet and tangy combination. Some want a tomato with a firm, smooth texture and few seeds. Russians like their tomatoes maroon colored; the Japanese like red tomatoes with green shoulders. Americans want them mostly smooth, round, and red and the size of a billiard ball. In taste tests, Californians picked a variety called 'Ace' for best flavor, while 'Better Boy' has won flavor tests in the Northeast. The All-America Selections winner 'Celebrity' generally appears high on every taste test no matter where it is grown.

Of course, growing conditions and the prevalence of disease can affect tomato flavor. Here are some common problems involving tomato cultivation, and what you can do to avoid or minimize these diseases and pests.

Anthracnose is a disfiguring fungal disease that generally occurs in late summer, causing black circular sunken patches on the skin and making the fruit inedible. There are resistant varieties, but any infected tomato plants should be burned. Plant disease-resistant varieties for the best control.

Blossom-end rot is a blackening of the tomato where the blossom fell off after pollination and fruit formation. Lack of water, infrequent watering, and lack of calcium in the soil are the prime causes. For prevention, lime heavily acid soil and avoid irregular watering during dry spells.

Cat-face describes a corky disfiguration of the fruit on mostly large-fruited tomatoes, usually caused by imperfect pollination. The corky imperfection is usually only skin deep and can be cut away to still leave an edible fruit. You can avoid cat faces by shaking the flower trusses to mix up the pollen.

Cracking is common on many varieties of cherry tomatoes like 'Sun Gold' and 'Sweet 100'. The cracking occurs most often when the fruit is overripe, so pick fruit as soon as ripeness occurs. Also, heavy rains or overwatering at the point of ripeness can increase the incidence of cracking.

Late ripening. Many heirloom varieties are naturally late ripening, a reason why they fell from favor. However, lateness is also caused by lack of phosphorus in the soil or too low a temperature at the start of the season. You can advance ripening by as much as 2 weeks by using black plastic as a mulch, which will warm the soil early and keep it warm.

Nematodes are eel-like microscopic worms that colonize a tomato's root system, stealing nourishment from it and causing a lackluster appearance and small, misshapen, or undersized fruit. Nematodes thrive in sandy soil mostly in southern states. Avoid nematode damage by growing your plants in containers or raised beds filled with a sterile potting soil, or sterilize your own by baking batches of topsoil in a deep, disposable aluminum roasting dish. Rich, compost-amended soils also deter nematodes.

Sunscald is a pale discoloration that can occur on the side of medium-size and large-fruited tomatoes, making them inedible. It is caused by exposure to too much sun, especially when the plants have insufficient foliage cover. To prevent sunscald, do not prune your tomato vines, and when tying to a stake, ensure some foliage shades the fruit clusters.

These are some of the varieties I recommend (the days-to-maturity figure begins on the day you set out 6- to 8-week-old transplants):

'Better Boy VFN Hybrid' (75 days) is a tall-growing derivative of the famous 'Big Boy' hybrid tomato but with added disease and nematode resistance. The large fruit of this variety can weigh up to 1 pound each. Charles H. Wilbur, an Alabama gardener, holds the world's record yield for a tomato plant—342 pounds. He has also grown the plants to exceed 25 feet high. He grew 1,368 pounds of fruit from just four plants. The fruits are smooth and round and have a meaty texture and good flavor. The original 'Big Boy' tomato was developed by the late Dr. Oved Shifriss at Burpee Seeds, while 'Better Boy' was produced by Petoseed using 'Big Boy' as a parent.

'Big Rainbow' (75 days) is a vining heirloom variety that is also known as 'Striped German' and may also be the same as 'Pineapple' and 'Flame' since they are all alike—with fruits weighing up to 3 pounds each and a yellow skin with red stripes. Slice through the center and the interior is also yellow, with red marbling. It's a meaty, fine-flavored variety that looks good sliced onto a salad plate.

'Celebrity' (72 days). It's not easy for a tomato to win an All-America award because it has to do well in a wide range of locations, from the Northeast and Northwest to the South and Southwest. 'Celebrity', a determinate hybrid, made it because of its handsome good looks (large globe shape), broad range of disease resistance, sweet meaty flavor, and productivity. Slice through it and you will see it is almost all meat with very few seeds and as red as red can be. Probably more home gardeners now grow 'Celebrity' than any other large tomato.

'Early Cascade Hybrid' (60 days) produces high yields of medium-size round fruits the size of a billiard ball, perfectly suited for cutting into wedges for salad. The scarlet red fruits are produced in clusters of six or more that hang down the tall-growing plants like a curtain. The vigorous vines will continue cropping into fall with continuous production after other tomato varieties have exhausted themselves.

'Paul Robeson' (70 days). Heirloom maroon tomatoes, such as 'Black Krim', 'Black Russian', and 'Black from Tula', come from Russia. They look alike and may even be the same variety. 'Paul Robeson' is a large, dark maroon variety that also came from Russia in a seed exchange, named for the American singer and civil rights advocate by Ukrainian farmers who wished to honor him for his visit to Russia championing the rights of oppressed groups in the country.

Born in Princeton, New Jersey, Robeson was a remarkably gifted person. A stage and screen actor with 11 movies to his credit and a charismatic speaker, Robeson was also a star athlete, particularly in professional football and basketball. The tomato named for him is a beauty: The large, smooth-skinned dark maroon fruits occur on indeterminate vines and can weigh almost a pound. They have a meaty, rich flavor, especially when sliced thin and eaten raw.

'Polbig' (62 days). A problem with many early-ripening large tomatoes is poor flavor. That's not the case with 'Polbig', a tomato from Poland that can produce big, red, juicy, ripe tomatoes by the Fourth of July. The round, smooth, deep red fruits are meaty and delicious, up to 1 pound each. Plants are vining and will yield all season until fall frost.

'Sun Gold' (58 days). The race is on to produce sweeter and sweeter tomatoes, following the phenomenal success of 'Sun Gold', a cherry-type golden yellow tomato from Japan. In my garden, 'Sun Gold' is the earliest to ripen of any tomato, and its sweetness is not sickly or cloying but delicious and juicy. The shiny round tomatoes hang in generous clusters, with up to a dozen fruits per stem and dozens of stem clusters hanging down the main stalk like a curtain—a total of a thousand fruits from a single vine.

'Burpee's Supersteak Hybrid' (72 days) is a remarkable giant-fruited vining tomato with perfectly smooth, almost-round fruits that can grow as big as a grapefruit. The fruits contain few seeds, creating meaty, firm slices and a flavor superior to other giant-fruited tomatoes. Developed by the late Ted Torrey, vegetable breeder for Burpee Seeds, he gave credit to David Burpee for picking the parents that produced 'Supersteak'.

BE AWARE! No tomato is treated with more disdain than supermarket varieties, such as QualiT 21, BHN 444, and Hybrid 882. Out of season, those sold at the grocery store often come from faraway places like Mexico, Israel, and Holland (where they are grown under glass). They are picked at a preripe stage called mature green in order to withstand rough handling during shipment, and, in order to hasten its red-ripe color, the fruit is then gassed for 3 days with ethylene, a colorless flammable gas derived from petroleum. Growers argue that the gassing is harmless because ethylene is a natural hormone produced by many fruit varieties including apples, and it shouldn't compromise the fruit's flavor. However, it's hard to believe that an artificially ripened tomato has the same flavor as one that's picked at the peak of ripeness. In addition, the varieties used by growers are chosen for a number of reasons, such as ease of mechanical harvesting, tendency to ripen all at one time, and ability to ship well without bruising.

These are not the same criteria used to choose a variety to grow in a home garden.

Supermarket tomatoes often endure long periods of cold. They are invariably shipped with lettuce at its ideal storage temperature of 37°F. Moreover, many people store tomatoes in the crisper section of the refrigerator, but as soon as the temperature drops below 55°F, a tomato stops ripening. A better place to store a tomato is at room temperature to allow it to ripen fully.

Occasionally in magazines and newspapers you will see advertised "the Amazing Tree Tomato" with an illustration showing a housewife on a short stepladder reaching up to gather tomatoes. In some of these advertisements, the product advertised is not a true tomato but a tamarillo, a small tropical, evil-smelling tree that produces oval red fruit with a sour yellow or orange interior. This plant generally requires 11 months of frost-free weather to ripen its fruit, and you wouldn't want to eat it raw. Its main use is as a salad dressing—like lemons, you would squeeze the fruit over lettuce. There is a genuine tomato-flavored tomato called 'The Tree', also known as 'Trip-L-Crop', which can grow to a bushy, treelike height and bear large tomatoes. This variety is worth growing, but the tamarillo is not, since it's suitable only for Zones 10 and 11 in the United States and then only as a substitute for lemon juice.

Different parts of the country favor different varieties. 'Florida 47', for example, is a tomato grown in Zone 10 during winter because it tolerates sandy soil and takes humid heat better than other varieties. 'Oregon Spring' is favored for the Pacific Northwest, where it tolerates cool summers and a maritime climate better than other kinds.

High-Nutrition Tomatoes

As soon as the health benefits of eating tomatoes became known, plant breeders began seeking varieties with high lycopene content for their antioxidant cancer-fighting properties and ability to promote healthy cell growth with high beta-carotene content and high vitamin A. The first of these was 'Caro-Rich', a scarlet orange variety especially high in beta-carotene, followed by 'Health Kick' (70 days), a red, high-lycopene variety from Burpee Seeds. Fruits are smooth, round, and produced in clusters on bushy plants that require no staking.

No grocery store tomato will give you as much nutrition as a garden-raised variety. According to the USDA, 100 grams of commercially raised tomatoes generally contain 30 percent less vitamin C, 30 percent less thiamin, 19 percent less niacin, and 62 percent less calcium than they did in the 1960s, plus they feature an undesirable 14 times increase in salt, mostly as a result of intensive chemical methods of propagation and varieties chosen for shipping qualities more than flavor.

There is a huge interest in heirloom tomato varieties, largely because they come in a wide range of shapes, colors, maturity times, and flavors. Since there are thousands of heirlooms (many with several names), a good way to check for flavor is to do an Internet search and see what other people think of a particular variety.

A tomato discussion could go on and on, but I'd like to add a few more tomatoes to my avoidance list: 'Sulpice' has poor flavor. All currant tomatoes, including 'Red Currant', 'Yellow Currant', 'Mexico Midget', 'Sweet Pea', and 'Golden Midget', are not worth growing since they are too small to impart a satisfying flavor and none can compare to the sweetness of the cherry-size 'Sun Gold'. All cream-colored and white tomatoes, such as 'Snowball' and 'Cream Sausage', have a watered-down flavor and look unappetizing on a salad plate. Neither 'Ponderosa Red' nor 'Ponderosa Pink' are as good as 'Delicious', which is a selection of 'Ponderosa Red'. All "cavern" tomatoes, such as 'Striped Cavern', are not worth space, since they are hollow like a pepper and have none of the crispness and flavor of a red bell pepper. 'Soldacki' from Poland develops ugly corrugated fruit and is highly susceptible to cracking. 'Cherokee Purple' ripens too late for Northern gardeners and needs a long Southern summer to develop a decent flavor.

Many of the tomatoes I avoid recommending are heirlooms. Most heirlooms give poor yields compared to modern home garden varieties. However, the yields of even worthwhile heirloom varieties like 'Brandywine' can be increased up to 10 times by choosing transplants that have been grafted onto a special rootstock. You can buy the grafts ready for transplanting or you can buy the rootstock and make the graft yourself on any heirloom of your choosing. Johnny's Selected Seeds sells the rootstocks and also instructions on how to make the grafts, which is not complicated.

PLANT PROFILE

ZONES: 5–9 as a summer and fall crop; 10–11 as a winter and spring crop

PROPAGATION: By seed started indoors 8 weeks before outdoor planting after frost danger

PLANTING: At least 2 feet apart in rows spaced 3 feet apart in full sun, using stakes to hold the vines erect

PESTS AND DISEASES: See above. Blossom-end rot, sunscald, blight, nematodes, and anthracnose are the main problems.

PERFECT PARTNERS: Cucumbers, eggplant, peppers, and tomatillos

Turnips

For extra-earliness and sweetest flavor, choose
'Tokyo Cross' that goes from seed to harvest in just 40 days.

GROW THIS! 'Purple Top White Globe', 'Tokyo Cross', and 'Just Right'

A loose soil, regular watering, and adequate spacing are needed to grow delicious turnips. Not many people would associate a turnip with sweetness, but a new family of golf ball–size white turnips by Japanese breeders has improved the flavor of turnips significantly from the tennis ball–size 'Purple Top White Globe' (an old favorite) and baseball-size turnip substitutes like rutabaga (also called Swede turnips). The all-white 'Tokyo Cross' from Takii Seeds is best harvested when it's the size of a golf ball. It won an All-America Selections award for its unique combination of earliness (40 days) and its moist, sweet flavor when cooked (they're best when steamed whole until tender). Takii also produced an All-American Selections award-winning turnip named 'Just Right' that's round, all-white, sweeter than 'Purple Top White Globe', and best harvested when the size of a tennis ball.

Sow turnip seed thinly in a broad row, thinning plants to stand at least 2 inches apart. Plants relish cool nights and tolerate mild frosts and are best grown as an early spring crop or for a fall harvest. All turnips store for long periods in the crisper section of a refrigerator, and the tops are edible as cooked greens. Indeed, nonbulbing varieties that are popular in southern states have been specially bred for their tender tops, sold as turnip greens. You'll find turnips in purple, white, red, and yellow.

BE AWARE! 'Gilfeather' is the name of a white turnip with green shoulders

that was bred in Vermont, and occasionally it is offered in seed catalogs. I tried it one year and found it mostly produced misshapen roots. I also considered its flavor inferior to Japanese turnips and the traditional favorite 'Purple Top White Globe'.

Speaking of 'Purple Top White Globe', some catalogs offer 'Purple Top Milan', which has the same coloration but a flattened shape. It looks attractive, but there's more good eating in the globe version.

PLANT PROFILE

ZONES: 5–8 as a summer and fall crop; 9–11 as a winter and spring crop

PROPAGATION: By seed direct-sown

PLANTING: At least 2 inches apart in a block planting with 8 inches between rows in full sun

PESTS AND DISEASES: Wireworms and flea beetles

PERFECT PARTNERS: Beets, carrots, celeriac, radishes, and rutabaga

Watermelons

'Yellow Baby' is early, supersweet, and almost seedless, requiring no pollinator to set fruit.

GROW THIS! 'Yellow Baby', 'Shiny Boy', 'Sweet Favorite', 'Sangria', 'Harvest Moon', and 'Crimson Sweet'

Watermelons are native to the arid Kalahari Desert, where they grow in sandy soil under a merciless sun, so the trick to growing good watermelons is to duplicate that environment—with as much direct sun as possible and a sandy or loam soil that is covered with black plastic to heat it up and keep it warm. With modern watermelon hybrids, aim for high soil fertility and regular watering to ensure full-size fruit, deep red color, and a middle that's solid and not hollow.

In addition to open-pollinated and hybrid red-fleshed watermelons, there are orange- and yellow-fleshed varieties (the Chinese pay premium prices for yellow-fleshed watermelons because they value their sweetness). The best of the yellows for US conditions was bred in a high-elevation region in Taiwan by Known-You Seed Company. It's an ice-box watermelon with a compact, round size called 'Yellow Baby', and it won an All-America Selections award for its earliness (70 days), sweetness, and low number of seeds (50 percent fewer than a regular ice-box watermelon like 'Sugar Baby'). Known-You more recently produced a red version of 'Yellow Baby', called 'Shiny Boy'. Similar in size and appearance to 'Sugar Baby', it is earlier and sweeter, and like 'Yellow Baby', it contains considerably fewer seeds.

Most northern gardeners prefer to grow the small ice-box watermelons because the larger oblong types like 'Jubilee' require too long a growing season. However, the All-America Selections winner and full-size watermelon 'Sweet Favorite', from Sakata Seeds, requires no more growing time than many ice-box watermelons.

There are two kinds of supersweet watermelons: a class called all-sweets, which contain seeds, and another class called seedless watermelons that may contain some edible, sterile white seeds and sometimes a few fertile black seeds. The leading variety among the all-sweets is 'Sangria'. It is the supreme standard for eating quality. The interior flesh is dark red, and the oblong fruits are striped dark green on a light green background. 'Sangria' is a hybrid, and nothing among open-pollinated watermelons can touch it for flavor and high yields. This is usually the seeded watermelon you'll see at grocery stores and farm stands alike.

A common question about seedless watermelons is "How is it possible to obtain seed of a seedless watermelon?" Most hybrid watermelons are diploids, but seedless watermelons are triploids (meaning they have triple the number of chromosomes). It's like crossing a jackass onto a mare to obtain a mule. The jackass is the male parent and the mare the female parent, and their progeny result in a sterile hybrid. It's the same with seedless watermelons—you have two parents but the offspring (the seed) is sterile. When you purchase a packet of seedless watermelon seed, you will find that the male is dyed a special color so the male parent can be recognized. To ensure that your planting produces a seedless variety, plant three female seeds for every one male seed, allowing bees to transfer pollen from the male to the females. You need a lot of space to grow a crop of seedless watermelons, and of all the vegetable fruits to grow, they are the most challenging. The results are worth your time, however; since a seeded watermelon can contain 1,000 seeds that can interfere with eating pleasure, and since spoilage occurs first around the seeds, you'll see why the seedless watermelons—with their tasty flesh and longer shelf life—are highly prized.

The first seedless watermelons were developed by a Japanese breeder, Dr. H. Kihara, in 1951, and his work was improved upon by an American breeder, the late Dr. Orie J. Eigsti, after Kihara's death. Eigsti's discovery that the drug colchicine, derived from a plant, could change the number of chromosomes in watermelons and was used to develop the first commercially successful seedless watermelon, 'Tri-X 313'. It's still the leading variety for sweetness, redness, and firm-fleshed consistency. He formed the American Seedless Watermelon Corporation in 1954 to supply the world with seed of his seedless watermelons. Unfortunately, home gardeners can no longer grow 'Tri-X 313' because the growing rights have been assigned to a select number of commercial growers who supply the nation's grocery stores.

However, there are a number of seedless watermelons suitable for home gardeners, notably 'Harvest Moon', the only seedless watermelon to win an All-America award. Weighing 18 to 20 pounds each, the round fruits are similar in appearance to the heirloom variety 'Moon & Stars', with a dark green skin covered in yellow spots that resemble a constellation of stars, and pink flesh. Not only is 'Harvest Moon' a sweeter flavor than 'Moon & Stars', but it is also earlier by 2 weeks (80 days compared to 100 days for 'Moon & Stars'). And because of its hybrid vigor, 'Harvest Moon' is higher yielding than 'Moon & Stars'.

When you're buying watermelon seed for commercial production, most suppliers now will ask you to sign a waiver that states they will not be responsible if you experience a crop failure due to watermelon blotch disease. This is because some South Carolina growers lost millions of dollars, claimed the disease occurred through contaminated seed, and sued the seed suppliers. Although most watermelon seed sold for commercial production is tested for the seed-borne disease, seed suppliers now take the precaution of requiring a waiver. The waiver is not required from home gardeners.

Be aware that some watermelons are regional in popularity. Florida, for example, is considered the best place in the United States to grow watermelons because of its long, hot summers, sandy soil, and frequent summer downpours. Florida, Texas, and Arizona are locales where home gardeners grow the monstrous open-pollinated 'Carolina Cross' (95 days), which holds the world's record for heaviest watermelon at 262 pounds.

BE AWARE! For a good analysis of heirloom watermelon varieties, I recommend Amy Goldman's book *Melons for the Passionate Grower*.

Interestingly, South Carolina State University conducted a taste test of modern and heirloom varieties, and hybrids won on flavor. Actually, two tests were made on the same varieties, one with the group blindfolded and the other with the blindfolds off. Blindfolded, the variety 'Crimson Sweet' won for sweetest flavor, but when the blindfolds were removed, seedless watermelons won for sweetest flavor.

The popular open-pollinated heirloom variety 'Moon & Stars' was recently used by All-America Selections to judge the benefits of a new look-alike seedless hybrid variety named 'Harvest Moon'—which proved to be heavier yielding, earlier by 2 weeks, and more sweetly flavored.

Other watermelons to avoid for poor flavor or too many seeds include 'Golden Midget' (small and seedy with golden skin but red flesh), 'Petite Yellow' (small size, pale yellow flesh, and poor flavor), and 'Citron', which has no flavor but can be used to make watermelon pickles.

Of course, when you're judging any watermelon, it must be picked at peak of ripeness. When picked too early, even the sweetest watermelons will lack flavor; when picked too late, they will taste like wet sawdust. For perfect ripeness, rap the skin with your knuckle. If it sounds like tapping your forehead (a dull sound), it is probably underripe; if it sounds like tapping your chest (a soft sound), it is probably overripe; if it sounds like tapping your knuckles (a ringing sound), then it is most likely ripe. Also look for the tendril closest to the fruit; if it is shriveled, that's a sign of ripeness.

 ## PLANT PROFILE

ZONES: 6–9 as a summer crop; 10 and 11 as a winter and early spring crop

PROPAGATION: By seed direct-sown after frost danger

PLANTING: At least 3 feet apart in rows spaced 3 feet apart, allowing vines to knit together, in full sun

PESTS AND DISEASES: Crows pecking into the immature fruit; anthracnose and fusarium wilt, for which there are resistant varieties

PERFECT PARTNERS: Cantaloupes, cucumbers, summer and winter squashes, and sweet potatoes

CHAPTER 6

BEST CHOICE ANNUALS

More annuals are sold at garden centers in spring than any other ornamental plant, including perennials, bulbs, and flowering woody plants. Because annuals produce the brightest colors in the plant kingdom, most germinate rapidly from seed and flower quickly, and many of them are everblooming, flowering nonstop until killed by frost or simply expiring from exhaustion.

When confronted with annuals at a garden center (usually flowering in six-packs) or presented in the pages of a seed catalog, it is often difficult to decide which varieties to grow. You can ask garden center personnel or try to contact customer service at a seed or nursery company, but often you must deal with temporary help who are not always qualified to provide an unbiased answer.

I feel qualified to guide you through variety selection of annuals because I conduct my own trials of annuals at my test gardens in Pennsylvania and Florida. I've visited hundreds of other test gardens, such as those conducted by Penn State University, and invariably I attend the California Pack Trials (also known as the California Spring Trials), where leading plant breeders display their introductions for evaluation.

It is not always easy among annuals to advise you what *not* to plant, because some of the poorer-performing annuals, like 'Rainbow Mixed Colors' coleus, 'Crackerjack' marigolds, and 'Thumbelina' zinnias, were bred to sell cheaply through mass-merchandising outlets, and so the old adage "You get what you pay for" applies. However, irrespective of how cheap a seed or plant is, my aim here is to advise you on varieties that are most likely to provide satisfaction and maximum enjoyment.

The following section of most popular annuals for garden display includes some biennials that have been turned into annuals by plant breeders, and also some perennials that have been annualized by breeders. These are the varieties you'll most commonly find displayed as transplants in garden centers during early spring and find available as seed from both seed catalogs and on the Internet.

PLANT CHARACTERISTICS

Throughout this chapter and the one that follows, these symbols identify a special benefit or preference for each plant. These attributes represent the main reasons why home gardeners choose annuals.

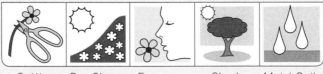

Cutting   Dry Slopes   Fragrance   Shade   Moist Soils

Asters, China

China asters make superb cut flowers, especially the long-stemmed varieties like 'Matsumoto' that have resistance to aster yellows disease.

GROW THIS! 'Matsumoto' and 'Serenade'

China asters make one of the finest cut flowers for indoor arrangements. The daisylike heads can be single like a Shasta daisy or doubled (two or more layers of petals). There are small button-size kinds called pompon asters, medium-size powder-puff kinds like the old-fashioned 'Crego', and large-flowered varieties such as 'Ostrich Plume' with reflexed petals and flower heads up to 6 inches across. The basic color range for China asters is red, pink, white, blue, and purple. There are dwarf varieties suitable for edging flowerbeds, but the long-stemmed varieties are the more desirable because a single plant in peak bloom can be cut at the soil line to create an instant bouquet. They can bloom for about 6 weeks in summer and have only one major fault—they are susceptible to a disfiguring disease called aster yellows spread by leafhopper insects.

The disease is so pervasive that it is inadvisable to grow asters in the same place twice, for if they avoid the disease the first season, they are likely to suffer from it in the second. Symptoms include a yellowing of the leaves and flower head and then a complete collapse of the entire plant.

Professional growers of asters for the cut-flower market grow the variety called 'Matsumoto' from Sakata Seeds. As with chrysanthemum breeding, the Japanese have always been leaders in aster breeding, and the 'Matsumoto' series grows masses of powder-puff flower heads with yellow centers on long stems up to 4 feet high. They have moderate resistance to aster yellows disease.

In addition to double-flowered asters, every cutting garden should feature a single or semidouble variety so the yellow button center is exposed and the flowers are more like daisies. 'Serenade' is an excellent 3-feet-tall mixture that includes singles and semidoubles in red, rose pink, crimson, deep blue, light blue, white, and maroon.

BE AWARE!
There are many dwarf varieties of asters suitable for edging beds and borders like 'Dwarf Queen' and 'Pot 'n Patio', but these are not long lived and look lost compared to taller kinds, blooming for only a short period

before turning brown in the heat. Stick with asters with long, strong stems suitable for cutting. They'll delight much more than the low, compact varieties.

 ## PLANT PROFILE

KNOWN BOTANICALLY AS: *Callistephus chinensis*

ZONES: All zones as a summer annual; winter flowering in Zones 9–11

PROPAGATION: By seed direct-sown or started 6 weeks before outdoor planting

SPACING: 12 inches apart in full sun

PESTS AND DISEASES: Mostly aster yellows and powdery mildew. Avoid planting in the same place twice.

PERFECT PARTNERS: Celosia, cosmos, marigolds, strawflowers, and zinnias

---

Begonias, Wax

Wax begonias are everblooming tender annuals useful for edging and for mass displays; try the larger-flowered variety named 'Big'.

GROW THIS! 'Cocktail' series, 'Big' Red with Bronze Leaf, 'Big' Red with Green Leaf, 'Dragon Wing', 'Bada Bing', and 'Bada Boom'

Benary is an old, established German seed company that has been responsible for some milestone breeding achievements among annuals and perennials, most notably for a strain of hybrid wax begonias called 'Tausandschone', meaning "thousand wonders." Growing just 10 inches high, they were good for sun or light shade, tolerated hot summers, and bloomed nonstop. In spite of their success and astonishing ability to bloom all season, they have been superseded by improved varieties, notably by the 'Cocktail' series, also bred by Benary. Although the pink, red, or white flowers on some varieties of wax begonias are individually small, they are crowded together so thickly on low-mounded plants that they create a bold splash of color. The foliage can be bronze or green. Ideal for massing in containers such as window boxes, hybrid wax begonias are also used for massed bedding in flowerbeds and borders, usually in a mix of colors.

Benary followed up the success of the 'Cocktail' series with yet another improvement—their 'Big' series that includes the color combinations red with a bronze leaf, red with a green leaf, and rose pink with a bronze leaf. Plants branch freely, and the amazing 3-inch-wide flowers create a column of color, planted in full sun or light shade. A competing variety is the 'Dragon Wing' series (from Burpee and Pan American Seed), with similar-size flowers and decorative pointed foliage shaped like a wing.

Another outstanding wax begonia series to intensify mass bedding displays is 'Bada Bing', a green-leaf series, and 'Bada Boom', a bronze-leaf series. Plants bloom within 11 weeks from seed and remain free flowering all summer until fall frost. The scarlet in both the green and bronze versions is particularly striking—the color so rich, it's like a flow of molten lava.

Unfortunately, garden centers rarely label wax begonias with a variety name and rely more on their pack appearance on the sales bench for impulse sales. Absent a label, look for wax begonias with big, bright colors and clean foliage.

Begonia seed requires light to germinate. The seed is tiny and should be simply pressed into the potting medium just to anchor it.

BE AWARE! Choose carefully when buying transplants from the sales bench. Stressed wax begonias can take a long time to recover. In particular, look for scorch marks on the leaves indicating irregular watering. They will bloom best in a peat-rich soil that remains relatively cool, so always cover the base of your begonias with an organic mulch such as shredded leaves or pine straw, which keeps the soil from overheating. Avoid using black plastic. See page 214 for a description of the seed-grown annual tuberous begonias.

PLANT PROFILE

KNOWN BOTANICALLY AS: *Begonia semperflorens*

ZONES: All zones as a warm-season annual; winter flowering in Zones 9–11

PROPAGATION: By seed started indoors 11 weeks before outdoor planting after frost danger. Barely cover with potting soil, as seed needs light to germinate.

SPACING: 12 inches apart in sun or light shade

PESTS AND DISEASES: None serious, just the usual slugs and other chewing insects

PERFECT PARTNERS: Coleus, French marigolds, impatiens, and ornamental kale

Black-Eyed Susans

The earliest everblooming annual
black-eyed Susan, 'Tiger Eye' is an
American-bred American native.

GROW THIS! 'Rustic Dwarfs', 'Tiger Eye', 'Prairie Sun', 'Cherokee Sunset', and 'Chim Chiminee'

Many plants are commonly called black-eyed Susans, but the native American hardy perennial prairie plant *Rudbeckia hirta* is the most deserving of the name. Black-eyed Susan, with its orange flowers with black button centers, is a common sight throughout the waysides of North America. It is from the wild kinds that plant breeders developed a popular free-flowering perennial variety 'Goldsturm' (German for "goldstorm"), and Burpee Seeds introduced an annual form, commonly called gloriosa daisies. 'Goldsturm' is so free flowering because its flowers are sterile and do not expend energy setting seed. Gloriosa daisies, however, have proven to be so easy to grow from seed that it is possible to scatter the seed on top of snow and expect it to germinate by dropping between cracks in the soil after the snow is melted.

The annual form of black-eyed Susan presents a spectacular display in midsummer, blooming riotously for several months and producing flowers up to three times the size of wayside black-eyed Susans. Some varieties have flowers up to 6 inches across, not only in the common orange but also in yellow, gold, rusty red, and maroon, plus bicolors. Moreover, there are golden yellow varieties with green button centers rather than black, such as 'Prairie Sun' with yellow petals and a vibrant orange zone around its green eye.

A common problem with traditional black-eyed Susans is that their tall stature makes them susceptible to wind damage, so many breeders set their sights on more compact plants. For many years, the variety 'Marmalade' from British breeder Ralph Gould was supreme. An orange flower with a black eye, it became popular for massed bedding displays and containers, blooming for 6 weeks in midsummer. This was followed by a mixture called 'Rustic Dwarfs' by the same breeder, containing mostly yellow and orange flowers with dark zones. An improvement over 'Marmalade' with its 6-week bloom period is the earlier, longer-blooming 'Tiger Eye', developed by Todd Perkins at Syngenta

Flowers. An All-America Selections award winner, it has good mildew resistance, and the plants are self-cleaning of spent blooms (meaning they cover faded blooms with fresh foliage and flower buds)—known humorously as "burying their dead." As many as 50 blooms can be open at any one time on a single plant. The 4-inch-wide blooms are a dazzling golden orange with a prominent dark brown button center.

Give 'Tiger Eye' at least 15-inch spacing so it can branch sideways and grow into its neighbor. It's terrific in containers, since the bushy plants grow to just 24 inches high. Allow at least 11 weeks from seeding to transplanting and first blooms. When buying nursery-grown potted plants for transplanting, pinch out the lead flower bud or bloom to encourage side branching. Use 'Tiger Eye' strictly as an annual. For perennial performance, grow 'Goldsturm'.

BE AWARE! Some annual black-eyed Susans have dark, all-maroon flowers that are okay in mixtures and when used for cutting, but they seem to recede into the background when planted alone. They do not make nearly the impact of the brighter yellow and orange varieties. For my taste, the double forms don't impress as much as the singles, with the exception of 'Cherokee Sunset' and the quilled 'Chim Chiminee'. A Burpee variety, 'Irish Eyes', used to be the only gloriosa daisy with a green button center, but its petals are plain yellow while 'Prairie Sun' has a golden zone inside the yellow, making it even more alluring in the landscape.

 ## PLANT PROFILE

KNOWN BOTANICALLY AS: *Rudbeckia* hybrid

ZONES: All zones as a summerlong, warm-season annual; winter flowering in Zones 9–11

PROPAGATION: By seed direct-sown or started 6 weeks before outdoor planting

SPACING: 12 inches apart in full sun

PESTS AND DISEASES: Mostly carefree, except for Japanese beetles

PERFECT PARTNERS: Cosmos, marigolds, sunflowers, and zinnias

Calendulas

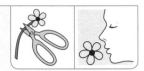

Valued for its early spring flowers and
spicy fragrance, 'Flashback' offers petals
with a unique metallic sheen.

GROW THIS! 'Calypso', 'Zen', 'Bon Bon', and 'Flashback'

Even though calendulas come from arid regions of North Africa, they are hardy,
cool-season plants that are often planted as companions to pansies. The daisylike flowers can be 3 inches across in orange, gold, yellow, and apricot, some
with appealing black centers. Plants grow bushy and may produce 30 or more
flowers fully open at any one time. The leaves and stems have a spicy fragrance,
and the edible petals are often sprinkled over omelets and mixed salads to provide a decorative touch. Commonly called pot marigolds, they are suitable for
containers and have stems long enough for cutting. When choosing varieties,
decide whether you want a tall kind like 'Calypso' for cutting or a short, bushy
mixture like 'Zen' for low bedding. If you like your blooms with black centers,
choose 'Bon Bon' (12 inches high) and 'Calypso' (18 inches) over 'Gitano', since
they bloom 10 days earlier.

Most calendulas have petals with solid colors, but a unique variety called
'Flashback' has a burgundy underside to the clear petals, giving the flowers a
unique metallic sheen. This makes them distinctive and especially appealing as
a cut flower.

Calendulas thrive in full sun and need good drainage. Flowering may dwin-
dle during the heat of summer, but if plants are cut back to almost the soil line,
fresh new growth will sprout to ensure a repeat bloom for fall. The plants tolerate mild frosts.

BE AWARE! There are many calendula mixtures available, mostly in clear
colors. An old variety, 'Radio' (24 inches high), is variable (some of the flowers
are small and others semidouble and crested). It used to be a popular mixture,
but I believe home gardeners today want their calendulas with a distinctive
brown center and uniformity of size, as you will expect from a variety like the
very popular 'Bon Bon' or 'Flashback', with its shimmering petals.

Carnations

When multicolored 'Can Can' starts to bloom, keep cutting to stimulate a continuous floral display.

GROW THIS! 'Can Can Cocktail Party'

Carnations are treasured for their delightful fragrance and long stems for cutting. Thousands of acres of special long-stemmed "perpetual flowering" carnations are grown under glass in Holland to supply the florist trade. They are produced in myriad colors, including all shades of red and pink plus purple, yellow, white, maroon, and bicolors, where the petal tips are rimmed with white.

The variety 'Can Can' was developed by Sakata Seeds, and 'Scarlet Can Can' not only won an All-America Selections award for its large flowers, basal-branching habit, and long-lasting garden display, but it also received a gold medal from Fleuroselect. More recently, Sakata has offered the long-awaited 'Cocktail' mixture (it invariably takes a while for a breeder to obtain enough colors to make a desirable mixture), and what a delight it is with its scented blooms. As many as 50 blooms will open all at one time on a single plant, and the more you pick them for arrangements, the more the plant is stimulated into producing new flower buds.

Carnations like full sun and a sandy soil for good drainage. In heavy clay soils, the crown may rot. They are a cool-season annual that likes to be transplanted in bud for a springtime display that lasts well into summer.

BE AWARE! For years, an open-pollinated mixture called 'Chabaud Giants' has been the leading variety for garden display, but they can make an untidy mess when the too-tall stems become heavy with rain or wind plays havoc with them. They don't have nearly the vigor or flowering longevity of hybrids like 'Can Can'. Another carnation variety with limited garden potential is the 'Lillipot' series. These grow just 8 to 10 inches high and look sensational on the display bench at the garden center, but they have been specially bred for pot culture as gift plants. The stems are simply not long enough to look good in the garden or for cutting.

 ## PLANT PROFILE

KNOWN BOTANICALLY AS: *Dianthus caryophyllus*

ZONES: 4–8 for early summer flowering; 9–11 for winter bloom

PROPAGATION: By seed started 8 weeks before outdoor planting. Plants are also propagated from division and stem cuttings.

SPACING: 12 inches apart in full sun

PESTS AND DISEASES: Root rot from poor drainage

PERFECT PARTNERS: Calendula, columbine, dwarf phlox, snapdragon, and sweet William

Celosias

For something completely different in cut flowers, grow shimmering pink 'Flamingo Feather'. And for the future, look for multicolored mixes with spiky flower plumes that resemble stalks of wheat.

GROW THIS! 'Century Mixed Colors', 'Chief', and 'Flamingo Feather'

There are three types of celosia popular in home gardens—the kind with feathery flower spikes (*Celosia argentea* Plumosa Group); those with flower heads resembling brain coral, commonly called crested cockscomb (*C. argentea* Cristata Group); and a third resembling wheatgrass (*C. argentea* Spicata Group).

Plumed celosia 'Century' type features handsome pyramid-shaped flower plumes.

Crested celosia shows how its high, ribbed flower clusters form a cockscomb shape, hence its common name.

One company—Sakata Seeds of Japan—has made the breeding of both plumosa and cristata types a specialty, and their introduction called 'Century Mixed Colors', with vibrant silky red, pink, yellow, and orange plumes, is so superior it won an All-America Selections award.

What the judges liked about the 'Century' series is the tall spirelike feathery clusters compared to other varieties and the ability of the plant to branch sideways. Also, the stems are long enough for cutting.

Among cockscomb types, the 'Chief' series is popular with home gardeners. With a color range similar to the feathery 'Century' series, the flower heads of 'Chief' are almost globular. Also consider planting the distinctly different *C. spicata* 'Flamingo Feather', with its myriad shimmering, spire-shaped flowers on long stems suitable for cutting. Among crested cockscombs, I also like to choose those with long stems for dramatic arrangements.

Plants are easy to grow, even direct-seeded into the garden, flowering in 80 days. Provide full sun and good drainage.

BE AWARE! Sakata tells me they sell more of the variety 'Kimono' than any other celosia, but that is because it flowers early on dwarf plants and looks good in the pack. I do not recommend it for garden display, though it can look good in patio containers. Some other dwarf cockscomb kinds that I do not recommend for garden display or cutting (because the foliage and stems are too compact) include the feathery 'Glow' series and spiky 'Kosmo' series. In general, the feathered celosias look more appealing massed in beds and borders than the cockscomb kinds.

 ## PLANT PROFILE

KNOWN BOTANICALLY AS: *Celosia argentea*

ZONES: 5–8 for summer bloom; 9–11 for winter and spring flowering

PROPAGATION: By seed direct-sown or started 6 weeks before outdoor planting after frost danger

SPACING: 12 inches apart in full sun

PESTS AND DISEASES: Mostly chewing insects such as slugs, greenfly, and Japanese beetles

PERFECT PARTNERS: Coleus for sun, marigolds, strawflowers, and zinnias

Coleus

Famous for its multicolored foliage and shade tolerance, the huge leaves of 'Kong' will be the envy of your neighborhood.

GROW THIS! 'Wizard', 'Kong', 'Trusty Rusty', 'Solar', and 'Fishnet Stockings'

Coleus is one of the best plant families for shade, since the leaves compare with flower colors in visual impact. What few people realize is that newer varieties are also suitable for planting in full sun. Native mostly to the jungles of Java, coleus is actually a tender perennial best treated as a tender annual.

Many varieties—especially older kinds—have a tendency to bolt to seed quickly and look weedy unless constantly deadheaded. An improvement is the 'Wizard' mixture, with a basal-branching habit and small, late flowers (if it flowers at all).

A series called 'Kong', introduced by Pan American Seeds, has extremely large leaves up to 6 inches across. Plants grow to 2 feet high, and one plant can fill a whiskey half barrel. 'Kong Rose' is an outstanding color combination: Its scalloped edge is chartreuse, while the leaf veins are mahogany and the center is a rose pink. When Anna Ball, owner of Pan American Seed, invited me to inspect the company's trial gardens in West Chicago, she pointed to containers of the 'Kong' series and declared: " 'Kong' knocks the socks off all those little-leaf coleus with its monster-size leaves." Anna is also head of Ball FloraPlant, a division of Ball Horticultural that offers plants grown vegetatively (meaning from cuttings) to garden centers. When I remarked how 'Trusty Rusty' was my favorite coleus for its seasonlong color, she agreed: "The copper leaf outlined in yellow is distinctive. Though it's not a 'Kong', it's still a big-leaf plant and thrives in sun as well as shade."

In 1994, Hatchett Creek Farms of Gainesville, Florida, set off a breeding frenzy when they introduced their 'Solar' series of coleus suitable for growing in full sun. These were followed by other sun-loving coleus, notably from Proven Winners, who made a big hit with their black-and-white–leaved variety 'Fishnet Stockings'. Many independent breeders continue to work on coleus, the most active of which is Dr. Bob Bors, assistant professor of the plant sciences department at the University of Saskatchewan, Canada, specializing in coleus with bizarre leaf shapes.

Soil for coleus must be warm, well-drained, and high in organic matter. They are thirsty plants and show when they need watering by wilting. Seed of coleus is tiny and must be started 10 weeks before outdoor planting after all danger of frost.

BE AWARE! The old 'Rainbow' coleus mixture quickly bolts to seed and looks weedy unless constantly deadheaded. Also, it can be variable in its color range, producing more of one color than others. It has been generally superseded by basal-branching, slow-to-bolt varieties pioneered by the American plant breeder the late Claude Hope and other independent breeders.

PLANT PROFILE

KNOWN BOTANICALLY AS: *Stolenostemon scutellaroides* or *Coleus blumei*

ZONES: All zones as a house plant; Zones 3–11 oudoors; plants perennialize in Zones 10 and 11

PROPAGATION: By seed sown indoors 10 weeks before outdoor planting after frost danger; and from cuttings rooted in plain water

SPACING: 12 inches apart in light shade or full sun with special sun-loving varieties

PESTS AND DISEASES: Whitefly, especially when grown indoors

PERFECT PARTNERS: Begonias, impatiens, petunias for shady areas, and wishbone flower

Columbines

Normally a perennial, new 'Origami' columbine is a mixture that will bloom reliably spring through summer from a March planting.

GROW THIS! 'Swan' and 'Origami'

Columbine is a hardy perennial North American wildflower. Some columbines are native to the Rocky Mountains, and others grow in woodland and rock outcrops of the Appalachians. Burpee Seeds was the first to introduce an annual variety, 'McKana's Giants', named for a home gardener who developed them. Annual varieties of columbine have a unique flower form, like a granny's bonnet, with a spur (nectar tube) extending backward. The nodding flowers are clustered at the top of 3-foot stems and are ideal for cutting. They have only one drawback—the bloom period is relatively short, confined to the cool months of spring, and the seed requires starting at least 10 weeks ahead of outdoor planting.

What is extraordinary is that two separate US companies produced improvements in columbines within a short period of each other. Pan American introduced their 'Swan' series in a wide color range and in a similar height to

'McKana's Giants', but with a larger flower size and longer blooming period. Goldsmith introduced a hybrid form called 'Origami', which is more dwarf than the 'Swan' series and with an even-longer blooming period. For mass plantings in beds and borders and for containers, I favor 'Origami'.

Colors of both kinds include yellow, red, pink, blue, purple, and white, plus bicolors.

BE AWARE! With the introduction of the tall 'Swan' series and the more compact 'Origami' series, the old 'McKana's Giants' are obsolete though still available. In general, they tend to be too tall and delicate, without the color impact of the newer varieties. In a container planting, I also favor the 'Origami' over the 'Swan' series.

 ## PLANT PROFILE

KNOWN BOTANICALLY AS: *Aquilegia* hybrids

ZONES: 3–8 for spring and early summer bloom; 9–11 for winter flowering

PROPAGATION: By seed started indoors 10 weeks before outdoor planting

SPACING: 12 inches apart in sun or light shade

PESTS AND DISEASES: None serious, though susceptible to powdery mildew

PERFECT PARTNERS: Calendulas, carnations, dianthus, pansies, and snapdragons

Cottage Pinks

Fragrant 'Amazon Neon' outshines traditional cottage pinks with generous flower clusters on strong stems, ideal for cutting.

GROW THIS! 'Magic Charms', 'Telstar' hybrids, 'Floral Laced', 'Neon' series, and 'Melody' series

According to the book *The Brother Gardeners* about the introduction of American plant species into the United Kingdom, the first man-made hybrid flower was a

An All-America award winner for long-lasting flowering performance, 'Telstar' cottage pinks continues flowering during cool weather.

cross between a cottage pink and sweet William, both species of dianthus that don't normally mate in nature. Ever since, the cottage gardens of England have become famous for their collections of pinks (the smaller-flowered dianthus) and carnations (the larger-flowered fragrant kind). A large number of dianthus are low growing and cushion shaped, with myriad blooms that can almost completely hide the foliage. In some species, the foliage is mostly blue or gray, so that even when not in bloom, the plants can be decorative, especially as an edging.

'Magic Charms', a series of low-growing, cushion-shaped annuals in mostly shades of red and pink (plus white), was the winner of an All-America Selections award for its ability to flower continuously during cool weather. This was followed with an award for 'Telstar' hybrids, a mixture that contains more bicolors than 'Magic Charms' and also flowers freely during cool weather. Sweet William has always been a popular sweetly scented cut flower, but it is a biennial, requiring two seasons to bloom. A big appeal of sweet William has been its habit of forming clusters of bicolored flowers like a bouquet. The colors include red, pink, and white, most of them with a contrasting throat. 'Floral Laced' cottage pinks are a unique mixture; the petal tips are fringed to produce a delicate lacelike effect.

If I had room for only one dianthus, it would be the tall 'Neon' series from Pan American. The variety 'Rose Magic' received an Award of Garden Merit. It is a superb cut flower and similar to Sakata's 'Melody' series, especially the pink color that produces some white flowers as well as light pink and deep pink on the same plant. Both produce long stems (up to 18 inches) and are excellent for cutting. They will also come back as a perennial in subsequent years.

Dianthus varieties can be annual or perennial. Mostly native to Europe and Asia, they relish a neutral or slightly alkaline soil, making them an excellent choice for rock gardens and growing out of dry walls.

Dianthus tolerate light frost and can be planted out several weeks before the last frost date in spring and in fall, a week or two before Labor Day for flowering into winter months. From a spring planting, they flower freely until hot summer nights occur. Start seed at least 10 weeks before transplanting outdoors.

BE AWARE! Avoid the annual form of sweet William called 'Wee Willie'. Its color range is limited, and the too-short stems do not allow it to make a satisfying display compared to the newer sweet William hybrids like the 'Neon' or 'Melody' series. Most bedding-type dianthus are unsuitable for cutting, so check plant heights when making a purchase.

 ## PLANT PROFILE

KNOWN BOTANICALLY AS: *Dianthus* species and hybrids

ZONES: 3–8 for spring and summer flowering; 9–11 for winter and early spring flowering

PROPAGATION: By seed started indoors 8 weeks before outdoor planting

SPACING: 12 inches apart in full sun

PESTS AND DISEASES: Chewing insects like slugs and foraging animals like deer

PERFECT PARTNERS: Calendulas, columbine, pansies, snapdragons, and violas

Dahlias

Grow 'Kelvin Floodlight' for dinner-plate-size yellow blooms, and 'Park Princess' for an everblooming, knee-high border of vibrant, pink-quilled flowers.

GROW THIS! 'Goldalia', 'Harlequin', 'Kelvin Floodlight', 'Park Princess', 'She Devil', the 'Mystic' series, and 'Mystic' hybrids

There are two kinds of dahlia suitable for making a big splash in home gardens: seed grown and tuber grown. Dinner-plate dahlias have individual flowers up to 12 inches across. These must be grown from tubers planted in a sunny position

'Bishop of Llandaff' dahlia is a tall heirloom variety valued for its long bloom period from early summer to fall frost and its decorative bronze foliage.

and well-drained soil in spring after frost danger. The seed-grown kinds are sometimes called Unwin types, and they'll flower the first year if seed is started indoors 8 weeks before outdoor planting.

In my judgment, the biggest bang for the buck has to be from seed with the 'Goldalia' and similar 'Harlequin' series that impress gardeners because their scarlet, orange, pink, and yellow flowers have a contrasting white or yellow collar around an orange seed disk. This bicoloration makes them stand out better than dahlias in solid colors.

'Kelvin Floodlight' is one of the biggest dinner-plate varieties grown from sausage-shaped tubers, with fully double bright yellow flowers on succulent stems that need staking to grow to 6 feet high. 'Park Princess' is another outstanding tuberous dahlia; it's smaller than 'Kelvin Floodlight' and amazingly free flowering, with a deep pink bloom and pointed petals. This creates a compact, uniform hedge effect when planted as a border, growing to 2½ feet by the end of the season. 'She Devil' grows up to 4 feet tall and is a hot pink cactus-flowered dahlia suffused with yellow at the center. Tuber-grown 'Bishop of Llandaff' is 3 to 4 feet high and eye-catching with its scarlet red daisy-flowered dahlia flowers on long stems above shiny bronze leaves. The new 'Mystic' series bred by New Zealand breeder Keith Hammett is similar in appearance and habit to 'Bishop of Llandaff' with its handsome bronze foliage, but 'Mystic' offers a wider color range (including bicolors). These tuberous dahlias are excellent for cutting, although the stems must be plunged up to their necks in water immediately after cutting to prevent their wilting.

BE AWARE! I prefer not to fuss with most 'Unwin'-type bedding dahlias. It's just too tedious having to go over the plants every day or so to remove ugly, browned spent blooms so the low, bushy plants can remain attractive and continue flowering.

PLANT PROFILE

KNOWN BOTANICALLY AS: *Dahlia* hybrids

ZONES: 3–8 for summer flowering; 9–11 for winter blooms

PROPAGATION: By seed started 8 weeks before outdoor planting, and also by tubers for the dinner-plate varieties

SPACING: 12 inches for dwarf, compact varieties; 3 feet for dinner-plate varieties; all in full sun

PESTS AND DISEASES: Mostly chewing insects such as slugs, and wind damage if the tall kinds are not securely staked

PERFECT PARTNERS: Seed kinds look good planted with celosia, marigolds, and zinnias; tuberous kinds make good companions with cannas, cosmos, gladiolus, and Oriental lilies. Bronze-leaf kinds are sensational against a background of tall, silvery artemisia.

Daisies, African

For shimmering flowers in electric colors
with distinctive black eyes, you'll rave about the 'Ravers'.

GROW THIS! 'Ravers' series, 'Zulu Prince', and 'Garden Gerbera'

A number of daisies native to South Africa are commonly called African daisies, including the botanical genera *Arctotis* (the original African daisy), *Dimorphotheca* (Cape daisy), and *Gerbera* (also called Transvaal daisy). One of the most memorable plant-finding trips I made was to South Africa in September (their springtime) to see the mass flowering of thousands of wildflowers northwest of Cape Town. It is the largest concentration of wildflowers in the world, especially around the farming community of Clanwilliam, where a vast nature preserve displays a huge selection above the Olifants River.

Sometimes it is difficult to tell the different African daisy species apart. When I first began gardening, the annual *Arctotis* and *Dimorphotheca* were the only ones available to grow from seed, usually as a mixture in shades of red, orange, and yellow. Recently, plant breeders have improved the color range and flower size through hybridizing, offering superior plants from cuttings rather than seed-grown starts. Proven Winners, a marketing organization that works with breeders worldwide, has a series of *Arctotis* called 'Ravers' developed by breeders at Sydney University in Australia.

The 'Ravers' have a bushy, compact habit and silvery indented foliage, bloom nonstop during cool weather, and especially like a coastal climate. They demand full sun and good drainage. 'Pink Sugar', a bright rose pink with black eye zone, is particularly attractive massed along a path and in containers.

Arctotis fastuosa is still listed by many seedsmen as *Venidium fastuosm*. It grows low, busy plants covered in orange daisy flowers with a prominent black eye zone and black button center. A white version, 'Zulu Prince', is white with a black eye zone and black button center, and it is my personal favorite of all African daisies, easily raised from seed. It's commonly called monarch of the veld.

Among gerbera daisies, I especially recommend 'Garden Gerbera', since it has mildew resistance and a vibrant color range that includes yellow, orange, red, pink, white, and apricot. Many other gerbera daisies have been bred for greenhouse production to satisfy demand from the cut-flower trade and so may not last as long outdoors as the 'Garden Gerbera', which is sensational clustered as a mixture in wide dish containers.

BE AWARE! In general, the vegetatively produced African daisies will flower more freely than those grown from seed. The seed varieties are fine if you wish to create a wildflower meadow or seed a dry slope where other flowers have difficulty growing. Be careful buying gerbera daisies, as these can look irresistible in pots with their huge, glimmering flowers up to 5 inches across, but many of the large-flowered varieties simply bend over when the flower head gets wet. It's better to plant the sturdier, small-flowered kinds like 'Garden Gerbera'.

 ## PLANT PROFILE

KNOWN BOTANICALLY AS: *Arctotis, Dimorphotheca,* and *Gerbera* hybrids

ZONES: 3–8 for summer bloom; 9–11 for winter flowering

PROPAGATION: Mostly meristem culture and cuttings and also from seed

SPACING: 12 inches to 2 feet apart, depending on variety, in full sun

PESTS AND DISEASES: Mostly chewing insects like slugs and foraging animals like deer; also mildew and root rot from excessive rainfall

PERFECT PARTNERS: California poppies, dianthus, freeway daisies, lavender, pansies, snapdragons, and violas

Daisies, Freeway

Look for unusual petal shapes, like spoons, of the sorts you'll find with 'Lilac Spoon'. Its unique flower form looks unreal, perfect for admiring close-up in containers.

GROW THIS! 'Voltage Yellow', 'Passion', 'Akila', 'Symphony' series, 'Serenity' series, 'Lavender Bliss', and 'White Bliss'

Not many years ago, I would have lumped the freeway daisy (*Osteospermum eklonis* and its hybrids) with the previous listing for African daisies because the *Dimorphotheca* species are closely related to *Osteospermum*. But the freeway daisies are now such a popular group that I feel it is better to treat them separately.

The newer hybrids bloom nonstop during cool nights, don't close up on cloudy days like the wild species, and will produce as many as 500 blooms all open at one time on a mounded plant that can be 2 feet high and 3 feet wide, ideal for filling a whiskey half barrel. The variety that has proven especially popular is 'Voltage Yellow', a plant that grows to 12 inches high and 2 feet wide, almost smothering itself with yellow daisy flowers day after day, for 3 months and more. Anna Ball, owner of Ball FloraPlant, recommends it in baskets and beds and confirmed my own experience—"It's the first osteo to bloom in spring and the longest lasting into summer." It was voted "Best Osteo" by Colorado State University. Plants require full sun and good drainage and produce stems long enough for cutting.

Other varieties of freeway daisies provide an amazing color range: not only the familiar lavender and purple shades of old varieties (evident in the 'Passion' mixture developed by Takii Seeds and the 'Akila' series) but also the vibrant red, orange, pink, lemon yellow, apricot, and snow white of the 'Symphony' and 'Serenity' series, the latter of which includes the sensational 'Lavender Bliss' and 'White Bliss', both with spoon-shaped petals.

'Voltage Yellow' is a free-flowering freeway daisy—with nonstop bloom from early spring until midsummer.

BE AWARE! In general, freeway daisies grown from cuttings will outperform seed-grown varieties and offer the richest color range. I used to be a big fan of the cheerful, small-flowered kingfisher daisy (*Felicia amelloides*), but the newer *Osteospermum* hybrids are not only larger flowered but freer flowering and longer lasting. Sakata Seeds recently registered the name Cape Daisy to describe their series of *Osteospermum*, requiring other seedsmen and nurserymen to use other common names in their promotions and on their seed packets and plant labels. Some have even resorted to calling their freeway daisy by the name marguerite daisy, which is a common name for a summer-flowering tender perennial chrysanthemum daisy.

 ## PLANT PROFILE

KNOWN BOTANICALLY AS: *Osteospermum* hybrids

ZONES: 3–8 for late spring and summer flowering; 9–11 for winter and early spring flowering

PROPAGATION: Although there are freeway daisies to grow from seed, by far the most vigorous and the most beautiful are propagated from cuttings and meristem culture for sale as potted plants or transplants.

SPACING: 12–18 inches in full sun

PESTS AND DISEASES: Mostly chewing insects like slugs and foraging animals like rabbits and deer

PERFECT PARTNERS: African daisies, California poppies, pansies, snapdragons, and violas

Marguerite Daisies

Once known as *Chrysanthemum frutescens* and now classified as *Argyranthemum frutescens,* these bushy daisylike plants are tender perennials that are often grown as annuals in areas with harsh winters. Left outdoors, they will overwinter in Zone 8 and south. They're great for container plantings, and they can be trained to a tree form with the top-knot of flowers and foliage creating a sphere, like a big lollipop.

Previously available in plain white with a yellow center, the color range now includes yellow, pink, and red. My favorite is the 'Madeira' series, with 'Madeira Deep Pink' being the most dramatic. The vigorous, mound-shaped plants almost suffocate themselves in flowers—much like a cushion chrysanthemum—for massing in beds and borders. Alternate the red, primrose-yellow, pink, and white for a sensational rainbow border or an eye-catching window-box planter.

Euphorbias

'Diamond Frost' looks like a cloud of mist and will enliven any color it is placed next to, like the shimmer in an Impressionist painting.

GROW THIS! 'Diamond Frost'

For a new plant species to gain acceptance in the crowded marketplace of flowering annuals, it needs a catchy common name, like larkspur, snapdragon, and morning glory. The term "euphorbia" is not a good common name for any plant, since there are hundreds of euphorbia species in cultivation, most of them perennial. *Euphorbia hypericifolia* has enjoyed worldwide recognition since 'Diamond Frost' won the designation of UK Plant of the Year. It's a cloudlike plant that produces a mass of small white bracts (pseudoflowers); several similar varieties are now available in garden centers. As a common name, I would propose "pixie dust," since the plant produces a shimmering or glittering effect. Planted among other annuals or perennials with solid colors, like red and blue, the airiness produces a misty or snowy effect and helps enliven any adjacent solid color.

Growing to just 8 inches high, 'Diamond Frost' is grown from cuttings and used mostly in combination containers, such as dish planters and hanging baskets, to enliven a mixed planting. Available only from transplants produced vegetatively, the plants bloom from spring until fall frost.

BE AWARE! Most kinds of euphorbia are tender perennials killed by frost, and 'Diamond Frost' is no exception, but it colors up quickly and remains decorative the entire season and is best treated as an annual. Many kinds of euphorbia exude a milky sap when cut, and this can cause a rash on bare skin. The common hardy groundcover *E. myrisinites* is an example of an invasive, short-flowered, succulent form of euphorbia that can cause a serious rash, and so you should avoid buying and planting this variety.

Another rogue among euphorbias is the so-called mole plant, *E. lathyris*. Though it's sold as a mole repellent, tests conducted in England have shown it is useless in repelling moles. It probably earned this reputation by growing where moles never venture anyway—in dry, stony soil devoid of earthworms!

PLANT PROFILE

KNOWN BOTANICALLY AS: *Euphorbia hypericifolia* and *E. graminea*

ZONES: 3–11 in a container planting through all seasons

PROPAGATION: Cuttings and meristem culture

SPACING: 12 inches apart in full sun

PESTS AND DISEASES: None serious

PERFECT PARTNERS: Just about any plant suitable for containers, such as calibrachoa, coleus, geraniums, lantana, lobelia, petunias, and verbena

Gazanias

Resembling a miniature sunflower, 'Sunbathers Totonaca' beats all other flowering annuals for a bold splash of color in a patio container.

GROW THIS! 'Kiss', 'Big Kiss', 'New Day', and 'Sunbathers Totonaca'

Gazanias are native to arid regions of South Africa, where they bloom riotously across thousands of acres following spring rains in September, the South African spring. They have shimmering daisy-type flowers that gleam like satin to attract pollinators. They generally close up on cloudy days and at night, but while the sun shines, the color combinations are astounding. The flower head consists of at least two, and sometimes four, colors. For example, a flower can have yellow petal tips, a red midsection, and a black eye zone around an orange button center.

The variety known as 'Kiss' has a wide color range, presently 15 colors, plus five specially blended mixtures, of which the most striking is the 'Frosty Flame' mix, made up of all striped flowers in the 'Kiss' series. A companion strain called 'Big Kiss' consists of a white with rose pink stripes and yellow with vivid red stripes. The 4- to 5-inch blooms are the biggest to be found among gazanias, with as many as 15 blooms open at any one time on bushy plants up to 12 inches high.

Another good gazania strain with a rich color assortment is the 'New Day' series from Pan American Seeds, by far the largest flowers I have ever seen in gazanias. Seek out the amazing 'Sunbathers', especially the variety 'Totonaca', bred in Israel by Danziger Farms. It is a dark red with yellow petal tips and a large crested yellow center. Its 5½-inch blooms look more like a sunflower than a gazania. These can be grown only from cuttings or meristem culture, as they produce no viable seed.

Gazanias relish full sun and enjoy summer heat. Use them as an edging to flowerbeds and for containers, especially window-box and dish planters.

Although gazania seed can be direct-sown, the hybrid seed is expensive, so plants are best started at least 8 weeks before outdoor planting after frost danger. Provide good drainage.

BE AWARE! Be aware that there are annual (*Gazania splendens*) and perennial gazanias (*G. rigida*) and that the perennial kinds not only require a second season to flower, but they also will not overwinter where there are frequent frosts. Perennial gazanias are used as a drought-tolerant groundcover for sandy soils in frost-free areas such as coastal California. There are trailing and clumping types. Choose trailing over clumping, as both are prone to winter dieback, but the trailing kind will quickly cover up its bare spots.

 ## PLANT PROFILE

KNOWN BOTANICALLY AS: *Gazania* hybrids

ZONES: 3–8 for summer flowering; 9–11 for winter and early spring flowers

PROPAGATION: By seed direct-sown or started 8 weeks before outdoor planting. The best new varieties are produced from meristem culture.

SPACING: 12 inches apart in full sun

PESTS AND DISEASES: None serious, except for the usual chewing insects such as slugs and foraging animals such as rabbits and deer

PERFECT PARTNERS: African daisies, California poppies, freeway daisies, marigolds, petunias, and zinnias

Geraniums, Bedding

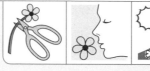

For sheer mass of flowers from spring through fall, plant 'Multibloom' geraniums. They seem to have one purpose in life—to bloom riotously.

GROW THIS! 'Calliope', 'Designer', and 'Aristo'

Ever since Penn State University produced 'Nittany Lion Red', a bedding geranium that bloomed the first season from seed, plant breeders have been trying to outdo each other with bigger and longer-lasting blooms from seed. A big advantage to growing bedding geraniums from seed is that the production cost is much less than growing them from cuttings. The 'Multibloom' series of seed-grown geraniums flowers in 10 to 11 weeks from seed and is available in 12 colors plus a mixture, but the flowers are fragile and susceptible to shattering after heavy rains (see the "Be Aware!" comment opposite).

Among geraniums grown from cuttings, the most popular variety and the most highly decorated with awards is 'Calliope', especially the variety 'Dark Red'. They represent a revolutionary breakthrough in breeding, combining the best features of their parents—vigor and sideways branching from ivy-leaf geraniums and large flower size from zonal geraniums. 'Dark Red' has been recognized with 10 awards in 2 years, including the Greenhouse Grower's Medal of Excellence.

Geraniums generally do not like hot, humid summers, but 'Calliope' is heat tolerant, and the breeder Syngenta is so confident 'Calliope' will bloom all summer that they sell plants with a guarantee of nonstop bloom.

There are many other fine, weather-resistant bedding geraniums, especially from geranium specialists Ball Horticultural, who introduced the phenomenally successful 'Carefree' series in the 1960s. Their best-selling variety today is the 'Designer' series, with 16 colors and deep green foliage, including a sprightly bicolor 'Peppermint Twist'. Anna Ball, owner of Ball FloraPlant, invariably recommends the company's 'Designer' series. She points out that "they size up quickly and flower all summer in sunny beds and containers, producing lots of rain-resistant flower heads—up to 5 inches across!"

BE AWARE! I do not recommend the 'Multibloom' seed-raised geraniums nor any other seed-raised bedding geraniums, in general, because they are not as robust as those raised vegetatively from cuttings. The flowers of seed-raised geraniums tend to be smaller and shatter more easily after rains, taking a week or more to recover their flowering display. Of course, if you live in an area like California where summer rains are seldom, this is not such a problem, but it only takes a good thunderstorm to strip the seed geraniums of their blooms. Be aware that several other classes of geraniums are offered in garden centers to grow as annuals, including cascading ivy-leaf geraniums (*Pelargonium peltatum*) and the Martha Washington or regal types (*P. domesticum*), which are especially popular in cool coastal areas like California for long-lasting displays. The 'Aristo' series has a particularly good color range, and the petals do not shatter easily after rain. However, they cannot take the high heat of most other areas of the United States. The ivy-leaf geraniums make sensational hanging basket plants. Both the ivy-leaf geraniums and Martha Washington types are perennial, but they will overwinter reliably in Zones 8 and 9.

 ## PLANT PROFILE

KNOWN BOTANICALLY AS: *Pelargonium* hybrid

ZONES: 3–8 for summer flowering; 9–11 for winter and early spring flowers

PROPAGATION: By seed started 10 weeks before outdoor planting after frost danger; also cuttings taken in fall and overwintered indoors

SPACING: 12 inches apart in full sun

PESTS AND DISEASES: Botrytis fungal disease can make geranium flowers turn to mush.

PERFECT PARTNERS: For combination container plants, mix with calibrachoa, dusty miller, euphorbia 'Diamond Frost', lantana, petunias, and verbena.

Hardy Hibiscus

The size of dinner plates, the flowers of 'Luna' are impressive enough, but this reliable flowering annual will come back as a hardy perennial year after year.

GROW THIS! 'Luna'

Many North American native wildflowers have been used by plant breeders to develop extraordinary garden-worthy varieties, including prairie wildflowers like rudbeckia, gaillardia, and lupines, either at the hands of American breeders or foreign breeders. The hardy North American swamp hibiscus is perhaps the best example of a native American wildflower that has astonished the gardening world after years of work by a foreign breeder to improve it for home gardens. The first annual varieties were called 'Southern Belle', which won an All-America Selections award for huge flowers and nonstop flowering from midsummer to fall frost, but this series is no longer available, replaced by the 'Luna' series that has flowers up to 8 inches across. Amazingly, seed to flowers takes only 13 weeks, with the plants growing quickly to 4 feet tall and sporting heart-shaped leaves. The color range includes white with a red eye, deep rose pink, light pink, and red.

This close-up shows the dinner plate–size 'Luna' hibiscus, developed from hardy wild North American swamp hibiscus.

BE AWARE! Do not confuse the hardy swamp hibiscus with other hardy hibiscus such as *Hibiscus trionum* (commonly called flower of the hour). Those flowers are white, sparse, and small, and the plant grows like a weed. Also don't confuse the swamp hibiscus with the tender tropical hibiscus (*H. rosa-sinensis*), whose flowers are only half the size of the hardy hibiscus hybrids. If you decide to grow tropical hibiscus, you'll find they flaunt a rich and varied color range, from white and shades of red and pink to yellow, orange, and apricot and a multitude of bicolors and tricolors that can include gray. They are often used as annuals to flower over one season; at the end of the season, you can uproot and discard them or take them indoors for protection over winter.

A tender hibiscus variety to avoid is the so-called mahoe (*H. tiliaceus*). It is one of the most aggressive trees known to man, and although the flowers are beautiful, changing color from yellow to red to maroon all in one day, in a frost-free location like southern Florida they will take over an entire garden.

 ## PLANT PROFILE

KNOWN BOTANICALLY AS: *Hibiscus moscheutos*

ZONES: 5–10 as a summer-flowering annual

PROPAGATION: By seed started indoors 10 weeks before outdoor planting

SPACING: 3 feet apart in full sun. May need staking, as stems can become top-heavy and brittle.

PESTS AND DISEASES: Mostly chewing insects such as caterpillars and Japanese beetles

PERFECT PARTNERS: Any equally large annual, such as castor bean plant. Also later-summer annuals and perennials such as asters, cannas, dinner-plate dahlias, and rudbeckia.

Impatiens (aka Patience Plant)

Nothing provides color for shaded areas like impatiens, especially 'Accent' and 'Super Elfins', but for the future, look for varieties specially bred for resistance to downy mildew.

GROW THIS! 'Super Elfins' and 'Accent' for shade

There are two kinds of impatiens commonly sold in garden centers: the patience plant, best grown in shade, and the larger-flowered New Guinea hybrids, bred for both sun and shade (see the next entry). The patience plant is the most widely used flowering annual for shade. For density of color, it beats other popular flowering shade plants like tuberous begonias and coleus. Two varieties of patience plant, the 'Super Elfins' and 'Accent', are at the forefront of sales. Both develop a spreading, mounded habit; large, overlapping, upward-facing blooms up to 2 inches across; and an extensive color range that includes solid colors (all shades of red, orange, and pink, plus white) and bicolors, usually with a contrasting eye color or a contrasting stripe running the length of each petal to create a shimmering effect. Anna Ball, owner of Pan America Seed, a plant breeding company, smiles whenever she sees her company's 'Elfins' extending like a floral carpet around the shaded perimeter of the company's extensive West Chicago trial garden. "When our breeders recommend the term 'Super' for a flower name, it means superior performance. And that's what the 'Elfins' provide in sun or shade, when massed in beds, or if spilling from baskets and planters."

BE AWARE! A new virulent mildew disease is spreading across North America and killing the familiar bedding-type impatiens by midsummer, but breeders are working to produce new resistant varieties of *Impatiens × walleriana*. Fortunately, New Guinea impatiens such as the 'Sun Patiens' are resistant (see next listing).

The 'Jungle' series of yellow and shades of orange impatiens are an oddity, but sparse flowering compared to 'Accent' and 'Super Elfins'.

Generally, the double-flowered varieties of impatiens are not as free flowering as the single flowered, although they can look charming in hanging baskets and patio planters. The flowers resemble miniature roses.

Whatever you do, avoid planting impatiens in a single color, like the common red or red-and-white mixed—the favorite motel parking lot color combination. Think in terms of vibrant color blends, such as orange, deep pink, and lavender.

 PLANT PROFILE

KNOWN BOTANICALLY AS: *Impatiens x walleriana*

ZONES: 3–11 as an annual; additionally, impatiens will perform as a perennial in Zones 10 and 11

PROPAGATION: By seed started indoors at least 8 weeks before outdoor planting after frost danger

SPACING: Minimum of 12 inches apart in light shade

PESTS AND DISEASES: Various chewing insects like caterpillars and Japanese beetles, but also the seed is susceptible to damping-off disease

PERFECT PARTNERS: Caladiums, coleus, petunias, and wishbone flower

Impatiens, New Guinea

Although early varieties are hard to keep alive during summer heat, new 'Sun Patiens' thrive in full sun under adverse conditions.

GROW THIS! 'Sun Patiens' for sun

'Sun Patiens' is a hybrid between bedding impatiens and New Guinea impatiens. In 1970, a plant-finding expedition to New Guinea, sponsored by Longwood Gardens and the USDA and led by the late Dr. Marc Cathey, returned with three new species of impatiens. These had larger flowers than any on the market, and when they were crossed with other impatiens species from Java and Celebes, they resulted in a series of large-flowered impatiens known as the New Guinea hybrids. In spite of their large size (twice as big as regular impatiens) and beautiful glossy green foliage (including variegated forms), the earliest introductions among New Guinea impatiens proved difficult to keep alive in home gardens. "I am at my wit's end with these things," wrote one frustrated gardener. "I keep trying and they keep dying on me." Another Internet complaint stated: "My last New Guinea impatiens has given up the ghost; never again!"

That kind of experience is typical of the original New Guinea impatiens, which need their roots kept cool, but the 'Sun Patiens' are much easier to grow because of genes from "patience plant" impatiens, resulting in a flower size and foliage display similar in appearance to the New Guineas. 'Sun Patiens' are available in three plant habits—compact, spreading, and tall, with the spreading types ideal for hanging baskets. The plants provide three seasons of color—spring through fall—and will even tolerate mild frosts. They relish full sun and produce a much deeper root system than previous New Guinea impatiens, allowing them to withstand weather extremes that can—and did—kill the older New Guineas. Indeed, if a 'Sun Patiens' shows signs of wilt from lack of water, instead of dropping its flower buds like previous New Guineas and dying, 'Sun Patiens' will revive. Some of the varieties have variegated foliage that makes them unusually attractive. In particular, 'Coral' among the tall types and white among the spreading types both have green and yellow serrated foliage.

Grown from cuttings rather than seed, 'Sun Patiens' relish full sun and an organically rich, well-drained soil mulched with pine straw or similar organic material to help deter weeds and keep the soil cool. They will also perform well in light shade.

BE AWARE! New Guinea impatiens are not susceptible to the mildew disease that is killing the bedding-type impatiens (*Impatiens × walleriana*). Since 'Sun Patiens' have mostly New Guinea blood in their genes, they are also tolerant of the disease.

 ## PLANT PROFILE

KNOWN BOTANICALLY AS: *Impatiens hawkeri* hybrids

ZONES: 3–11 for summer flowering as annuals; in Zones 9–11, they may overwinter as a tender perennial

PROPAGATION: Seed varieties generally are unreliable; choose only those plants that have been grown from cuttings or meristem culture.

SPACING: 2 feet apart in light shade for most varieties, full sun for 'Sun Patiens'

PESTS AND DISEASES: Nematodes, chewing insects such as Japanese beetles, and caterpillars

PERFECT PARTNERS: Coleus, petunias, and wishbone flower in shade; callas, cannas, marigolds, Persian shield, and zinnias in sun

Lantana

For long-lasting, drought-resistant displays through to fall frost, grow low-branching 'Bandana' and 'Landmark'.

GROW THIS! 'Bandana' and 'Landmark'

The orange-flowering species *Lantana camara* is a woody perennial commonly grown as a tender shrub for frost-free locations like southern California and southern Florida. It is popular as a tree form growing in tubs on decks and patios. There is a vigorous pink species, *L. montevidensis*, that has a beautiful weeping habit ideal for cascading down slopes and over retaining walls. However, since it is everblooming, lantana is also widely sold and used as an annual in northern gardens. The leaves have a pleasant spicy aroma, and the flower clusters resemble verbena, composed of dome-shaped clusters of small flowers.

The 'Bandanas' are grown from cuttings or meristem culture and have been selected for extra-large flower size and strong vigor. Since they have long stems that can creep across the ground, they are especially good for low bedding as a seasonlong groundcover and planted in window boxes and hanging baskets so the pliable stems hang down to create a curtain of blooms. The color range is extensive, rich in hot colors such as red, yellow, and orange, but also in pink, white, and bicolors. Several colors in the 'Bandana' series have won awards at various institutions: the pink at Colorado State and the gold at Cornell University and Penn State University.

Similar to 'Bandana', the 'Landmark' series from Ball FloraPlant is a free-flowering strain—also grown from cuttings—that can spread to 2 feet.

BE AWARE! You may find lantana varieties with an erect habit. These erect forms are mostly offered for sale as gift plants. For home gardens, stick with the lantanas with spreading, mounded, and free-flowering habits because they make great groundcovers and beautiful hanging baskets.

 PLANT PROFILE

KNOWN BOTANICALLY AS: *Lantana* hybrids

ZONES: 3–11 as a summer-flowering annual; 9–11 for winter and spring flowering and to grow as a tender perennial

PROPAGATION: By seed started 8 weeks before outdoor planting, although the best varieties are grown from cuttings

SPACING: 18–24 inches apart for the spreading kinds so they knit together, in full sun

PESTS AND DISEASES: Whiteflies, spider mites, and nematodes, though mostly carefree

PERFECT PARTNERS: Calibrachoa, petunias, and verbena

Larkspur and Delphiniums

Annual larkspur is easier to grow than perennial delphinium, especially the tall, erect 'Giant Imperial' mixed colors.

GROW THIS! Larkspur 'Giant Imperial' mixed colors and 'Sublime' mixed colors; delphinium 'Aurora', 'Pacific Giants', and 'Magic Fountains Mix'

Larkspur is an annual closely related to perennial delphinium, and it is much easier to grow than the temperamental tall delphiniums of Gertrude Jekyll and Claude Monet fame. Some coastal locations in California, the Pacific Northwest, and Maine can grow delphinium like those displayed at the Chelsea Flower Show, but for the rest of the country, summers are too hot and humid and winters too cold for delphinium to be reliably perennial.

Turn to larkspur instead. Larkspur grows spires of star-shaped flowers closely packed around a tall stem, up to 5 feet high. They can be single-flowered florets or doubles like the ones in the florist shops, and the color range can include blue, red, pink, violet, and white. They are best sown into their flowering positions in fall and allowed to sprout before freezing weather makes them dormant. Then a warming trend in spring will give them a spurt of energy and an early bloom. They can also bloom from an extra-early spring sowing, as soon as the soil can be worked. Larkspur will flower continuously until hot summer days arrive. Generally the plants need staking to help them stay upright, and this is best done by stretching some nylon reach-through garden netting across the bed to a height of 2 feet. The larkspur will then grow through the netting to become self-supporting. 'Giant Imperial' hybrids have the thickest, tallest flowerstalks. Also recommended is the 'Sublime' mixture for its double, star-shaped florets.

In addition to garden display, larkspur is valued as a cut flower and as a component of meadow mixtures. The blue is a particularly striking color and often planted with coreopsis to create a pleasant yellow-blue color harmony. Provide the plants with full sun and good drainage.

However, if you have the right climate and would like the challenge of growing larkspur's kissing cousin, the delphinium, consider the really tall 'Aurora' series from Takii Seeds or the standard mixture known as 'Pacific Giants', originally bred by the California plant breeding house of Waller Flowerseeds. Both of these varieties generally require staking. 'Magic Fountains' grows spikes half the height of the 'Aurora' and 'Pacific Giants' and doesn't require staking. Both kinds are generally purchased as transplants and transferred to their flowering positions early in spring. By cutting the spent flowering stems back and mulching heavily with straw or shredded leaves, it's possible that a third of them may come back to bloom the following season, but alternate freezing and thawing generally rots the roots.

BE AWARE! Larkspur and delphinium choices can sometimes be confusing to sort out. Larkspur are native to the Pacific Northwest, while delphinium come from Siberia. The wild American larkspur is blue and is fine for wildflower meadow plantings, but it does not have the color range of the garden varieties named above. There's a type of delphinium called the belladonna group that grows bushy. The most common variety is 'Connecticut Yankees', developed by the famous 20th-century painter and photographer Edward Steichen. Don't confuse this bushy type with regular tall larkspur or tall delphinium; these low plants rarely grow more than 2 feet high and produce a brief flowering display, in shades of blue, purple, and white, in cool weather. They are good, however, to partner with dwarf yellow perennials such as coreopsis for a low bedding display, but they cannot compare in stature with regular larkspur, the tall 'Pacific Giant'–type delphiniums (with closely spaced florets), or the very tall 'Aurora' series.

 PLANT PROFILE

KNOWN BOTANICALLY AS: *Delphinium ajacis* and *D. elatum*

ZONES: 3–8 as a summer-flowering annual; 9–11 for winter and early spring flowering

PROPAGATION: By seed direct-sown or started indoors 6–8 weeks before outdoor planting

SPACING: 12 inches apart in full sun

PESTS AND DISEASES: Mostly chewing insects such as slugs. Delphiniums especially are relished by slugs, rabbits, and deer.

PERFECT PARTNERS: Bachelor's buttons, coreopsis, poppies, snapdragons, and sweet peas

Marigolds, American

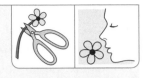

Also called African marigold, 'Perfection' is my preference for its generous everblooming flower display, medium height, and large, globular heads.

GROW THIS! 'Lady' series, 'Perfection', 'French Vanilla', 'Discovery', 'Antigua', 'Inca II', and 'Moonstruck'

Common plant names for annuals can be confusing. In the United Kingdom, American marigolds are called African marigolds because they were a popular flowering annual for gardens in Morocco, where they bloom freely during the dry heat of summer. This created the impression that the tall, erect, large-flowered kinds came from Africa—when in fact they are native to the Americas, mostly Mexico. In France, American marigolds are called Indian marigolds because in India they cherish the color gold and use marigolds as garlands at special celebrations such as weddings and religious holidays. Another marigold, the French marigold, also comes from Mexico, but when it became popular among the French, a new common name was created.

In regards to the true American marigold, the 'Lady' series was developed by Burpee Seeds in response to the public's need for a bushy, low-growing plant, since the taller, large-flowered kinds like Burpee's 'Climax' hybrids have a tendency to grow too tall and topple over in windstorms or break their necks when heavy with rain.

The 'Ladies' are extremely free flowering, with as many as 50 tennis ball–size blooms open at any one time. Colors include yellow, primrose, gold, and orange, with 'Lady Primrose' the cream of the crop.

Even more vigorous than the 'Ladies' are the 'Perfection' series, developed by Syngenta. Eventually, I hope to see a white added to both series. Indeed, the white marigold was so elusive that the dean of seedsmen, David Burpee, offered $10,000 to the first person to send him seeds that could grow a white as white as 'Snowstorm' petunia. The prize was awarded to an Iowa housewife, Alice Vonk, and Burpee went on to introduce several whites, including 'French Vanilla', which I rate the best among the whites. One drawback of all the white varieties is a tendency for the flowers to fade into an ugly black ball, so rigorous deadheading is needed to keep the plants looking clean.

Variety names like the 'Discovery' series, 'Antigua' series, 'Inca II' series, and 'Moonstruck' series are all excellent, large-flowered compact varieties—not as good as the 'Lady' series and 'Perfection' series for garden display, in my opinion, but better suited for container plantings like dish planters and whiskey half barrels because of their shorter height.

When you transplant an American marigold with a bloom showing, cut it off. This stimulates the plant into branching sideways and producing more blooms. Moreover, the pruned plant will soon overtake any unpruned plants for a much more impressive floral display.

BE AWARE! Avoid "odorless" marigolds. Yes, marigolds can have a strong scent, but without their spicy aroma, they attract pests and foragers.

One of the most common color mixtures offered in seed racks is 'Crackerjack', a cheap-to-produce open-pollinated mixture that offers yellow, gold, and orange in its color range. But it is highly variable in performance, flower height, and size, depending on the seed source. Many plants in the mixture grow too tall, and flowers rarely form a tight globular head like the 'Perfection' series. They often look stressed, and one color will usually predominate. Another variety name sometimes encountered in seed racks is an untidy mixture called 'Marigolds on Parade'. The packet includes seed of many different varieties, often differing in stem height and flower size. Next to a mixture of uniform height, like the 'Lady' and 'Perfection' series, they look ragged and untidy.

 ## PLANT PROFILE

KNOWN BOTANICALLY AS: *Tagetes erecta*

ZONES: 3–9 for summer flowering; 9–11 for winter and early spring blooms

PROPAGATION: By seed direct-sown or started indoors 6 weeks before outdoor planting

SPACING: 12 inches apart in sun

PESTS AND DISEASES: None serious. Sometimes afflicted with aster yellows. Japanese beetles can attack the flower heads.

PERFECT PARTNERS: Blue sage, cockscomb, cosmos, dusty miller, petunias, sunflowers, and zinnias

Marigolds, French

'Queen Sophia' set a new standard in dwarf marigolds with its unique flower form—called anemone flowered—and its stamina to bloom all season until fall frost. Though now discontinued, several newer varieties provide a similar never-ending display.

GROW THIS! 'Durango Flame', 'Safari Red', and 'Zenith'

French marigolds are much more compact than American marigolds, and although smaller flowered, they can create a ribbon of color as an edging to flowerbeds or a blanket of color when massed as bedding plants. They are also dazzling grouped in containers such as window boxes and dish planters. 'Queen Sophia'—an All-America Selections winner—was bred by the French seed company Gaboreau, who sold production rights to Bodger Seeds, which has since ceased to exist, and so 'Queen Sophia' has disappeared from the market. You may still see transplants labeled as 'Queen Sophia' because of its overwhelming popularity, but they are most likely 'Durango Flame' or 'Safari Red', two very suitable substitutes.

When I was catalog manager for Burpee, I helped to introduce a remarkable series of marigolds called triploid hybrids. Called the 'Nugget' series, they were truly remarkable, and you could tell them apart from a trial planting of hundreds of other French marigolds by the sheer density of bloom. An interspecific cross between the American and French marigolds, they were mules. In other words, they were sterile and could not set viable seed but would keep on trying. None of these varieties are around today because they proved too expensive to produce, and seed germination was always substandard. However, Floranova seed breeders have developed a triploid hybrid called 'Zenith' with a germination rate of 75 percent. The series includes two carnation-flowered types and three crested types. Until the germination rate on triploids can be improved, you are unlikely to find them at garden centers, but they are sold in seed catalogs.

French marigolds like full sun and a well-drained soil.

BE AWARE! I avoid nonhybrid mixtures such as 'Petite' and 'Spry'. The flowers are variable, and plant heights generally are not uniform, often growing too untidy. Also, I don't like the bicolored signet marigold called 'Mr. Majestic'. Although it has been recognized as a novelty by Fleuroselect, it looks identical to 'Harlequin', an heirloom variety dating to the 1870s. Neither 'Mr. Majestic' nor 'Harlequin' produces a free-flowering display like the 'Durango' and 'Safari' series.

 ## PLANT PROFILE

KNOWN BOTANICALLY AS: *Tagetes patula*

ZONES: 3–9 for summer flowering; 9–11 for winter and early spring flowers

PROPAGATION: By seed direct-sown or started indoors 6–8 weeks before outdoor planting after frost danger

SPACING: 12 inches apart in sun

PESTS AND DISEASES: None serious. Like American marigolds, French marigolds are often used to repel nematodes from infected soils.

PLANT PARTNERS: Dwarf petunias, dwarf zinnias, and scarlet sage

Morning Glories

The old favorite 'Heavenly Blue' creates a curtain of saucer-shaped sky blue flowers on vigorous vines. It is still the most popular morning glory for covering a fence or trellis.

GROW THIS! 'Heavenly Blue', 'Scarlet O'Hara', 'Grandpa Ott's', 'Mt. Fuji', and 'Tie Dye'

Think of flowering vines that have impressed you, and two will probably spring to mind: wisteria and morning glory. Wisteria is a woody plant with a limited color range (blue and white), and it's a 1,000-pound gorilla in the garden. Left to its own devices, it will strangle anything in its path and climb to the top of 100-foot-high pines. Morning glories, on the other hand, are much better behaved, especially 'Heavenly Blue', with its sky blue trumpet-shaped flowers and heart-shaped leaves. An old-fashioned variety whose origins are obscure, 'Heavenly Blue' is still the most popular morning glory for home gardens, because it is the most generous with its flowers, quickly growing skyward from seed direct-sown into the garden and blooming riotously nonstop all summer until fall frosts.

There are other colors in morning glories, including a red ('Scarlet O'Hara'), and a violet blue, small-flowered variety called 'Grandpa Ott's'. There is also a white, but it is not one I would grow (see below under "Be Aware!").

More recent breeding achievements have been made with bicolors, including 'Mt. Fuji', a mixture that has its petals ringed at the edges in a contrasting color, and 'Tie Dye', a striped mixture.

Plant morning glories against any kind of support such as a trellis or garden netting and they will climb by twining. They grow fast, up to 10 feet high by midsummer, if given full sun and good drainage. As the name suggests, the floral display is best in the morning and under cloud cover.

BE AWARE! Morning glories like to present a pillar of blooms on fast growing vines. Some breeders have dwarfed them for containers, but these dwarf kinds are shy bloomers, so choose the large-flowered varieties above for the most colorful display. There is a white called 'Pearly Gates' that is weak flowering, and also a washed-out pale blue called 'Flying Saucers'. If you would like a white morning glory, choose the related moonflower vine. It has pleasantly fragrant flowers up to 5 inches across that open in the late afternoon and flower all night.

In addition, there are variegated foliage forms that tend to look anemic with their streaks of white that appear as if the plant is covered in bird droppings. You may also see promotions for a recent morning glory introduction called 'Star of Yalta'; it appears to be identical to the heirloom 'Grandpa Ott's'.

The cardinal climber (*Ipomoea multifida*) is also a type of morning glory, but the flowers are tiny and the color range is limited to mostly red, pink, and white. It attracts hummingbirds, but that's its only good quality, in my experience.

PLANT PROFILE

KNOWN BOTANICALLY AS: *Ipomoea purpurea*

ZONES: 3–11 as a flowering annual; 9–11 for winter and early spring flowers

PROPAGATION: By seed direct-sown, as plants resent transplanting. Soak seeds in lukewarm water overnight to aid germination.

SPACING: 2 feet apart when grown up trellis or garden netting so the vines knit together, in full sun

PESTS AND DISEASES: None serious, except for chewing insects like Japanese beetles, which can skeletonize the leaves

PERFECT PARTNERS: Climbing nasturtiums, hyacinth vine, Mexican firecracker vine, moonflower vine, and vining sweet peas

Nasturtiums

The dwarf 'Whirlybird' nasturtium provides the most colorful floral display for low bedding, but the old-fashioned 'Climbing Mixed Colors' are my favorite for covering fences and trellises.

GROW THIS! 'Climbing Mixed Colors' and 'Whirlybird'

Nasturtiums are tender annuals that can be climbing or bedding kinds. They have mostly trumpet-shaped blooms with spurs (nectar tubes) containing a sweet nectar for hummingbirds to visit. The flowers are edible, have a peppery flavor, and are used mostly to decorate fresh salads. The best use for the vining kinds can be seen each summer in the restored garden of Impressionist painter Claude Monet, north of Paris. From opposite ends of a broad path leading from the front of his house to a water garden, the vines are allowed to creep across the ground from parallel beds and meet in the middle. A variety sold as 'Climbing Mixed Colors' knits together to create a carpet of hot colors, including red, yellow, orange, pink, and maroon.

For mass bedding or edging, a variety of bushy, compact nasturtiums known as 'Whirlybird' is a preferred choice since the flowers have no spurs, forcing the flowers to face up and create a more colorful display than old-fashioned varieties. The 'Whirlybirds' form low mounds up to 12 inches high and are suitable for containers such as window-box planters and hanging baskets.

Nasturtiums bloom best during cool weather and prefer a sandy or well-drained soil. The climbing kinds will twine to climb up any kind of support, such as a trellis or netting, extending 8 feet in a season.

BE AWARE! I do not recommend the beautiful perennial form of climbing nasturtium known as the flame nasturtium (*Tropaeolum speciosum*) from Chile. It grows a column of scarlet red flowers and under ideal conditions looks like a pillar of fire. Unfortunately, it cannot tolerate heat and humidity and prefers a maritime climate. I have seen it growing spectacularly in the Shetland Islands north of Scotland and also in the Pacific Northwest, but I haven't seen it grown successfully in too many other locales.

The canary-bird flower is also a type of nasturtium (*T. peregrinum*), but the flowering display is usually sparse and the flowers too small to make a decent display.

 ## PLANT PROFILE

KNOWN BOTANICALLY AS: *Tropaeolum majus*

ZONES: 3–8 as a summer-flowering annual; 8–11 as a winter- and early-spring-flowering annual

PROPAGATION: By seed direct-sown after frost danger or started indoors 4 weeks before outdoor planting. Sterile kinds, like doubles, can be propagated by cuttings.

SPACING: 12 inches apart, so the plants knit together, in sun

PESTS AND DISEASES: Mostly whiteflies, aphids, slugs, caterpillars, and flea beetles

PERFECT PARTNERS: Hyacinth bean, moonflower, morning glories, and sweet peas

Pansies

'Majestic Giants' from Japan are larger flowered
than the famous 'Swiss Giants' and 'Yellow with Black
Blotch' the firm favorite.

GROW THIS! 'Majestic Giants II' and 'Delta'

Pansies have developed from violas, which grow wild in the Swiss Alps, and
which is why the Rudolf Roggli AG firm near Thun, Switzerland, for many years
dominated the breeding of garden kinds of pansies and why the mixture of large-
flowered pansies called 'Swiss Giants' became very popular. Unfortunately, with
the demise of the Roggli firm as plant breeders, the 'Swiss Giants' are now difficult to obtain, though still propagated by a Dutch company, Hem Seeds.

For sheer size of flowers, nothing can compare with the 'Majestic Giants',
now renamed 'Majestic II' since the original 'Majestics' have been improved by
the Japanese breeder Sakata Seeds, using 'Swiss Giants' as a parent. The
'Majestics' are the largest-flowered pansies, and they have become the preferred
variety for fall planting—not only to bloom in fall, but also to overwinter and
bloom extra early in spring. Although flower size varies among individual colors, the variety 'White with Blotch' is the biggest, measuring up to 4 inches
across. 'Yellow with Blotch' is only slightly smaller and outsells every other
pansy variety. The plants have good heat tolerance, lasting well into summer.

Not quite as large as the 'Majestic' series, but with stronger flowering and
quicker recovery after inclement weather, is the pansy 'Delta' series. My favorite is 'Delta Fire', with burnt orange petal edges, a yellow throat area, and a
handsome black blotch.

Although pansies prefer full sun, they will tolerate light shade. Give them
good drainage and water freely during dry or hot periods. Mulching to keep the
soil cool also helps extend the bloom period. Grow them massed in beds and
borders and in containers. Pansies are the most popular bedding plant for fall
and early spring color.

BE AWARE! Surely part of the charm of growing pansies are the black
markings surrounding the throat of each flower—a handsome black blotch
in some varieties and black whiskers in others, giving them almost human

characteristics. Like black stipple applied to a canvas by an artist, a pansy's black markings within a solid color have a twinkling effect. Then why breed out the black blotch and whiskers to obtain a clear plain color? That's the case with a variety sold as 'Clear Crystals'. It's an appealing name, but it's lacking in visual interest, in my opinion, compared to those with traditional black markings.

 ## PLANT PROFILE

KNOWN BOTANICALLY AS: *Viola* x *wittrockiana*

ZONES: 3–8 for spring, early summer, and fall flowering; 8–11 for winter flowering

PROPAGATION: By seed started indoors 10 weeks before outdoor planting. Pansies are hardy and will tolerate frost and even frozen soil if mulched.

SPACING: 8 inches apart in sun or light shade

PESTS AND DISEASES: None serious, except chewing insects like slugs and foraging animals such as rabbits

PERFECT PARTNERS: Calendulas, daffodils, snapdragons, tulips, and violas

Petunias, Large-Flowered

Rain-resistant 'Wave' petunias produce so many flowers they almost completely hide the foliage, and like the Duracell bunny, they just keep on going and going, spreading sideways to create a carpet of color.

GROW THIS! 'Surfinia', 'Cascadia', 'Storm', 'Cadenza', 'Wave', 'Explorer', 'Supertunia', and 'Phantom'

Before you purchase any petunia, it's important to realize that the popular kinds can be classified as grandiflora (meaning large flowered); milliflora (meaning small flowered); and multiflora (meaning many flowered), with flowers that are medium size. The grandifloras can have blooms up to 4 inches across, while the multifloras rarely exceed 2½ inches and the millifloras 1½ inches. They can be *mounded* in habit for flowerbeds, *spreading* for a groundcover effect, and *cascading* to tumble down a hanging basket or from window-box planters, like a curtain. The multifloras and the millifloras hold up better after rain than the grandifloras, and given the choice, I always prefer multifloras for both beds and containers. When buying plants from a garden center, you'll find the botanical designations probably missing, but when you're buying from a seed catalog, they are usually identified correctly.

Most petunias are grown from seed, but some of the best are vegetative and available only from garden centers. That is the case with the free-flowering small-flowered 'Surfinia', bred by Suntory breeders, and 'Cascadia', bred by Israeli breeder Danziger Farms (usually plant labels will identify them correctly). Each major breeding establishment has its own series of petunias. For sheer flower power and vigor, I especially like the 'Storm' series of grandifloras from Syngenta, the 'Cadenza' series of spreading multiflora petunias from Takii, the 'Wave' series from Pan American, and the 'Explorer' spreading multiflora series from Sakata.

The 'Supertunias' are another remarkably free-flowering medium-size petunia made popular by Proven Winners. They are so vigorous and loaded with flowers that a single plant will extend its spreading stems vertically up a wall, and if its opposite stems meet a terrace, it will create a cascading curtain of vibrant blooms, such as when grown in a window-box planter. The variety 'Vista Bubblegum', a Proven Winner, is especially free flowering, and 'Pretty Much Picasso' (a pink flower edged with green) is one of the most unusual color combinations.

BE AWARE! A variety of extra-large petunia called 'Can Can' occasionally makes its appearance, but in spite of the fact that home gardeners want large-size blooms, these are not long lasting and suffer from heavy rains and sunscald (bleaching of the flowers). They were developed from a strain called 'Superbissima', growing up to 7 inches across, originally bred by a home gardener, the late Theodosia Burr Shepherd, but her original flower forms are no longer available.

Another variety to avoid is 'Petunias on Parade', as this is generally a mixture of different kinds (including grandifloras and multifloras), so heights and flower sizes can vary considerably, and it's hard to keep them looking tidy.

Both multiflora and grandiflora double-flowered petunias produce a poor show compared to single-flowered varieties. The doubling reduces the wow factor by covering up the brightest part of the flower—the throat with its contrasting white, yellow, or green eye.

I also turn thumbs down to so-called black petunias like 'Black Velvet' because they become invisible among the shadows cast by foliage. If you want a deep, rich color to match your outdoor decor or complement other blooms, choose the deep maroon variety 'Phantom' for its bicoloration that includes slender yellow petal stripes that form a star; use it in a patio planter where you can admire its unusual color combination more readily than in the garden. It's one of Anna Ball's favorites, producing gasps of surprise from visitors to her Ball FloraPlant test plots. "Make it a solo performer in a planter or mix it with other sun-loving annuals, and it meshes beauty with drama," she advises.

 ## PLANT PROFILE

KNOWN BOTANICALLY AS: *Petunia* x *grandiflora*, *P.* x *milliflora*, and *P.* x *multiflora*

ZONES: All zones as an annual, though best for winter flowering in Zones 9–11

PROPAGATION: Seed and cuttings

SPACING: 8 inches for multifloras and millifloras; 12 inches for grandifloras

PESTS AND DISEASES: Mostly chewing insects like slugs and snails

PERFECT PARTNERS: Marigolds, scarlet and blue sage, and zinnias

Petunias, Mini-

Once difficult to keep flowering all season, mini-petunias in the 'Super Cal' series are more forgiving of adverse conditions.

GROW THIS! 'Million Bells', 'Superbells', and 'SuperCal'

The plant known simply as calibrachoa was first introduced by Park Seeds, a trailing type that has long since disappeared from the market, overshadowed by 'Million Bells'—a hanging-basket and window-box plant whose name is now commonly used to describe all forms of calibrachoa. A prolific flowering annual from South America that looks like a miniature petunia, its common name is now mini-petunia. What it lacks in flower size it makes up for in sheer quantity of bloom and an amazing color range not found in real petunias. Some of the

'Superbells' series—from the same breeding program as 'Million Bells'—have rich veining and a more extensive color range, particularly in bicolors such as 'Blackberry Punch' (black with red petal tips) and 'Coralberry Punch' (coral salmon with a dark center). Also, the 'Superbells' tend to be more vigorous than 'Million Bells' and other calibrachoa varieties.

All calibrachoas have several shortcomings in differing degrees, depending on variety—they are generally short lived, providing a bold burst of color at the start of the season, but dwindling as the soil pH changes from acid to alkaline from fertilizing. If you allow the soil to dry out just briefly, they will die, and you may find it difficult to keep the roots moist during summer heat and humidity without moisture crystals in the potting mix.

These problems have been solved by crossing calibrachoas with multiflora petunias, resulting in larger flowers than the original calibrachoas, and they've been able to retain the distinctive color range of calibrachoas that includes terra-cotta, gold, and cherry red. Called petchoas, the plants tolerate alkaline soil and are more forgiving of irregular watering. Sakata Seed's 'SuperCal' series of petchoas are the leader. Moreover, the leaves are not sticky like those of petunias, and so when the petals drop, they fall through the foliage to the ground—this makes the plants self-cleaning. The plants withstand temperature fluctuations and look sensational in containers, especially window-box planters and hanging baskets, located in full sun.

In the entertainment world, it is said that "If it plays in Peoria," the act will be a success. In the world of horticulture, there is a similar saying: "If it plays in Dallas," meaning a plant can be expected to grow just about anywhere if it grows in Dallas with its poor soils and viciously hot summers with long periods of drought. Here's what Jimmy Turner, director of the Dallas Arboretum, had to say about petchoas: "To be truthful, neither petunias nor calibrachoas really excel in the Dallas area. Well, after 3 years of testing, 'SuperCal' has become one of our favorite cool-season hanging-basket and container plants, outlasting both parents every year . . . [and] seldom do they suffer from that bane of all Texas gardeners—powdery mildew."

Plants grow up to 16 inches high and spread up to 30 inches. They are grown from cuttings, not from seed, so you'll find them at various stages of maturity in garden centers, but especially as hanging baskets and large container compositions.

BE AWARE! Ever since 'Million Bells' was introduced by Proven Winners, the plant family has met aggressive competition from other breeders. Gradually, the number of colors offered in the 'Million Bells' series has dwindled now that Proven Winners is promoting its 'Superbells' as an improved selection of 'Million Bells'. I have also seen 'Million Bells' offered as 'Mission Bells', but they are one and the same.

 ## PLANT PROFILE

KNOWN BOTANICALLY AS: *Calibrachoa* x hybrid

ZONES: 3–8 as a summer-flowering annual; 9–11 as a winter- and spring-flowering annual

PROPAGATION: Only from vegetative reproduction (cuttings and meristem culture)

SPACING: 12 inches apart, so they knit into each other, in sun or light shade

PESTS AND DISEASES: None serious. Some chewing insects like slugs, aphids, and caterpillars can be a problem.

PERFECT PARTNERS: All manner of container plants, such as coleus, French marigolds, lantana, verbena, and especially euphorbia 'Diamond Frost'

Sage, Blue

For a misty blue background effect
behind yellow marigolds, grow tall, bushy 'Mystic Spires'.

GROW THIS! 'Evolution Blue', 'Evolution White', and 'Mystic Spires'

Few blue-flowering annuals have the intense blueness of blue sage. Moreover, blue sage is everblooming from early summer to fall frost, and the stems are ideal for cutting—the more you cut, the more the plant produces new flower buds. The standard of excellence among blue sage used to be 'Victoria', but using 'Victoria' as a comparison, All-America Selections found 'Evolution Blue' deserving of an award for its extralong flower spikes. It has a companion, 'Evolution White', that has silvery white flower spikes.

Plants start to bloom within 10 weeks of sowing seed and grow bushy to

Annual blue salvia 'Evolution Blue' won an All-America award for its deep blue color and long-lasting flower display.

20 inches high. Use them in mixed borders, especially partnered with yellow annuals like gloriosa daisies, zinnias, and marigolds massed in a bed and grouped in containers. Ensure good drainage. Plants tolerate heat, drought, and poor soil.

The tall variety 'Mystic Spires' (3 feet) is unique in that it stands head and shoulders above other varieties. In addition to mass bedding, it can be used as a dramatic background, especially behind low-growing yellow and orange flowers like marigolds and dwarf zinnias. As Anna Ball, owner of Ball FloraPlant, describes it: "An outstanding heat-resistant blue annual that flowers all season, its myriad blue flower spikes command attention."

BE AWARE! Early forms of annual blue sage, such as 'Blue Bedder', tend to be too tall and a lighter blue than newer varieties like 'Victoria' and 'Evolution Blue'. Be careful how you use the whites. They can be so dazzling that when they're massed together, they will tend to punch a big hole in the landscape. Rather, sprinkle them lightly among the blues for a shimmering effect, or salt them among hot colors like African marigolds and dahlia-flowered zinnias to enliven the solid colors.

PLANT PROFILE

KNOWN BOTANICALLY AS: *Salvia farinacea*

ZONES: 4–11 as summer-flowering annuals; 9–11 as winter flowering

PROPAGATION: By seed started indoors 8 weeks before outdoor planting after frost danger

SPACING: 12 inches apart in full sun

PESTS AND DISEASES: None serious

PERFECT PARTNERS: Asters, cosmos, gloriosa daisies, marigolds, ornamental grasses, scarlet sage, and zinnias

Sage, Scarlet

Once available only in fire-engine red, new 'Salsa' salvias offer myriad colors, including purple, apricot, orange, pink, white, and bicolors.

GROW THIS! 'Strawberry', 'Salsa', 'Sangria', and 'Summer Jewel Red'

Although the color range of scarlet sage has been extended from scarlet red to violet blue, purple, pink, orange, and white, nothing—not even red geraniums—produces such a dramatically intense accent in the garden as the reds in scarlet sage. For mass bedding, the tubular flowers, arranged in a triangular spike against dark green leaves, make a dazzling display in beds and borders whether out in full sun or in light shade. (In hot southern states, you can extend the flowering period right through summer by planting them in shade.) With adequate water, scarlet sage will shrug off the heat and maintain a continuous flowering display into fall. Varieties vary in height from just 12 inches to 3 feet. 'Strawberry' is an early, red-flowering dwarf that branches freely with densely packed flower spikes.

The finest planting of scarlet sage I ever saw was at Leaming's Run Gardens in Cape May, New Jersey, where a serpentine bed leading up a lawn to a Victorian-style white gingerbread gazebo was planted entirely with red salvia.

The flowers of annual sage are made up of two prominent parts—an outer circle of petals called bracts and an inner trumpet that extends out from the bracts. Syngenta Flowers, of California, has a series called 'Salsa' that has several bicolors; when planted as a mixture, the effect is distinctive. Takii Seeds is responsible for another outstanding bicolor, 'Sangria', where the bracts and the trumpet are different colors; for example, the bracts can be creamy white and the flower trumpet a scarlet red.

Scarlet sage prefers an organically rich, well-drained soil and tolerates close planting in containers to produce a vivid display. Plants grow to just 12 inches high, the flower spike often extending another 6 inches above the mounded foliage.

BE AWARE! Many wild perennial scarlet sages are native to California, and gardeners there should visit native plant nurseries to select the best, as they are drought resistant as well as attractive. An annual red sage (*Salvia coccinea*) bred from a North American native species is named 'Lady in Red'. It won an All-America Selections award for its penstemon-like scarlet red flower spikes and ability to bloom all season; but an even brighter form, 'Summer Jewel Red', received an All-America award for its improvement over 'Lady in Red', which was used as a comparison in the All-America Selections trials. So when you have the choice, go with 'Summer Jewel Red'.

 ## PLANT PROFILE

KNOWN BOTANICALLY AS: *Salvia splendens* and *S. coccinea*

ZONES: 3–8 as a summer-flowering annual; 9–11 for winter flowering

PROPAGATION: By seed sown indoors 8 weeks before planting outdoors after frost danger

SPACING: At least 8 inches apart in sun

PESTS AND DISEASES: The usual chewing insects like slugs and Japanese beetles

PERFECT PARTNERS: Marigolds, petunias, and zinnias

Snapdragons

The 'Sonnet' and 'Liberty' medium-tall snapdragon varieties make good bedding displays during cool weather and are superb for cutting.

GROW THIS! 'Liberty' and 'Sonnet'

The old-fashioned snapdragon has an unusual flower formation. Tubular florets crowd around an erect stem, forming a spire, with the top of each floret hinged with an upper lip that closes the entrance. By pinching the base of the flower, the "mouth" can open and close. Although newer forms of snapdragon have been bred with open mouths (called butterfly flowered), other open-mouth varieties have been doubled (called azalea flowered).

At one time, it was the tall 'Topper' and 'Rocket' series that home gardeners favored, but today it is the intermediate height 'Liberty' and 'Sonnet' series that outsell other varieties since they are tall, but not too tall, and require no staking. Their flower spikes can be 3 feet high and branch freely, so that a parade of color is assured from early spring until the heat of midsummer exhausts them.

'Sonnet' snapdragons, bred by Sakata Seeds, are so popular in California that sales in that state outsell all other states combined, partly because in the mild coastal valleys, snapdragons can be grown all through the winter as well as in spring, summer, and fall.

Although snapdragons are a cool-season annual, if the spent stems are cut back to within 4 inches of the soil and kept watered, they will rejuvenate to flower again spectacularly during cool fall weather.

Snapdragons have a spicy fragrance, and they demand full sun plus good drainage. The tall kinds benefit from staking, especially from wide-mesh garden netting stretched across the bed so they poke their stems up through the netting to become self-supporting.

BE AWARE! The whole point of growing snapdragons, in my experience, is to grow strong, towering spikes studded with vibrant flowers, especially yellow, orange, and red. But breeders have introduced a whole series of low-growing forms suitable for low bedding, such as 'Flower Carpet' (in solid colors) and 'Floral Showers' (in bicolors). These are amazing breeding accomplishments,

but the short stems are unsuitable for cutting to make arrangements, and at garden centers they are usually the last to be purchased.

 ## PLANT PROFILE

KNOWN BOTANICALLY AS: *Antirrhinum majus*

ZONES: 3–8 for summer and fall flowering; 9–11 for winter and early spring flowering

PROPAGATION: By seed started indoors 8 weeks before outdoor planting

SPACING: 12 inches apart in sun or light shade. Tall kinds may need staking.

PESTS AND DISEASES: Rust (a fungal disease) and the usual chewing insects like slugs and aphids

PERFECT PARTNERS: Larkspur, marigolds, petunias, trumpet lilies, and zinnias

Spider Flowers

Each season the bushy, compact 'Sparkler' series adds a distinctive new color and has rapidly made all other spider flowers obsolete.

GROW THIS! 'Sparkler' series

Spider flowers grow wild in arid parts of Texas and Mexico, and traditionally cultivated kinds have provided gardeners with a host of benefits (like drought resistance and a long blooming period). But there's one big disadvantage—the older the plant gets, the more rangy it looks, because older varieties tend to produce one long, naked flowerstalk. 'Sparkler' is different. Instead of a tall, swaying flower stem, it grows bushy, producing multiple short side branches. It maintains an explosion of globular, spidery flower heads in four distinct colors—white, rose pink, blush pink, and lavender—plus a mixture (and more colors in the pipeline). Easily grown from seed, plant height is 42 to 48 inches with a 36-inch spread. On a rainy day, all spider flowers tend to give off a spicy odor some people find unpleasant (like sweaty socks), and, of course, be careful you do not snag skin on the small spines that run along the stems.

Glenn Goldsmith, president of the California seed company that developed 'Sparkler', told me that he used a technique for dwarfing wheat on spider flowers. The breeder Todd Spencer was subsequently honored by All-America Selections with a Breeder's Cup award.

BE AWARE! Unless you want to use them for tall backgrounds, avoid old, traditional spider flowers such as white 'Helen Campbell' and the old 'Queen' series, since these soon grow tall and gangly. Also, you'll find good reviews of the variety 'Rosalita' because it doesn't self-sow to create a nuisance in subsequent years, but, unfortunately, it is small flowered compared to the 'Sparkler' series and can be weedy looking.

 ## PLANT PROFILE

KNOWN BOTANICALLY AS: *Cleome hassleriana*

ZONES: 3–11 as a summer-flowering annual; 9–11 as a winter- and early-spring-flowering annual

PROPAGATION: By seed direct-sown or started 6 weeks before outdoor planting after frost danger

SPACING: Older, tall varieties can be spaced 12 inches apart in full sun, but the new dwarf kinds need 2–3 feet for their natural branching habit.

PESTS AND DISEASES: None serious

PERFECT PARTNERS: Asters, bedding geraniums, marigolds, ornamental grasses, sunflowers, and zinnias

Plants Recommended for Tall Backgrounds

Spider flowers are often chosen for planting at the back of a border as a backdrop for lower-growing annuals and perennials. Here's a list of other tall, flowering plants you'll find featured: asters, tall annual varieties (such as 'Matsumoto') and tall perennial varieties (such as 'Monch'); celosia 'Flamingo Feather'; dahlia, tall tuberous varieties (such as 'Bishop of Llandaff'); delphinium, tall varieties (such as 'Pacific Giants'); hardy hibiscus 'Luna' series' larkspur 'Giant Imperial'; moonflower (when trellised); morning glories (such as 'Heavenly Blue', when trellised); nasturtiums, climbing (when trellised); salvia 'Mystic Spires'; sunflower 'Autumn Beauty'; sweet peas, tall varieties (such as 'Galaxy' when trellised); verbena, tall varieties (such as *V. bonariensis*); zinnias, tall varieties (such as Benary's Giant Dahlia-Flowered)

Sunflowers

The nonstop bloom in a wide range of
bicolors and tricolors makes 'Autumn Beauty'
my favorite tall, branching sunflower.

GROW THIS! 'Sunrich', 'Sunbright Supreme', and 'Autumn Beauty'

The rise in popularity of the sunflower has been spectacular. It used to be that garden centers and seed catalogs would offer one kind—the giant-size 'Mammoth Russian' variety with heads up to 15 inches across, the flower composed of yellow petals around a black disk filled with black and gray-striped seeds used for birdseed and snacks. These sunflowers, developed from wild North American species, became popular in Russia as a source of oil. But for ornamental purposes, they are not long lived, and the heads soon shed their petals and drop their seeds to the ground.

Today, home gardeners are mostly interested in growing sunflowers to use as cut flowers and also for long-lasting summer-to-fall flowering. Two varieties—the 'Sunrich' and 'Sunbright Supreme' series—are very similar in appearance and are both from Japanese breeders. These produce medium-size yellow or orange heads, one to a stem for cutting. They are fast growing and flower within 60 days from seed. A little-known fact about sunflowers is that the flowering occurs during short days, and so greenhouse growers can produce a winter crop, while home gardeners generally will see flowering occur after midsummer when daylength shortens. Growth will not stop during long daylight hours: The stems will simply grow taller. Both 'Sunrich' and 'Sunbright Supreme' are pollenless because florists complained that the pollen makes a mess indoors and stains clothing; breeders obliged by eliminating the gene that produces the powdery yellow pollen.

Of the 11 colors in the 'Sunrich' series, growers particularly like the one known as 'Tiffany' because in addition to golden yellow petals and a black seed disk, it has a brown rim between the petals and the seed disk, giving it an eye-catching tricolor effect.

For garden display, home gardeners find the multistemmed kinds more appealing than single-stemmed varieties since they are everblooming, especially the mixture 'Autumn Beauty', which has flowers up to 4 inches across in a diverse range of bicolors and tricolors. Moreover, the more you cut 'Autumn Beauty', the more the plant is stimulated into producing new flower buds until fall frost.

BE AWARE! Under the heading "Sunflowers" in seed catalogs and also in seed racks at garden centers, you will find a huge assortment of varieties, some listed as a sunflower that are not deserving of the name. For example, the "Mexican sunflower" (*Tithonia angustifolia*) is a weedy-looking plant that blooms late, producing more foliage than flowers. Growing to 8 feet high, the sparse, orange flowers are no bigger than a cosmos, and they even look like orange cosmos. So that's one to avoid, in my opinion.

Then there are the giant, tall 'Mammoth Russian' sunflowers that can grow to 12 feet tall, topped by a single, top-heavy ugly flower that is mostly composed of a black seed disk and tiny yellow or orange petals. Grow it for seeds to make a snack or to feed the birds, but don't give it much space as an ornamental.

 ## PLANT PROFILE

KNOWN BOTANICALLY AS: *Helianthus annuus*

ZONES: 3–11 for summer-flowering annuals

PROPAGATION: By seed direct-sown or started indoors 4 weeks before outdoor planting after frost danger

SPACING: Minimum of 12 inches apart in full sun. Tall plants may need staking.

PESTS AND DISEASES: The usual chewing insects like slugs and Japanese beetles; birds will feast on the seed disks.

PERFECT PARTNERS: Tall celosia, tall cosmos, marigolds, morning glories, and zinnias

Sweet Peas

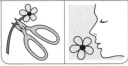

Keith Hammett's modern 'Streamers'
series includes new color combinations, while the late Henry
Eckford's 'Eckford's Finest Mix' offers the best fragrance.

GROW THIS! 'Galaxy', 'Bijou', 'Eckford's Finest Mix', and 'Streamers'

There is a revival of interest in growing sweet peas. The tragedy is that for all their beauty and honey-sweet fragrance, they ever fell from grace. Before World War II, the sweet pea was the most popular flowering annual in North American gardens. Such was the demand for sweet peas that thousands of acres were grown in the Lompoc Valley, California, where cool coastal mists and sandy soil with excellent drainage produce ideal growing conditions.

It was a soil fungus that finally brought about the demise of the annual sweet pea, turning the stems and leaves brown before they have a chance to flower. By planting sweet peas in a different location each season, or planting in containers with sterile soil, it's still possible to grow them and enjoy armloads of flowers for indoor floral arrangements. They offer an extensive color range that includes all shades of red, blue, pink, orange, maroon, and purple, plus white. There are climbing types like 'Galaxy' and dwarf, compact kinds like 'Bijou' that require no staking, but these modern kinds have sacrificed fragrance for large flowers and vigor.

Where intense fragrance is important, choose 'Eckford's Finest Mix'. Henry Eckford was a Scotsman who began hybridizing sweet peas at his farm in Shropshire on the Welsh border. He collaborated with US seedsman W. Atlee Burpee to introduce his best varieties into North America.

Keith Hammett, a New Zealand sweet pea breeder, has produced some sensational newer varieties that retain fragrance, notably his 'Streamers' mixture. 'Streamers' display a range of striped varieties that give them a charming old-fashioned appearance. Plants are summer flowering (most sweet peas require 12 hours of daylight to begin flowering) and have long stems suitable for cutting.

BE AWARE! 'Little Sweetheart' and 'Cupid' are pathetic-looking, low-growing, mounded varieties with small, pink flowers. They look like aberrations,

since we expect our sweet peas to be either bushy and erect like the 'Bijou' series or tall and climbing like the 'Royals'. Beware of vendors selling perennial sweet pea plants as annual sweet peas. The perennial sweet pea is a tall, vigorous, disease-resistant plant with a limited color range (mostly rose pink and white). Flowers are half the size of annual sweet peas and lack fragrance. Actually, I find that the perennial sweet pea has merit as a hardy flowering vine that is easy to grow and comes back every year, but its lack of fragrance and small flower size will disappoint you if you expected the fragrance and more vibrant color range of annual sweet peas. In the transplant stage, annual sweet peas and perennial sweet peas are hard to tell apart, so ask a customer service rep which kind they have on display.

Unless you live in the Pacific Northwest, do not follow the advice in some books that suggest the European method of propagation: a fall sowing. Much of the United States experiences winters that are too cold for sweet peas to survive a fall planting.

 ## PLANT PROFILE

KNOWN BOTANICALLY AS: *Lathyrus odoratus*

ZONES: 3–7 for spring and summer flowering; 8–11 for winter and early spring flowering

PROPAGATION: By seed direct-sown 1 inch deep in early spring or from seed started indoors 4–6 weeks before outdoor planting. Soak seeds overnight to speed germination.

SPACING: 12 inches apart in full sun. Stake tall kinds.

PESTS AND DISEASES: Fungus root rots that prevent plants from growing twice in the same general area; the usual chewing insects such as slugs and foraging animals such as rabbits

PERFECT PARTNERS: Calendulas, coreopsis, cosmos, and poppies

Texas Bluebells
(aka Lisianthus)

When you grow the 'Echo' series, you'll discover why this is now the florist's favorite cut flower. The Japanese have turned this inconspicuous native American prairie wildflower, also known as *Eustoma,* into a glamour girl.

GROW THIS! 'Echo Blue', 'Mariachi', 'Forever Blue', and 'Forever White'

Foreign breeders often recognize the commercial potential for a North American wildflower before a US breeder does. Perfect examples are the Yorkshireman George Russell, who developed 'Russell Hybrid' lupines from North American species, and Sakata Seeds of Yokohama, Japan, who used the wild North American hardy swamp mallow to develop the award-winning 'Southern Belle' and 'Disco' series (both now superseded by the 'Luna' series).

What farsightedness it must have taken to believe that the desert wildflower known as Texas bluebell could become a garden-worthy annual that's a favorite cut flower among florists because some of the flowers resemble roses with their multiple layers of petals. In the wild, the Texas bluebell looks like a small, pathetic evening primrose. Sakata's breeders, however, have made a beautiful swan from this ugly duckling.

Sakata's most popular series is their double-flowered 'Echo'. The color range includes all shades of blue plus yellow, white, pink, and bicolors. Plant height is up to 3 feet, with the plants freely branching at the base to send up a dozen strong, slender flowerstalks that are suitable for cutting during summer. Many gardeners now prefer the 'Mariachi' series, from the same breeder, for its extra row of petals and even more similarity to a rose bloom.

Another appealing flower form is the single-flowered lisianthus because the urn shape resembles a tulip. 'Forever Blue' and 'Forever White' both received All-America Selections awards for their ability to bloom all season and throw new flower stems after cutting.

Texas bluebells require full sun and good drainage, and the flowers are easily damaged by inclement weather, especially heavy rains. The brittle stems generally need staking to keep them erect and the flowers facing up.

BE AWARE! Some wildflower catalogs offer seed of the native Texas blue-bell. If you're mass-sowing into an arid prairie or desert landscape, these seeds are fine; for garden display, the flowers of the native plant are pretty, yet easily overshadowed by the cultivated kinds.

 ## PLANT PROFILE

KNOWN BOTANICALLY AS: *Eustoma grandiflora*; also *Lisianthus russulanus*

ZONES: 4–8 as a summer-flowering annual; 9–11 for winter flowering

PROPAGATION: By seed started indoors at least 10 weeks before outdoor planting. Press seeds into the soil surface just barely far enough to anchor them, as they need light to germinate.

SPACING: 12 inches apart in full sun. Plants are best staked to keep the stems erect.

PESTS AND DISEASES: Soil fungal diseases such as damping-off; slugs and foraging animals such as rabbits

PERFECT PARTNERS: Texas bluebells should be a part of every cutting garden, along with asters, celosia, cosmos, lilies, marigolds, sunflowers, sweet peas, and zinnias.

Verbenas

For a low, spreading carpet of flowers all season, grow 'Homestead Purple'. Want a unique color? Grow 'Lanai Twister Pink' verbena hybrid.

GROW THIS! 'Homestead Purple', 'Tapien' series, and 'Lanai' series (especially 'Lanai Twister Pink')

Verbenas are tender annuals available as spreading kinds and upright forms. The spreading kinds not only look good massed in beds and borders, but they are also exquisite in hanging baskets and window-box planters. Each flower of a verbena is a cluster of a dozen or more florets that overlap to create a dome of color in mostly shades of red, pink, and blue, plus white and bicolors.

'Homestead Purple' is an unusually vigorous variety. Although the flowers individually are smaller than newer hybrid varieties, the sheer quantity and repeat bloom creates a carpet of color for months during the heat of summer. Anna Ball, owner of Ball FloraPlant, always has plenty of this spreading groundcover in her test plots. "Each plant is packed with enough vigor to keep it flowering and spreading to 2 feet and more across—a pool of deep purple color," she notes. And it doesn't create bald spots, starting in the center, like many other verbenas, I might add.

The 'Tapien' and 'Lanai' series are outstanding for their rich assortment of colors and resistance to powdery mildew. The 'Lanai' series, in particular, has received a number of awards, including Best of the Best from the University of Georgia and Top 10 Annual Performers from the University of Tennessee. My top color pick among the 17 current color choices is 'Lanai Twister Pink', because it has a unique color combination—an outer ring of petals that is apple blossom pink and an inner ring that is deep rosy red. Examine a flower closely and you will see that this is unique because the inner ring of flowers is literally cut in half by the color contrast.

When choosing varieties, be sure to check whether the plants are tall growing or spreading. Some verbenas—like *Verbena hastata* and *V. bonariensis*—grow tall and erect—up to 5 feet high—while the spreading kinds rarely exceed 8 to 10 inches in height and extend 3 feet wide. Plant spreading varieties like the 'Quartz' series when you desire a greater density of color or are planting in patio containers. Give verbena full sun and an organic-rich soil with good drainage. For a patriotic color combination, it's possible to choose among several shades of red, blue, and a snow white.

BE AWARE! Tall varieties of verbena—such as *V. corymbosa*, *V. hastate*, and *V. stricta*—are

Verbena 'Lanai' mixed colors create a low-spreading carpet, blooming nonstop all season; it's ideal for hanging baskets.

perennials and weedy looking. If you would like a tall verbena that will flower the first season from seed, choose *V. bonariensis*, with its masses of perky purple flower clusters on stems suitable for cutting.

 ## PLANT PROFILE

KNOWN BOTANICALLY AS: *Verbena* x *hybrida*

ZONES: 3–8 as summer-flowering annuals; 9–11 as winter- and early-spring-flowering annuals

PROPAGATION: By seed started indoors 8 weeks before outdoor planting after frost danger

SPACING: At least 12 inches apart in full sun, allowing stems to knit together

PESTS AND DISEASES: Usual chewing insects such as slugs, and foraging animals such as rabbits

PERFECT PARTNERS: Calibrachoa, dusty miller, lantana, marigolds, petunias, and zinnias

Vincas (aka Periwinkle)

For drought resistance where little else will grow, try the disease-resistant 'Cora' in a multitude of pastel colors.

GROW THIS! 'Cora', 'Cobra', and 'Titan'

Annual vinca (also known by its botanical name, *Catharanthus*, and by another common name, Madagascar periwinkle) is a sun-loving, drought-resistant plant with glossy dark green leaves. Its flowers are star shaped. The color range is extensive, including red, pink, purple, white, and bicolors—including a very popular white with red eye and a pink with red eye. Growing outside their native Madagascar, annual vinca encountered a serious problem—a virulent airborne fungal disease, *Phytophthora*, which turns the plant brown. All that has changed through work by the California plant breeder Syngenta Flowers using genetic material collected from the wild. Called 'Cora', to honor the wife of a leading US bedding plant grower, the 14- to 16-inch-high plants spread up to 25 inches and are covered in impatiens-like blooms in eight dazzling colors, including red, pink, violet, lavender, apricot, and white with red eye zone known as 'Polka Dot'. In addition to low bedding, the plants are suitable for growing in containers, such as dish planters and hanging baskets.

For the home gardener, 'Cora' vinca is everblooming from spring through fall frost. Indeed, in my Zone 10 garden on Sanibel Island, Florida, I have had 'Cora' in continuous bloom *for 3 years*, since it will perform as a perennial if not killed by frost. It thrives in heat and humidity and tolerates a wide range of soils, including poor, impoverished soil and almost pure sand. There are two conditions it doesn't like—a cold soil (therefore delay outdoor planting until the soil has thoroughly warmed up in spring) and poor drainage. Where drainage is poor, grow in raised beds or containers.

'Cobra' and 'Titan' are two other vincas with varying degrees of disease resistance. They are generally less costly to buy than 'Cora'.

Some of the colors in the 'Cora' mixture of annual vinca have a distinctive red eye zone. The variety is disease resistant and everblooming until fall frost.

BE AWARE! With their superior disease resistance, 'Cora', 'Cobra', and 'Titan' make other annual vincas obsolete. Although some other varieties of annual vinca are still sold, I'd suggest you avoid 'Pretty' and 'Little Linda' because they tend to be short lived and are likely to soon disappear from the market.

PLANT PROFILE

KNOWN BOTANICALLY AS: *Catharanthus roseus*

ZONES: 3–11 as a summer-flowering annual; 9–11 as a winter- and early-spring-flowering annual. In frost-free areas, vinca is a perennial.

PROPAGATION: By seed sown indoors 8 weeks before outdoor planting after frost danger

SPACING: 12 inches apart in full sun

PESTS AND DISEASES: Old annual vincas are so susceptible to *Phytophthora* fungus disease they are hardly worth growing anymore. 'Cora' is virtually immune.

PERFECT PARTNERS: Calibrachoa, coleus, impatiens, lantana, marigolds, petunias, verbena, and zinnias

Violas

Also called Johnny-jump-ups, new 'Penny' and 'Sorbet' bloom nonstop all season from early spring to fall frost in sun or light shade.

GROW THIS! 'Sorbet' and 'Penny'

Violas are closely related to pansies, and one of the most popular varieties for years has been a compact, free-flowering yellow-and-blue bicolor commonly called Johnny-jump-ups. The popularity of violas has risen dramatically with the introduction of the 'Sorbet' series, a strain developed by Pan American Seeds, and the similar 'Penny' series from Goldsmith Seeds. They are so vigorous and carefree that they bloom continuously all season from spring through fall frost, nonstop—providing they are watered during dry periods. The 'Penny' and 'Sorbet' violas grow to just 8 inches high and branch freely at the base, so they do not stretch during warm weather like many older varieties. Planted in spring, they are hardy and will bloom all through the summer until hard fall frosts. Planted in fall (usually after Labor Day), the plants will bloom until hard frosts but often still have enough vigor to survive the winter and repeat-bloom in spring. Although the individual plants are small, they keep branching from the base, and what they lack in size they make up for in sheer quantity of bloom. The color range is extensive, including blue, yellow, orange, red, and white, but it is the bicolors that are most appealing, many of them with "whiskered" faces. A viola flower is made up of five petals—the two uppermost known as wings because they flare out. These wings can be a different color than the lower petals, and so some of the most eye-catching color combinations are yellow with purple wings, yellow with blue wings, and even yellow with red wings. 'Orange Duet', a yellow-and-orange-whiskered bicolor, won a Fleuroselect award.

Breeding work on the 'Sorbet' series was initiated by my friend Juggy Sharma (now retired) for Pan American Seeds. An especially beautiful variety in this strain is called 'Yesterday, Today, and Tomorrow' since it displays three colors on one plant—white, changing to light blue as the flower matures, changing to deep blue. Juggy's father was a ranger for the sacred wildflower valley, known as the Valley of the Flowers, in India's Himalayas. We still cherish a goal to travel there together, camp in the valley, and do some plant exploring.

Anna Ball, owner of Pan American Seeds, advises replacing summer annuals past their prime with 'Sorbet' violas in fall. "You'll enjoy flowers right up to hard frost, then as spring arrives, you get another big show right along with your crocuses and tulips," she says.

BE AWARE! Old-fashioned varieties, such as Johnny-jump-ups (*Viola × williamsiana*), soon exhaust themselves when spring turns to summer. The same is true with the old deep purple variety 'Helen Mount' and the black 'Bowles' Black' (both *V. tricolor*). Stick with the 'Penny' and 'Sorbet' series for the longest-lasting bedding displays.

 ## PLANT PROFILE

KNOWN BOTANICALLY AS: *Viola tricolor and V. cornuta*

ZONES: 3–8 as a spring-, summer-, and fall-flowering annual; 9–11 as a winter-flowering annual

PROPAGATION: By seed started indoors 8 weeks before outdoor planting

SPACING: 9–12 inches apart in sun or light shade

PESTS AND DISEASES: Usual chewing insects such as slugs, and foraging animals such as rabbits

PERFECT PARTNERS: African daisies, calendulas, forget-me-nots, lobelia pansies, and snapdragons

Zinnias, Daisy-Flowered

Whoever would have thought that a single-flowered zinnia series called 'Profusion' could be so colorful that it could outsell the giant-flowered kinds for a long-lasting display?

GROW THIS! 'Profusion' single flowered and 'Zahara' double flowered

Basically, there are three kinds of zinnias popular among home gardeners: The first group, *Zinnia elegans*, has the largest flowers, usually classified as dahlia

Zinnia 'Zahara Fire' won awards from All-America Selections and a Fleuroselect award for its vibrant color and profuse flowering on low, compact plants.

flowered and cactus flowered. The dahlia flowered have doubled, flat, rounded petals, while the cactus flowered are quilled, with pointed and twisted petals resembling cactus spines. Both are popular for mass plantings and cutting, especially planted in a rainbow of colors that might include red, yellow, orange, pink, white, purple, and even green, plus bicolors. A second group is *Z. haageana* (also called narrow-leaved zinnia), forming low, bushy plants covered with small, double multicolored flowers with pointed petals. The third group has *Z. angustifolia* in its blood, mostly single flowered, resembling a daisy, but also double flowered.

Most zinnias have a common problem. They are desert plants from Mexico, and they are accustomed to dry summers; during wet seasons, they often succumb to mildew and botrytis fungal diseases. Although there are fungicides that will help control these diseases, most home gardeners do not want to use them.

'Profusion' zinnias are to zinnias what cushion mums are to chrysanthemums—they create a dome of daisylike flowers and dark green foliage. The daisylike flowers are so profuse that they can almost completely hide the foliage. They are so disease resistant that they can flower nonstop from late spring until heavy fall frost. Such is the success of 'Profusion' zinnias for mass bedding and containers that the breeder Sakata Seeds has introduced a diverse range of habits and flower forms, including the original dwarf cushion types, plus knee-high types suitable for cutting and double-flowered kinds. Plants of the original 'Profusion' grow to 12 inches high, flower within 8 weeks from seed, and self-clean by covering faded flowers with new flower buds and foliage. The color range includes red, orange, cherry, coral pink, yellow, white, and a mixture. The orange, white, and cherry are All-America Selections award winners. Mass them in low beds, in containers, and as edging plants, since the uniform height can create a hedge effect.

I am not so enthusiastic over a similar single-flowered series called 'Zahara', but the double form is superior to the 'Profusion' doubles; if you want to light up your garden with an intense blaze of color, make it 'Zahara Fire', an All-America Selections and Fleuroselect winner.

BE AWARE! There are certain flowering annuals that look sensational in color photographs but are disappointing when you actually grow them. One is zinnia 'Red Spider', which has pointed petals, but the plant grows more leaves than flowers, and they are pathetically small. Also too small to be of any ornamental value is 'Red Cap'.

 PLANT PROFILE

KNOWN BOTANICALLY AS: *Zinnia angustifolia*

ZONES: 4–8 as a summer-flowering annual; 9–11 as a winter- and early-spring-flowering annual

PROPAGATION: By seed either direct-sown or started indoors 6 weeks before outdoor flowering

SPACING: Minimum of 12 inches apart in full sun

PESTS AND DISEASES: Mildew and botrytis disease and usual chewing insects such as slugs, grasshoppers, and Japanese beetles

PERFECT PARTNERS: Dwarf celosia, dwarf nasturtiums, dwarf verbena, French marigolds, and petunias

Zinnias, Dahlia- and Cactus-Flowered

Benary's 'Giant Dahlia Flowered Zinnias', in a mixture of vivid colors, have mildew resistance. This makes them the most desirable of all large-flowered zinnias.

GROW THIS! Benary's 'Giant Dahlia Flowered Zinnias', 'Burpeeana Giants Mixed', 'Burpee's Big Tetra', 'Magellan', 'Dreamland', 'Zowie', 'Swizzle', and 'Giant Lime'

The 'Magellan' series of dahlia-flowered zinnias are compact and vigorous.

Many gardeners are drawn to zinnias for their large blooms and strong stems, suitable for both dramatic garden display and cutting. They have a rich color range, making them popular as a rainbow mixture and ideal for massing in beds and borders. Among the tall kinds, it's hard to choose between a number of famous names—'Burpeeana Giants Mixed' cactus-flowered hybrids (with huge quilled petals pointed like cactus spines) and 'Burpee's Big Tetra' giant dahlia-flowered (double flowers with flat, rounded petals), both with individual flowers up to 6 inches across on 3-foot-high plants.

A much more vivid color impact is possible by choosing among bushy, low-growing types, such as the 'Magellan' series, developed by Syngenta, and 'Dreamland', developed by Takii. Both have won All-America Selections awards, and it's hard to tell the two apart, although 'Magellan' is a little more uniform in height and slightly larger flowered. Plants grow to just 14 inches high, almost smother themselves in blooms, and flower within 8 weeks from seed. Plant them in full sun with good drainage.

Several new dahlia-flowered bicolored zinnias outshine other bicolors. These include 'Zowie', a 3-foot-high yellow variety with a red eye zone bred by Syngenta Flowers. Winner of an All-America Selections award for its vigor and free-flowering nature, it makes an exceptional cut flower. From the same breeding program came the 'Swizzle' series—a cherry with ivory petal tips and a red with yellow petal tips. Both create a low mound of leaves and picture-perfect double flowers especially suitable for growing in containers.

BE AWARE! There are flowering annuals that seem to sell on the name alone. The dwarf, compact zinnia called 'Thumbelina' won an All-America award for its cushion shape and 1-inch flowers in a wide color range. It's supposed to be double flowered, but it is an unstable mixture growing many singles with an ugly cob (raised) center and with very few true doubles on the same plant. The packet copy generally recommends it for edging beds and borders, but it needs constant deadheading to keep it flowering. Most of us want zinnias with stems long enough for cutting, but the stems of 'Thumbelina' are too short.

There are too few green flowers among annuals, because flowers must contrast with green foliage to attract pollinators, and green 'Envy' has been one of the best. But more recently, it has been superseded by Benary's larger-flowered 'Giant Lime'.

 ## PLANT PROFILE

KNOWN BOTANICALLY AS: *Zinnia elegans*

ZONES: 4–8 as a summer-flowering annual; 9–11 for winter and early spring flowering

PROPAGATION: By seed either direct-sown or started indoors 6 weeks before outdoor planting

SPACING: 12 inches apart in full sun

PESTS AND DISEASES: Susceptible to damping-off disease, also botrytis and mildew, and usual chewing insects such as slugs, Japanese beetles, and grasshoppers

PERFECT PARTNERS: Asters, celosia, gloriosa daisies, marigolds, petunias, and spider flowers

CHAPTER 7

BEST CHOICE PERENNIALS

Perennials are a huge family of plants that mostly produce green foliage growth the first season, then go dormant over winter and flower the next season, usually in spring, summer, or fall. Some perennials, like peonies, can outlive their owners, blooming reliably year after year; others, like cottage tulips, can be short lived and need planting from flowering-size bulbs each year.

The following pages contain my personal favorites. Many are popular hardy varieties like daylilies, hostas, and bearded irises. They are relatively easy to grow and command attention in the garden. They produce a big bang for the buck. Some others I have included are tender perennials and are not so well known, like caladiums, calla lilies, and bromeliads. Although they are unlikely to overwinter in northern gardens with frequent frosts, they make good patio plants for taking indoors during winter.

This choice selection I have grown myself at Cedaridge Farm. And in many cases, I have visited the breeders responsible for the choicest varieties, such as Paul Aden, a preeminent hosta breeder on Long Island who produced the very popular chartreuse 'Sum & Substance' and slate blue 'Blue Angel' hostas, both of which have such large leaves that they look tropical. I was a good friend of the late Jan de Graaff, breeder of hardy garden lilies at his farm in Oregon, and still am of Dr. Darrell Apps, famous for his repeat-flowering daylilies such as 'Happy Returns'. I have even traveled abroad, to Holland, England, and France, to meet with Europe's leading perennial breeders, and in France, I interviewed Mr. and Mrs. Daniel Lawson, who continue to breed 'Barnhaven' primroses, a mostly hardy strain that originated from breeding work by an Oregon plant breeder named Florence Bellis.

So, yes, my choice of perennials is deliberately selective, since I would rather provide a lot of good information about outstanding varieties I know you will find worth growing than provide small reviews about a lot of plant families that I don't feel make that big an impact.

Seed of popular perennials is available from seed racks in garden centers, but the majority of perennials are purchased as potted plants ready to bloom the first season. The same is true of biennials such as columbine, hardy hibiscus, and sweet William, but since these have been encouraged to bloom the first season, they are described in the annuals chapter.

Some perennials are purchased as raw bulbs, such as lilies and daffodils. The daffodils are generally planted in fall for blooming the following spring and the lilies in spring for blooming later that summer season, depending on the variety. The spring-planted bulbs, such as dinner-plate dahlias, are often too tender to survive frozen soil, and so where winters are severe, these are either treated as annuals to die down after frost, or they are dug up, cleaned of soil, and stored in a frost-free location such as a basement or heated garage.

PLANT CHARACTERISTICS

Throughout this chapter, these symbols identify a special benefit or preference for each plant. These attributes represent the main reasons why home gardeners choose perennials.

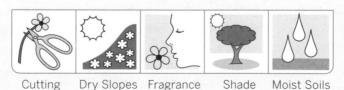

Cutting   Dry Slopes   Fragrance   Shade   Moist Soils

Amaryllis

The butterfly amaryllis 'Papilio' has an
amazing petal pattern, as though painted by an artist,
with maroon veins on a white background and green throat.

GROW THIS! Naked ladies, 'Charmeur', 'Ambiance', and 'Papilio'

The name "amaryllis" can apply to several fall-, winter-, and spring-blooming flowering bulbs with big trumpet-shaped blooms. It can apply to the tender *Amaryllis belladonna*, a beautiful pale pink perennial that comes from South Africa, and also its hardy look-alike, *Lycoris squamigera*, that comes from Asia. Both are commonly called naked ladies because in summer they produce flowers on naked stems without leaves. The straplike leaves occur earlier in spring and then die back and disappear by early summer. All prefer full sun. Among the amaryllis known as *Hippeastrum*, I personally like the reds and the red-and-white bicolored varieties. Among the reds, my favorite is 'Charmeur', because it is a soft orange red and not the harsh crimson red of most other red amaryllis. For a red-and-white bicolor, I recommend 'Ambiance', since it is a little more dramatic in its color contrasts than the old favorite called 'Apple Blossom'. To get an indoor amaryllis to rebloom in areas where the ground freezes, keep the leaves healthy by watering the pot and transplant to the garden after frost danger. In fall, after frost kills the top, repot and take indoors for a repeat bloom.

The most eye-catching of amaryllis is 'Papilio', also called butterfly amaryllis. This has trumpet-shaped flowers up to 8 inches across with pointed white petals that are delicately striped dark red. Plants thrive in sun or light shade and will overwinter outdoors in Zones 7 to 11 providing they are given a fertile soil with good drainage. The two kinds of naked ladies amaryllis are summer-flowering and multiply readily by making more bulbs. They include the tender *Amaryllis belladonna* (Zones 8 to 11) and the hardy *Lycoris squamigera* (Zones 5 to 9). The latter will survive frost and even frozen soil.

BE AWARE! Be careful when choosing double-flowered amaryllis, for the petals of most of them resemble crumpled paper, including red 'Ragtime' and the red-and-white bicolor 'Dancing Queen'.

The most coveted of all amaryllis is the blue amaryllis (*Worsleya rayneri*) from the Organ Mountains of Brazil. It is rarely seen in gardens because it is difficult to obtain flowering-size bulbs. One day, I searched on eBay to see if anyone had the blue amaryllis for sale, and a lady in the Midwest offered 10 bulbs to the highest bidder. Her photograph showing a close-up of one bloom was just like the plant I had seen near Rio de Janeiro during a visit to Brazil, and the highest bid was $30. A bargain! I would gladly have paid $50 and was about to enter my bid when I decided to click on the link giving more information. This showed another photo of a group of flowers with leaves too slender to be the genuine article. I read further and saw that the Latin name was for a small blue wayside weed that grows in China. I looked in a bulb catalog and saw that I could buy 10 bulbs of these for $3. Buyer beware!

PLANT PROFILE

KNOWN BOTANICALLY AS: *Hippeastrum* hybrids and *Lycoris* and *Amaryllis* species

ZONES: All zones as a houseplant to bloom during winter months; perennial in Zones 7–11. The naked lady–type *L. squamigera* is outdoor hardy in Zones 5–9.

PROPAGATION: Mostly from flowering-size bulbs. Amaryllis from seed can take 7 years to flower.

SPACING: Shoulder to shoulder in pots; 6–8 inches apart in the garden, in sun or shade

PESTS AND DISEASES: Several viruses and the usual chewing insects such as slugs and grasshoppers

PERFECT PARTNERS: Caladiums outdoors, paperwhite narcissus indoors. The naked lady–types look good with rudbeckia 'Goldsturm', summer phlox, and ornamental grasses.

Anemones, French

With the largest flowers of all the French anemones and the kind sold by most florists, 'Mona Lisa' can be mostly blue, red, pink, and white—all with contrasting eye zones and a powdery black center.

GROW THIS! 'Harmony Mix' and 'Mona Lisa'

French anemones, also called poppy anemones and windflowers, were made popular by cut-flower growers around the French city of Caen who bred special large-flowered varieties of *Anemone coronaria*. They are grown from seed or from corms, depending on the variety. The flowers are cup shaped and up to 5 inches across and have a powdery dome of black stamens at the center like an Oriental poppy. The colors include poppy red, pink, blue, purple, and white. The best strain for bedding is 'Harmony Mix', since it is naturally low growing and ideal for low beds, especially partnered with pansies and primroses. Approximately 25 percent of the blue blooms will be double flowers. A larger-flowered and taller variety (18 inches), 'Mona Lisa' was introduced by Pan American Seed. It has the widest color range and is best grown from seed, producing blooms up to 5 inches across when grown in greenhouses. Though temperamental for outdoor bedding, they flower well in coastal locations such as coastal California and the Pacific Northwest.

For outdoor display, anemone corms are best planted in the fall in sheltered positions for early spring flowering. Ready-to-bloom transplants are also sold in early spring for spring flowering after frost danger. They will naturalize in Zones 7 to 9, but their best flowering outdoors occurs in Zone 8 and in cold-frames farther north. Standard varieties grow to 12 inches high and require full sun and a well-drained soil, but they will tolerate light shade.

BE AWARE! French anemones for spring flowering can be temperamental and fail to return after the first season of bloom, even within their zones of hardiness. Moreover, they are often confused with the much hardier fall-flowering white or pink Japanese anemones, largely because the best French anemones now come from Japan.

PLANT PROFILE

KNOWN BOTANICALLY AS: *Anemone coronaria*

ZONES: 7–9 as a perennial; 3–6 as an annual except in sheltered locations, such as along a house foundation in excellent drainage

PROPAGATION: Mostly from dormant bulbs, but also from seed started indoors 10 weeks before outdoor planting

SPACING: 6 inches apart in sun or light shade

PESTS AND DISEASES: Mostly greenfly and aphids, especially when grown indoors as a potted plant, but also powdery mildew and rot induced by poor drainage and alternate freezing and thawing

PERFECT PARTNERS: Daffodils, pansies, Spanish bluebells, star of Bethlehem, tulips, and violas

Angel's Trumpets

The orange variety 'Charles Grimaldi', named for a San Francisco nurseryman, has large, pendent, honey-scented flowers and it blooms several times each season.

GROW THIS! 'Charles Grimaldi'

The botanical name for angel's trumpets, *Brugmansia*, used to be *Datura*, but taxonomists decided that *Datura*, whose flowers hang down (instead of facing up), should be given a different appellation. The late Charles Grimaldi was a San Francisco nurseryman who hybridized a series of angel's trumpets, the best of which is a fragrant, large-flowered orange variety that he named for himself.

'Charles Grimaldi' is a fast-growing woody plant that will bloom the first year from cuttings that are extremely easy to root in warm temperatures above 60°F. Simply cut a 6-inch section of stem and place one end in water to quickly establish a root system. Or insert tip cuttings into a peat-based, moist potting soil. Within one season, that 6-inch cutting will grow into a tree up to 5 feet high, and if protected during winter from freezing weather, it will continue to grow to 30 feet and higher in subsequent years. The fragrance is honey scented, and the plants bloom in several flushes throughout the year, usually in spring, midsummer, and fall. The plants look good in a whiskey half barrel and can be trained to a tree form, with a slender, straight trunk and a topknot of leaves and flowers. Plants tolerate moist soil and should never be allowed to dry out or they will wilt. Also, they are heavy feeders and require a balanced granular or liquid organic fertilizer every 3 weeks.

To overwinter, the plant can be cut back to 3 feet high, the roots dug up, and transferred to a pot. It may drop all its leaves and look dead, but at the onset of warm weather it will invariably leaf out with large, lance-shaped leaves.

BE AWARE! There are several species of *Brugmansia* and its look-alike, *Datura*, offered by nurseries as angel's trumpets; all should be considered poisonous, producing hallucinogenic effects if ingested. Although offered by nurserymen and seedsmen, *D. metel* should never be planted. An annual form of angel's trumpet known as jimsonweed, it takes its common name from Jamestown, a town in Virginia where British soldiers during the Revolutionary War were poisoned after American patriots sneaked *Datura* leaves into cauldrons of their soup. Since *Brugmansias* grow treelike with masses of big, pendent flowers, they have good ornamental value, whereas *Daturas* in general remain bushy and sparse flowering and—to my sensitivity—evil looking.

 PLANT PROFILE

KNOWN BOTANICALLY AS: *Brugmansia* hybrids

ZONES: All zones as a potted houseplant and as an annual, moved indoors for protection against freezing during winter. Plants will overwinter outdoors in Zones 10 and 11.

PROPAGATION: Mostly by cuttings, which will root in plain water

SPACING: At least 4 feet apart in sun or light shade

PESTS AND DISEASES: Whitefly, aphids, slugs, and other chewing insects; also rust disease

PERFECT PARTNERS: Any member of the tobacco family, to which they are related, such as blue potato vine, nicotiana, and petunias; also hibiscus (tropical and hardy kinds), hydrangea, and Oriental lilies

Asters, Perennial

If I had to pick just one perennial aster, I would agree with perennial expert Graham Stuart Thomas and choose the Swiss-bred, sky blue 'Monch'.

GROW THIS! 'Monch', 'Wood's Blue', Wood's Pink', and 'Wood's Purple'

There are many varieties of aster for late summer and fall flowering, including those known as New England asters (*Aster nova-angliae*) and a look-alike group called New York asters (*A. nova-belgii*). They bloom mostly in shades of red, pink, and blue, plus white, all with yellow button centers. The most popular color is blue, and for sheer flower power, the most desirable fall aster is a hybrid between two European species, *A. amellus* and *A. thomsonii*. Originating at the perennial plant nursery of Frikart in Switzerland, 'Monch' (*A. × frikartii* 'Monch') is a beautiful sky blue with a yellow center that blooms nonstop from late August through October. 'Monch' is a better plant than 'Wonder of Staffa' from the same Swiss breeding program. It is a deeper blue with more symmetrical flowers, described by the perennial plant expert the

Perennial aster 'Monch' cascades down a retaining wall. It blooms riotously from midsummer to fall frost.

late Graham Stuart Thomas as "Without doubt . . . the finest aster for long display. It is the last word in elegance, in poise and form." Both plants produce 2½-inch flowers that overlap each other. They grow to 4 feet high, doubling in sideways spread each year. Recipient of an Award of Garden Merit from the prestigious Royal Horticultural Society, 'Monch' prefers full sun and soil with good drainage. Propagate by division or stem cuttings taken from the base of the plant.

The Wood's series of hardy perennial asters—such as 'Wood's Blue', 'Wood's Pink', and 'Wood's Purple'—are mounded and compact selections of *A. dumosus*, up to 18 inches high, and vigorous and disease resistant. The late Ed Wood of Portland, Oregon, was an apple breeder, but he worked on breeding perennial asters as a sideline.

BE AWARE! Don't confuse perennial asters with annual asters—commonly called China asters (*Callistephus chinensis*). Avoid Tatarian asters (*A. tataricus*). They are too tall (6 feet), extremely invasive, and difficult to get rid of once established. Every small piece of broken root will grow a new plant, so even digging them up doesn't necessarily eradicate them.

 PLANT PROFILE

KNOWN BOTANICALLY AS: *Aster x frikartii*

ZONES: Zones 5–8 for summer and fall flowering, depending on variety

PROPAGATION: Mostly from root division and also from cuttings taken in spring and early summer before plants bloom. Also from seed, but seed-raised plants may not breed true.

SPACING: At least 3 feet apart for tall kinds; 18 inches apart for compact varieties; in sun

PESTS AND DISEASES: None serious, except for foraging animals like rabbits and deer

PERFECT PARTNERS: Japanese anemones, ornamental grasses, Russian sage, sedum 'Autumn Joy', and wormwood

Astilbes

Although the late Georg Arends,
a German perennial breeder, developed some
superb astilbes, the new 'Visions' series are
more drought resistant.

GROW THIS! 'Visions' and 'Hennie Graafland'

Certain flowers can make a garden's reputation. At Magnolia Plantation, South Carolina, thousands of tourists flock to see the flowering southern azaleas in March and April. At Longwood Gardens, Pennsylvania, it is thousands of chrysanthemums that draw the crowds in fall, while at Keukenhof, Holland, one million visitors trek to see tulips in peak bloom during April and May. At Hodnet Hall in Shropshire, England, I saw an entire valley planted with all colors of astilbe, and a similar planting around a lake at Maple Glen, South Island, New Zealand. Only after seeing these two examples of astilbe used generously in moist soil did I appreciate its value as a summer perennial with a big wow factor.

Astilbe (commonly called false spiraea) is a hardy perennial that can create a crowd-pleasing display with its large, feathery plumes, especially massed along a stream bank or beside a pond, as the plants like a moist soil. The color range includes many shades of red, pink, and mauve, plus white.

The 'Visions' series prefer a moist soil but will tolerate periods of drought. Also drought tolerant is the low-growing 'Pumila' (*Astilbe chinensis* var. *pumila*), a deep pink suitable for groundcover effect. The light pink 'Sprite' won a Perennial Plant of the Year award from the Perennial Plant Association, although 'Hennie Graafland' has a similar dwarf habit and more prominent pink flower spikes. 'Fanal' is a brilliant crimson red variety produced by the late Georg Arends, a German nurseryman who also introduced pinks (like 'Rhineland') and a white ('Deutschland'). The spirelike flower plumes of 'Fanal' stand erect, and when massed in a border or island bed for early summer display, it can outshine every other perennial in the garden.

The strong, wiry stems of astilbes are suitable for cutting, and the plants are easily propagated by division. In humus-rich, moisture-retentive soils, plants will thrive in full sun or light shade. Astilbes are especially beautiful when partnered with blue hostas like 'Blue Angel'.

BE AWARE! The Arends hybrids, such as red 'Fanal' and white 'Deutschland', are beautiful but are unforgiving of dry soils. There are also several annualized astilbe on the market, such as 'Astary', 'Bella', and 'Showstar', but I have only seen these perform well in pots and in containers, such as whiskey half barrels. So for the most vivid displays, I still recommend the 'Visions' series.

 PLANT PROFILE

KNOWN BOTANICALLY AS: *Astilbe* x *arendsii* and *A. chinensis*

ZONES: 3–8 depending on variety, for summer flowering; *A. chinensis* varieties 4–8

PROPAGATION: Mostly division before and after flowering

SPACING: At least 12 inches apart in sun or light shade

PESTS AND DISEASES: None serious; occasional deer damage

PERFECT PARTNERS: Carex sedge and other compact ornamental grasses, hostas, Japanese iris, ligularia, and ostrich ferns

Bee Balm

For mildew resistance, pick these
two—pink 'Marshall's Delight' and scarlet 'Jacob Cline'.

GROW THIS! 'Jacob Cline', 'Marshall's Delight', and 'Bergamo'

A relative of the mint family and native to North America, bee balm has pleasantly aromatic leaves that are the main ingredient in Earl Grey tea. For several weeks in midsummer, the bushy, erect plants flower spectacularly with red, pink, white, or purple tubular flowers that resemble a crown and attract hummingbirds. A big problem with bee balm, however, is its tendency to suffer from powdery mildew disease that discolors the leaves.

Perennial growers have introduced several mildew-resistant kinds. One of the best is 'Jacob Cline' on account of its bushy dome of extra-large scarlet red flowers and disease resistance. A good disease-resistant pink is the taller

'Marshall's Delight', capable of flowering for 3 months from late June through early September. For those who like to grow perennials from seed, try rose purple 'Bergamo'; it is mildew resistant and flowers the first year, and it won a Fleuroselect award.

Also known as monarda, bee balm likes full sun and good drainage, although it is tolerant of wet soil. The long, strong stems are suitable for cutting.

BE AWARE! Monarda is so susceptible to mildew disease that where the disease is a problem, only resistant varieties should be considered. 'Croftway Pink' is very susceptible, and the popular 'Cambridge Scarlet' also suffers.

 ## PLANT PROFILE

KNOWN BOTANICALLY AS: *Monarda didyma*

ZONES: 4–8 for summer flowering

Flowering Herbs

Bergamot is one of an elite group of herbs that provide both attractive flowers and good flavors. Here are some other flowering herbs to consider for perennial beds, and their culinary value.

Agastache (also called hyssop) imparts a licorice scent and flavor suitable for making an herbal tea.

Basil 'Siam Queen' has beautiful deep dusky pink flower clusters and aromatic leaves that help to enliven the flavor of tomatoes.

Chamomile has an apple fragrance and makes a refreshing herbal tea.

Chives produce beautiful globe-shaped pink flowers and narrow, hollow leaves for flavoring cream cheese and omelets.

Dill grows large, yellow flower umbels; its feathery foliage can be chopped finely to flavor fish dishes.

Garlic chives produce masses of white flower clusters in summer, while the leaves add a pleasant onion flavor to soups and stews.

Lavender displays beautiful blue flower spikes in summer. Both the flowers and the leaves make a refreshing tea.

Rosemary (especially the weeping form) covers itself in blue flower clusters in early summer. The needlelike leaves are ideal for flavoring meat dishes such as pork and lamb.

Thyme forms a dense mass of flowers. Several varieties form a low-growing groundcover that releases a spicy fragrance if walked on. The leaves add a memorable flavor to soups and stews.

CHAPTER 1

BE INFORMED BEFORE YOU BUY

Author Derek Fell visits a production hoop house at Bud's Bromeliads, near Ft. Myers, Florida.

This bedding plant grower's production greenhouse features an almost endless view of 'Accent' impatiens, one of the best annuals for shade gardens.

Dependable white and purple coneflowers *(Echinacea purpurea)* grow in the test plots of Burpee Seeds at Fordhook Farm in Doylestown, Pennsylvania.

At my own home, Cedaridge Farm, I plant hundreds of flowering annuals to evaluate the performance of new—and beloved—varieties in a home-garden setting.

Expanding the color range of a flower often takes years; here the newest colors of spider flower *(Cleome hassleriana)* are tested for uniformity of habit and longevity of the flowering display at a Syngenta production farm in Gilroy, California.

During the California Pack Trials in spring, the test plots at Syngenta Flowers in Gilroy, California, bloom in wide swaths of brilliant color, giving buyers the opportunity to evaluate their outdoor performance.

At Ball Horticultural in West Chicago, various annuals are grown in hanging baskets and evaluated for long-lasting bloom.

Longwood Gardens in Kennett Square, Pennsylvania, dazzles visitors with garden-style test plots for summer-flowering annuals.

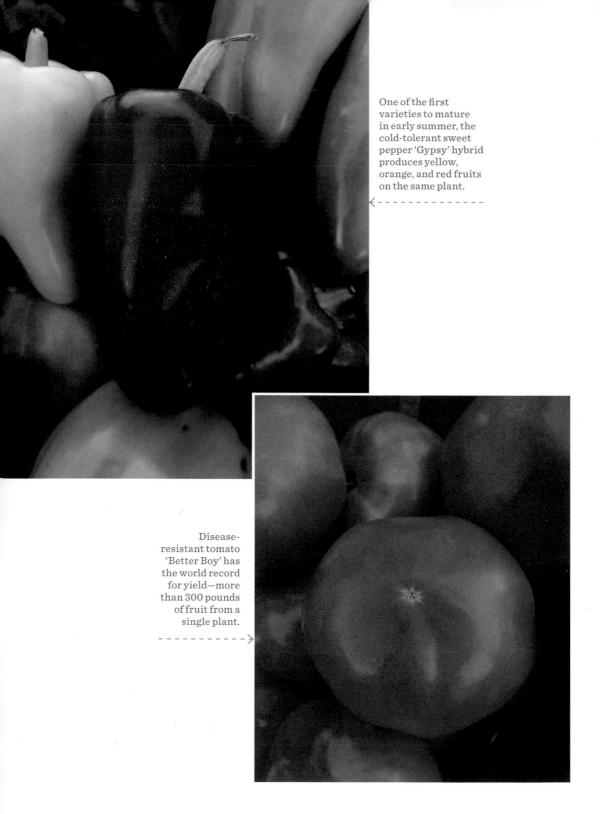

One of the first varieties to mature in early summer, the cold-tolerant sweet pepper 'Gypsy' hybrid produces yellow, orange, and red fruits on the same plant.

Disease-resistant tomato 'Better Boy' has the world record for yield—more than 300 pounds of fruit from a single plant.

CHAPTER 2

WHAT EVERY GARDEN NEEDS

'Detroit Dark Red' beets are carefully spaced for round root development and mulched to deter weeds at the Rodale Institute in Kutztown, Pennsylvania.

These flats of transplants, including zinnias, petunias, and dahlias, are ready to be placed into a test garden to evaluate their flowering performance.

At Cedaridge Farm, the 'Lady' series of American marigolds is grown through black plastic and mulched with straw to deter weeds.

Turnip 'Just Right' is watered by an irrigation hose to maintain consistent moisture, which speeds maturity and ensures sweet flavor.

Spider mites on a potted Mandevilla vine can discolor the leaves and produce a lackluster appearance. To discourage insect pests on most container plants, wipe the leaves with rubbing alcohol.

This overhead sprinkler system at Cedaridge Farm can be moved from one planting area to another so various sections of the garden can be watered on an as-needed basis.

CHAPTER 3

SPACE-SAVING IDEAS

This Syngenta test plot is actually a trial of hanging baskets, even though the pots are displayed on the ground. These mini petunias (*Calibrachoa* varieties) are being evaluated for bloom longevity in a container.

Squash vines are notorious for sprawling throughout the garden. Try growing bottle gourds up a metal or wooden arch to create a dense cover of foliage and an intriguing overhead display of fruit.

A "green wall" of living plants extends along a corridor at Longwood Gardens in Kennett Square, Pennsylvania, showcasing how vertical growing can save space, look beautiful, and create privacy.

Rex begonia with English
ivy and impatiens brighten
and decorate stout
containers on a patio.

Coleus 'Trusty Rusty'
and 'Limelight' make
colorful companions
in a compact
container planting.

Japanese hakone grass (*Hakonechloa macra* 'Aureola') overflows a trio of urns with its bowed leaf blades and cascading habit, perfect for filling an unplanted area of the garden.

Swiss chard 'Ruby' grows thick with colorful stalks in a space-saving Earth Box, which features a water reservoir to avoid rapid moisture loss.

A hanging pouch planter means salad greens are ready for harvesting right outside the kitchen.

Free-flowering 'Wave' petunias mingle their vibrant colors in a hanging basket.

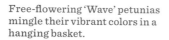

Tiny white flowers of *Euphorbia* 'Diamond Frost' create a sparkling effect among pansies in a basket planter.

CHAPTER 4

ENJOY THE HARVEST

Radish 'Cherry Belle' is the earliest-maturing radish, ready to eat just 20 days after direct seeding.

Cherry tomato 'Sun Gold' is not only extra sweet and heavy yielding, it is also extra early.

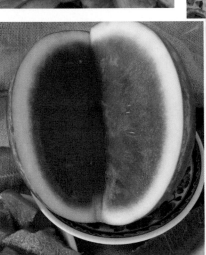

Because seed production in watermelons typically robs fruit of its flavor, seedless varieties consistently win taste tests for best flavor.

223

Although 'Iceberg' is a tasty Burpee crisphead lettuce variety, it is often confused with the generic series of lettuces with crisp green outer leaves and a white interior mass produced for supermarket sales.

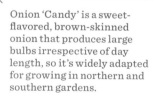

 Onion 'Candy' is a sweet-flavored, brown-skinned onion that produces large bulbs irrespective of day length, so it's widely adapted for growing in northern and southern gardens.

Red cabbage 'Ruby Ball' won an All-America award for extra-earliness and tight heads. A tight head generally resists bolting and provides more flavor.

CHAPTER 5

BEST CHOICE VEGETABLES

Heirloom pole snap bean 'Lazy Wife' is a late-season variety that is at the top of the list for melt-in-the-mouth flavor.

'Musica' Spanish runner bean has flat pods and is more heat resistant than its look-alike English runner beans (also called scarlet runners), but its biggest attributes are its tenderness and incredible flavor.

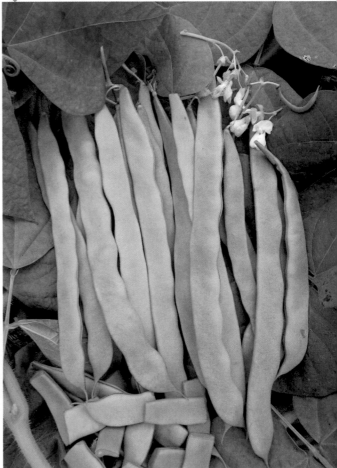

Yellow wax snap bean 'Gold Crop' won an All-America award for its attractive, crisp, pencil-straight pods and delicious flavor.

'King of the Garden' produces large beans on a climbing vine. Called butter beans when shelled, they are meaty and delicious.

The edible spiraling bud clusters of Romanesco broccoli are delicious cooked or raw, tasting more like cauliflower than broccoli; it's loaded with vitamin C, fiber, and carotenoids.

'Ace' hybrid beets are less fibrous than nonhybrids, and they produce round, dark red, uniform roots that are tender and delicious when cooked.

'Early Market' cabbage is prized for its extra-earliness.

'Stonehead' won an All-America award because it holds its heads longer than other spring cabbage, remaining edible when other cabbage varieties have bolted to seed.

Chinese cabbage 'Pagoda' grows tall, tight heads (with better taste than other varieties) and features a crisp yellow heart.

Cabbage 'Savoy King' won an All-America award for its handsome dark green, tight heads that are slow to bolt and delicious as a cooked side dish.

Carrots are now sold as mixtures of red, purple, orange, yellow, and white, so look for 'Kaleidoscope', which has a good balance of colors.

'Snow Crown' cauliflower won an All-America award for its huge white heads and delicious flavor raw or cooked.

'Golden Bantam' is an heirloom sweet corn variety that is famous for sweetness, but it must be cooked soon after it is separated from the stalk in order to retain its sugary sweetness.

Sweet corn 'Honey & Pearls' won an All-America award for its delicious sweet flavor and ability to fill the cob with edible bicolored kernels right to the tip.

The round yellow fruits of 'Lemon' cucumber are more attractive than its white counterpart 'Crystal Wax'. The center slices are large enough to fill a sandwich.

The Japanese cucumber 'Orient Express' is suitable for growing up a trellis to save space and features a tender, bitter-free skin that doesn't need peeling.

The shiny green basil 'Siam Queen' won an All-America award for its strong, pleasant flavor and the ornamental value of its purple flower clusters.

'Purple Rain' eggplant has an attractive striped purple-and-white skin. Its shape and size make it ideal for slicing into rounds for grilling.

'Titan' is one of the largest leeks you can grow. Its mild onion flavor is perfect for stews and soups.

Many seed suppliers now sell lettuce as mixtures, usually composed of a cos type, loose-leaf type, and butterhead type as well as different colors like red and green.

Lettuce 'Buttercrunch' was developed by Cornell University and is noted for dark outer succulent leaves and a crisp, buttery center. You can eat it out of hand like an apple.

231

'Tigger' melon is similar in appearance to the popular 'Queen Anne's Pocket Melon', but it offers much better flavor.

A type of annual hibiscus, 'Clemson Spineless' okra won an All-America award not only for its vigor, but also for its spine-free stalks and leaves.

Burpee's 'Ambrosia' hybrid cantaloupe not only produces the sweetest flavor, it also offers more edible flesh than similar-size cantaloupes.

The football-shaped 'Red Torpedo' onion produces more slices per bulb than round onions, so it's perfect for small-space gardens.

Shelling pea 'Green Arrow' can contain 11 tasty sweet peas per pod. Bred in Britain by the late pea breeder George Beavin, it is known by the name 'Green Shaft' in Europe.

The edible-podded pea 'Oregon Sugar Pod' produces large, sweet, flat pods and delicious sweet peas; it's best when picked before the peas swell the pod.

Renee's Garden and many other seed suppliers now offer packets containing a mixture of bell pepper colors at less cost than buying colors separately.

'Big Bertha' sweet bell pepper ripens from green to red. Fruits can measure up to 10 inches long, with thick walls and seeds conveniently clustered at the stem end for easy removal.

Not only is 'Cayenne' hot pepper fiery hot, it is also popular for braiding into decorative wreaths.

Hot pepper 'Hungarian Wax' produces medium-hot red, orange, and yellow slender peppers all on the same plant.

'Red Pontiac' is a favorite red Irish potato, growing extra-large tubers. It's also the variety generally used for the Tomato-Potato graft, which produces tomatoes on the vine and potatoes among the roots.

'Beauregard' has replaced 'Centennial' as the most popular sweet potato variety because of its good disease resistance, large size, and good flavor.

French fingerling potato 'La Ratte' is the variety most often used by gourmet chefs to make potato salad because of its creamy flavor.

Among giant pumpkins, 'Prizewinner' is a favorite to win giant pumpkin contests. It has a deeper color and more uniform shape than the other popular giant, 'Big Max'.

These 'Pennsylvania Neck Pumpkins' are the preferred variety to make pumpkin pie filling and pumpkin soup because the flavor is so rich. The neck is solid meat, and the small seed cavity is clustered inside the bulbous end, making it easy to remove seeds.

Seed companies are now offering seed packets containing a mixture of radish colors, such as the variety 'Easter Egg'.

‹- - - - - - - - - - - - - - ›

Malabar spinach isn't a true spinach, but its climbing, heat-tolerant vines produce succulent, spinachlike leaves. Everbearing from spring through frost, the more you pick the leaves, the more the plant produces. The edible flower clusters can be sautéed or steamed like asparagus.

‹- - - - - - - - - - - - - - -

Pattypan squash can be purchased as a mixture of green, yellow, and white to create a beautiful and delicious side dish. Stuff them with a rice, corn, or sausage mixture and bake them for a summer meal.

Summer squash 'Early Prolific' is the heaviest-bearing summer squash, and the young fruits are tender enough to eat raw.

'Ronde de Nice' is a round type of zucchini squash that can be hollowed out and stuffed or sliced into rounds to grill.

'Delicata' winter squash has a flavor and interior color similar to a sweet potato when cooked. It is extra delicious when the seed cavity is filled with maple syrup.

Vegetable spaghetti squash are often yellow or white, but certain varieties have a marbled orange, green, and white skin. The spaghetti-like interior is a low-calorie substitute for spaghetti pasta.

239

Strawberry 'Tristar' is a day-neutral variety developed by Dr. Gene Galletta at the USDA's Agricultural Research Station. Unlike other strawberries, its fruiting ability is not affected by day length, so it can fruit several times a season, in spring, summer, and fall.

'Earliglow's' king berry (which is the first berry to ripen on a fruit cluster) can be the biggest among strawberries—often as big as a small peach.

Stems of Swiss chard 'Bright Lights' are not only brightly colored, but the leaf is also so tender it can serve as a heat-tolerant spinach substitute.

'Paul Robeson' is a large-fruited Russian heirloom tomato named for the famous American actor, singer, athlete, and civil rights activist. The meaty slices have a hearty flavor and can cover a round of bread.

'Early Cascade' is a popular tomato variety for cool-season areas like the Pacific Northwest. The vining plants will easily produce 300 fruit per plant on vigorous vines that bear until frost.

Given proper spacing and no interruption in growth, 'Purple Top Globe' turnip produces attractive rounded roots and a sweet flavor.

Most large, oblong watermelons need a long growing season to ripen, but 'Sweet Favorite' hybrid ripens within 79 days, making it suitable for northern gardens.

CHAPTER 6

BEST CHOICE ANNUALS

Wax begonia 'Big Green Leaf'
produces large flowers in a
nonstop display from early
summer to fall frost.

The annual aster
variety 'Matsumoto'
mixed colors is a
tall-stemmed variety
treasured by florists
as a cut flower, with a
noticeable resistance to
yellows disease.

The annual black-eyed Susan (*Rudbeckia hirta*) named 'Becky' is a low-growing mixture with a mounded cushion habit—perfect for low bedding, containers, and edgings.

Black-eyed Susan 'Tiger Eye' is self-cleaning, covering its faded flowers with fresh foliage and flower buds; it's a bushy plant that partners well with neighboring plants like zinnias and marigolds.

Black-eyed Susan 'Indian Summer' has the largest flowers and longest-lasting display among annual *Rudbeckias*.

'Rustic Dwarfs' black-eyed Susan is a beautiful mixture of bushy, compact, bicolored annual *Rudbeckias*, developed by Britain's leading breeder of flowering annuals, the late Ralph Gould.

Calendula 'Flashback' mixed colors features petals that have maroon undersides, making each flower shine as though it were metallic.

Calendula 'Bon Bon' is the best of traditional pot marigolds for the symmetry of its flowers and eye-catching dark center.

The spiked celosia 'Flamingo Feather' is well named for its feathery appearance. It will soon be available in a mixture of colors.

Carnation 'Can Can Red' won an All-America award for its large and fragrant flowers, strong stems suitable for cutting, and everblooming quality.

'Big Chief' is a crested type of celosia, producing globe-shaped heads in a more vibrant color range than other varieties.

Coleus 'Trusty Rusty' is an eye-catching, ginger-colored variety that stands out in a container because of its unique color.

"Annual" columbines that bloom their first year are sometimes unreliable when grown from seed. Choose 'Origami Red' columbine and other 'Origami' colors for your best chance at seeing beautiful bell-shaped blooms the first season.

This coleus, named 'Fishnet Stockings', must be seen to be believed. The dark veining appears to be etched with a fine pencil. It makes a nice contrast to plants with solid petal colors in mixed container plantings.

The fragrant flowers of *Dianthus* 'Melody Pink' are composed of several colors in different shades of pink (plus a white); the long stems are suitable for cutting.

Cottage pinks 'Telstar' mixed won an All-America award for its vibrant color range and long-lasting floral display.

Cottage pinks (*Dianthus*) 'Laced' mixed colors displays large, distinctive, fringed flower petals.

Cactus-flowered dahlia 'She Devil' is an eye-catching tuberous dahlia that flowers the first year.

The 'Outdoor' series of gerbera daisies offers a wide range of hot colors for bedding display and massing in containers.

Seed-raised dahlia 'Goldalia Scarlet' has a distinctive crown of yellow inner petals that sets it apart from other seed-raised annual dahlias with plainer petals.

Osteospermum freeway daisies have been improved more than any other class of flowering annual in recent years. 'Passion' mixed colors is a selection of violet and purple shades, blooming all summer.

Osteospermum 'Voltage Yellow' is an extremely free-flowering freeway daisy, sometimes sold as a marguerite daisy. It flowers early and lasts well into summer.

African daisy 'Lilac Spoon' seems to be spinning like a pinwheel with distinctive spoon-shaped petals that are sure to attract attention in containers.

Euphorbia 'Diamond Frost' fills in containers or hanging baskets with little bursts of glitter from its airy habit. It is best planted with other flowers in a container or hanging basket to produce a shimmering or sparkling effect.

The 'Asti' series of African daisies offers a dazzling color range, never more beautiful than when massed as a mixed color border.

This sensational sun-loving gazania, 'Sunbathers Totonaca', is like no other gazania in flower form and color. Indeed, it seems to think it is a sunflower. Plants can only be grown from cuttings.

Gazania 'Kiss' is a new series of sun-loving annuals with prominent stripes running the length of each petal, quite distinct from anything previously seen in gazanias.

The new hybrid bedding geranium mixture 'Calliope' is free flowering and maintains a dense flowering display after other geraniums exhaust themselves.

The tropical hibiscus 'Fifth Dimension' displays three distinct colors: bright yellow, gray, and red. Though tender to frost, plants are everblooming during summer and ideal for containers.

253

Although impatiens 'Accent' mixed colors is susceptible to the new mildew disease that is killing bedding impatiens across the United States, it has amazing vigor, a compact habit, and superior uniformity.

'Sun Patiens Red' is a hybrid between bedding impatiens and New Guinea-type impatiens. It does well in hot sun or light shade and blooms for three seasons—spring through fall.

Lantana 'Bandana' mixed colors is a mound-forming, everblooming annual that attracts hummingbirds and butterflies.

Delphinium 'Aurora' mixed colors includes this lavender blue with white centers. It's a favorite cut flower and an improvement over the old 'Pacific Giants', but be sure to stake it so it doesn't flop over.

The 'Lady' series of American marigolds is noted for compact plants, an improvement over tall marigolds that topple in bad weather. 'Lady' features masses of globe-shaped flowers, almost the size of tennis balls, in yellow, gold, orange, and primrose.

'Perfection' orange is an early, free-flowering American marigold with stems long enough for cutting. Flowering is continuous from early summer to fall frost.

'Bonanza Bolero' is the French marigold that many growers consider to be the best replacement for the extremely popular 'Queen Sophia', which is no longer available.

'Durango Flame' is the closest to a true red you will find in French marigolds. The color is intensified after a rain shower.

Morning glory 'Heavenly Blue' is the most popular annual flowering vine. Even though color mixtures are available, 'Heavenly Blue' reigns supreme.

The climbing types of nasturtium can be grown up a trellis to mingle their hot colors with other climbers like morning glories and sweet peas.

I nominate the 'Ultimo Morpho' pansy the most beautiful of all flowering annuals for bedding and container display. Bred by the Japanese seed breeder Sakata, it is named for the magnificent blue morpho rain forest butterfly of Costa Rica.

'Delta Fire' is an outstanding pansy for its distinctive orange and yellow petals and black throat, and it recovers quickly after inclement weather.

'Majestic Giants' are the largest-flowered pansies, developed from the famous, but difficult to obtain, 'Swiss Giants' series originally bred by the seed house of Roggli in Switzerland. This yellow variety with black blotch is the most popular pansy by sales volume worldwide.

259

'Supertunia Shades of Blue' is an excellent mixture to grow in a lightly shaded area where the muted light will display the blue tones to perfection.

Tired of the same old pastel petunia colors? Grow petunia 'Picasso' with its unique deep pink petals edged in emerald green. Use it in containers and hanging baskets to impress visitors.

Petunia 'Peach Flare' is the largest grandiflora petunia you can grow. Use it in containers where its impressive large size can be appreciated up close.

Of all the mini-petunias (*Calibrachoa* spp.), I find the variety 'Terracotta' to be the most desirable because it is a color not found in other flowering annuals.

Mini-petunia 'SuperCal Petchoa' mixed colors are crosses between regular petunias and the smaller-flowered *Calibrachoa*. This results in larger flowers than regular calibrachoa and more vibrant colors than regular petunias.

'Sonnet' snapdragons in mixed colors are tall and produce multiple strong stems prized by flower arrangers.

Salvia splendens 'Salsa' has the widest color range of all bedding salvias, with not only the common red color, but also pink, purple, orange, white, and bicolors.

A highly unusual bicolor flower, *Salvia splendens* 'Sangria' displays white and red trumpet-shaped flowers on a sturdy flower spike.

The heirloom sweet pea 'Cupani' is small-flowered but highly fragrant and the forerunner of all modern sweet peas. It has a distinctive blue keel and purple wings.

Spider flower (*Cleome hassleriana*) 'Sparkler' won an All-America award for its compact habit and multiple side branches.

'Mammoth Russian' produces humongous flower heads, up to 15 inches across, filled with striped seeds for birds on 12-foot-tall stems. Its flowerhead is short-lived, so don't plant it in an ornamental bed. But it's perfectly fine for areas where backyard birds can find the seed. For an everblooming sunflower, plant 'Autumn Beauty'.

The hardy perennial sweet pea (*Lathyrus latifolius*) resembles the annual sweet pea except the color range is limited to shades of pink and purple, plus white. Although the flowers are slightly smaller and lack fragrance, the plants bloom continuously from spring until fall frost if the flower clusters are picked regularly.

The Texas bluebell (*Lisianthus*) is now available in pink and white. 'Mariachi Blue' is favored by florists as a cut flower because its double row of petals gives it the appearance of a blue rose.

Verbena 'Homestead Purple' is the most free-flowering verbena you can grow. Spreading to 3 feet wide, it makes a continuous flowering groundcover.

The everblooming annual verbena 'Lanai Twister Pink' stands out in a crowd because of its pink and white bicolored petals and everblooming quality.

Viola 'Sorbet Yellow-with-Purple-Wings' will bloom non-stop all season, providing it is watered during dry spells.

Vinca was on its way out as a popular flowering annual because of its disease susceptibility, but the variety 'Cora' has such good disease resistance it has re-established its popularity among home gardeners, especially for sunny, dry locations. In frost-free areas, it will perform as a perennial, and at my Florida property, it has bloomed riotously for 3 years without a stop.

The 'Profusion' series of daisy-flowered zinnias forms mounds of flowers so dense they almost completely hide the foliage.

'Profusion' zinnias in mixed colors are massed in a container at the test garden of Sakata Seeds in Salinas, California. The series is well named as the plants bloom profusely until fall frost.

Benary's 'Giant Lime' dahlia-flowered zinnia is prized by flower arrangers and has largely replaced Burpee's 'Envy' because of its larger flower size.

Zinnia hybrid 'Swizzle Cherry' is the best of the bicolored zinnias, outclassing varieties like 'Candy Cane' and 'Whirligig', which tend to be variable in their bicoloration.

Zinnia 'Dreamland Pink' ended the reign of 'Peter Pan' dwarf large-flowered zinnias. 'Dreamland Pink' has a more robust growth habit and longer flower displays.

CHAPTER 7

BEST CHOICE PERENNIALS

The hardy *Lycoris squamigera* is commonly called naked ladies because the flowers occur on naked stems months after the strap-like green leaves have disappeared.

Amaryllis 'Christmas Red' has been conditioned to bloom indoors during the Christmas holiday season.

Aster 'Wood's Pink' honors the memory of its breeder, an Oregon fruit tree breeder.

The hybrid angel's trumpet 'Charles Grimaldi' honors the memory of its breeder, a San Francisco nurseryman. The orange, honey-scented, pendant trumpet-shaped flowers occur in several flushes during spring, summer, and fall.

The *Astilbe* hybrid mixture 'Visions' will tolerate drier soil than older *Astilbe* varieties.

The 'Rieger' series of hybrid begonias from Germany produces masses of flowers that resemble carnations, more suitable for a conservatory or sunroom than the outdoors.

Monarda didyma 'Cambridge Scarlet' will light up a perennial border with its scarlet blooms that attract hummingbirds.

Begonia bolivienses 'Santa Cruz Sunset' won an American Garden Award for its ability to produce a never-ending display of pendant scarlet blooms that resemble a fuchsia. The display continues until fall frost.

The hybrid bromeliad *Aechmea* 'Blue Tango' can remain in flower for 6 months.

This new calla lily, called 'Green Slipper', is a future introduction from Golden State Growers in California. It's expected to be a big hit with flower arrangers.

Chrysanthemum 'Igloo' mixed varieties are sufficiently hardy to overwinter in northern states.

273

The Shasta daisy (*Chrysanthemum × superbum*) was developed by the late Luther Burbank at his breeding facility in Santa Rosa, California.

Clematis 'Jackmanii' is a vigorous climber that likes to grow with its feet in the shade and its flowers in the sun.

The coneflower variety 'Magnus' (*Echinacea purpurea*) was discovered in Norway. The flowers can be dramatic—up to 6 inches across.

Heuchera and related species can be cross-pollinated to produce a variety of foliage shapes and colors, including purple, yellow, red, and orange, often with contrasting leaf veins. *Heuchera*'s common name is coral bells, which refers to its dainty reddish flower spires.

The miniature daylily 'Pardon Me' was developed by Dr. Darrell Apps, American daylily breeder. A repeat-flowering variety, it resembles the popular 'Stella d'Oro' in flower size but produces mahogany blooms instead of orange ones.

Confused by all the daffodil varieties? Then choose 'Fortissimo' since it is not only the largest-flowered daffodil you can grow, but it also naturalizes easily and will multiply in sun or partial shade.

Foxtail lilies (*Eremurus* species) are mostly white, yellow, and orange. They come from the deserts of Afghanistan; they're hardy but they resent poor drainage, so grow them on slopes in gravel soil. Never supply supplemental water; instead, let natural rainfall be the only source of moisture.

The Japanese painted fern (*Athyrium niponicum pictum*) has silver foliage and makes a distinctive edging along woodland paths.

Even though the newer blue variety of hardy perennial geranium 'Rozanne' blooms over a longer period, 'Johnson's Blue' is my favorite among the many kinds because of its large blue flowers.

Called Lenten roses, *Helleborus orientalis* plants resemble pachysandra, flowering from February through May. They self-seed freely into bare soil. This assortment of colors is from evergreen plants at Cedaridge Farm.

Variegated maiden grass (*Miscanthus sinensis* 'Variegatus') is hardy and produces silky pink flower plumes that rise erect above the foliage in fall.

The giant-leafed hosta 'Sum & Substance' was introduced by Long Island hosta breeder Paul Aden, who also developed the similar large-size 'Blue Angel'. Both produce flower spikes with white flowers as big as foxgloves.

Bearded iris 'Gracchus' is an heirloom variety that has distinctive yellow standards and purple falls; it produces masses of flowerstalks in spring in full sun.

Siberian irises will take a moist soil. The blue varieties like 'Wedgewood Blue' make good companions to yellow flag irises since they flower at the same time in late spring.

Gaillardia 'Arizona Sun' (commonly called Indian blanket) won an All-America award for its ability to flower the first year from seed and to repeat-bloom.

Lavender 'Munstead' is hardier than the deeper blue 'Hidcote' and looks stunning when paired with a white variety of lavender. Even hardier than 'Munstead' and a deeper blue is 'Phenomenal', a mutation discovered by Peace Tree Farm in Pennsylvania. It's hardy to Zone 4.

Never has there been a hardy garden lily as beautiful as 'Scheherazade' with its pendant blooms that seem to glow like embers. An Oriental strain, it multiplies freely in sun or light shade, producing long stems suitable for cutting.

Hardy Asiatic lily 'Grand Cru' features bright orange petals with a ring of red flashes. It is valued for cutting as well as for garden display.

The hybrid Oriental lily 'Casa Blanca' is not only heavily fragrant, but it is also the most popular lily for cutting—and a "must" for an all-white theme garden.

The vigorous, free-flowering herbaceous peony 'Barrington Belle' was developed by US peony breeders Klehm. As many as 50 blooms can be crowded together on a single plant at any one time.

The lupinelike flowers of *Baptisia australis* are eye-catching. Tolerant of poor soil (and native to Texas, since *australis* means southern), it has a vigorous root system that tolerates drought and severe cold.

The 'Volcano' family of summer phlox (*Phlox paniculata*) has good mildew resistance and the ability to produce extra-large florets and large flower clusters.

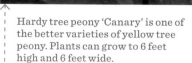

Hardy tree peony 'Canary' is one of the better varieties of yellow tree peony. Plants can grow to 6 feet high and 6 feet wide.

Ranunculus 'Tecolote' mixed colors (also known as Persian buttercups) are related to poppies and will overwinter in Zone 8 and south.

282

This black pincushion flower (*Scabiosa atropurpurea*) is actually an annual, part of a common mixture that is easily raised from seed. Blue perennial pincushion flower 'Fama' will bloom the first year from seed.

The famous blue poppy (*Meconopsis betonicifolia*) comes from the Himalayas and burns up in summer heat. At Cedaridge Farm, I plant it in the fall because it will overwinter and flower the following spring.

'Barnhaven' primroses are a hardy, drought-tolerant, and bunch-flowered series, developed by Oregon housewife Florence Bellis and now propagated by an English couple living in France.

'Barnhaven' primroses winter over in northern gardens and also withstand long periods of drought. They are much hardier than bedding primroses sold in the spring at garden centers and that last only until summer heat puts an end to the display.

'Knock Out' roses in mixed colors make a stunning hedge. A big flush of flowers in spring is followed by repeat-blooms throughout summer until fall frost.

This mixed border of *Caladiums* is showcased at my Sanibel Island Zone 10 garden. Also called rainbow plant, they are mostly grown from bulbs. The multicolored heart-shaped foliage remains decorative all season. The bulbs can be lifted and stored in a frost-free area where frosts occur.

The heavily fragrant heirloom rose 'Belle de Crecy' has a distinct swirling petal pattern and a "button" center admired by flower arrangers.

Blue perennial sage (*Salvia nemerosa*) 'May Night' has the deepest blue flowers and an ability to bloom throughout the season.

287

Stonecrop (*Sedum spectabile*) 'Brilliant' flowers in fall and is a magnet for butterflies. It is one of the most drought-tolerant hardy perennials you can grow.

Coreopsis tinctoria, commonly called tickseed, has been bred to create an extensive range of colors on dwarf plants, but 'Zagreb' is still the one to grow if you desire an explosion of yellow in your perennial borders.

In the tulip trials at Cedaridge Farm, the orange Triumph variety 'Cairo' always steals the show with a hint of ginger in its shining petals.

'Albert Greenberg' is a large day-blooming tropical water lily with mottled leaves. It will continue blooming after hardy water lilies have finished, but it needs to overwinter in a frost-free location.

Hardy water lily 'Atropurpurea' was developed in France and displays the darkest red among hardy water lilies.

Yarrow (*Achillea* hybrid) 'Summer Pastels' is an All-America award winner. It has the most extensive range of colors among yarrow grown from seed.

Hardy *Yucca filamentosa* 'Color Guard' is among the most drought-resistant perennials you can grow. In addition to bright variegated foliage, it produces tall white flower clusters in summer.

BEST CHOICE LAWN GRASSES

Bentgrass is a fine-bladed grass that is used for putting greens and is the most beautiful of all lawn surfaces, but it requires almost daily irrigation during summer to keep it healthy.

Prairie dropseed (*Sporobolus heterolepis*) is used at Chanticleer Garden in Wayne, Pennsylvania, as a labor-saving "no-mow" lawn.

Lawns seeded with improved perennial ryegrass are indistinguishable from bluegrass lawns, and they are more hardy and drought tolerant, often staying evergreen even when covered in frost and snow.

St. Augustine is a heat-resistant lawn grass grown mostly from plugs and sod in southern states. It spreads by vigorous subsurface roots that will crowd out weeds. It requires less mowing than bluegrass and other temperate lawns, but it will turn brown in areas with persistent frost.

PROPAGATION: Division of the roots at any time. Can be invasive unless divided every year.

SPACING: 2–3 feet apart in full sun

PESTS AND DISEASES: Mildew disease, which is most problematic in a dry season

PERFECT PARTNERS: Asiatic lilies, astilbe, echinacea, rudbeckia, and ornamental grasses such as helianthus, summer phlox, and variegated maiden grass

Begonias, Tuberous

Choose American-grown 'AmeriHybrids' for stunning multicolored displays in light shade and 'Santa Cruz' for a mounded container planting dripping with scarlet red flowers.

GROW THIS! 'AmeriHybrids', 'Nonstop', 'Go-Go', and 'Santa Cruz'

Tuberous begonias come from South America and have been hybridized to produce several kinds, the most popular of which are the giant-flowered picotee types with large, double, ruffled yellow flowers and a frilly pink petal edge up to 8 inches across. Also available are smaller-flowered pendula, or hanging basket, types, and scented kinds. 'AmeriHybrids' are the only strain still produced in the United States.

Tuberous begonias are tender, and they like to be well established in their flowering positions before hot weather sets in. To achieve this, the tubers must first be planted in a seedling tray filled with a peat-based potting soil and kept lightly shaded and watered to produce a flush of green, serrated leaves

'Nonstop Yellow' tuberous begonia flowers from seed the first season and tolerates shade.

reaching to 4 inches high. When planting, place the round, flat tubers hollow side up. An organic fertilizer, such as fish emulsion, is ideal for keeping the plants healthy and flowering continuously until fall frosts. Start the tubers 8 weeks before outdoor planting after frost danger in spring. Although noted for shade, they do not like deep shade, preferring a location that receives morning sun or filtered shade.

Begonias prefer cool, moist conditions, so spraying plants with water on very hot days will help them through the heat, but avoid saturating the soil, as this can promote rot. In the fall, after the leaves turn yellow, withhold water and lift the tubers. Clean them of soil and store them in a cool, dry, dark frost-free place until planting time the following spring. Use the giant picotee kinds (these are bicolors with a contrasting color around the petal perimeter) massed in beds in semishade and in containers such as dish planters. Use the pendula hanging-basket types in baskets and window-box planters, where the cascading stems and flowers can drape like a curtain.

A special class of tuberous begonia, pioneered by the leading German plant breeder Benary, are the 'Nonstop' hybrids. Bred as annuals to flower the first year within 10 weeks from seed, the short, stocky plants produce fully double, ruffled flowers up to 4 inches across in a wide range of hot colors, including bright red, deep pink, canary yellow, snow white, and a pink picotee. The American-bred 'Go-Go' series from Syngenta Flowers is similar in appearance but does not produce the smaller female flowers that surround the larger males like the 'Nonstops'.

A free-flowering red species, *Begonia boliviensis*, has recently made an impact for container growing under several names. My favorite is 'Santa Cruz', a scarlet red introduced by Benary. It is sensational used in a hanging basket or urn, flowering freely all summer until fall frost.

BE AWARE! The begonia family is large, with many varieties grown for foliage effect. This includes some used as houseplants, including the Rieger and rex series of tropical begonias, of which the variety 'Iron Cross' is the most popular. The Riegers are a cross between wax begonias and the tuberous kinds by Otto Rieger, a German plant breeder, and they have their good and bad points. They look sensational on the sales bench, in pots, and in hanging baskets. They're covered in medium-size flowers that look like miniature roses, in a hot color range of mostly red, orange, yellow, and white, but they are temperamental, preferring light shade and a moist, cool soil. The flowers turn to mush in too warm or too cold a temperature, as well as when they're overwatered or overfed. Many people consider them "toss out" plants, meaning they are thrown away after flowering, but they are actually perennial and, if cut back, can be induced to rebloom in cool, shady, frost-free conditions.

 ## PLANT PROFILE

KNOWN BOTANICALLY AS: *Begonia* x *tuberhybrida*

ZONES: All zones as a houseplant or for conservatory display. Otherwise, not suitable for overwintering in any USDA Hardiness Zone, with one exception: *B. grandis* is a shade-loving hardy perennial in Zones 6–8, growing leaves shaped like angel's wings and small pink flower clusters.

PROPAGATION: Tuberous begonias are mostly propagated from bulbs planted in early spring for transplanting outdoors after frost danger. Rex begonias can be propagated from leaf cuttings.

SPACING: At least 12 inches apart in light shade

PESTS AND DISEASES: Slugs, spider mites, and thrips

PERFECT PARTNERS: Brunnera, caladiums, carex grasses, ferns, heucheras, and hostas

Bromeliads

The sapphire blue flower spikes of Florida-bred *Aechmea* 'Blue Tango' can last for up to 6 months. Grow it in a container for a stunning patio highlight.

GROW THIS! *Aechmea* 'Blue Tango', *Neoregelia* 'Tres Colores', *Alcantarea imperialis,* and *Billbergia pyramidalis*

In many popular plant families, the rise to fame can be traced to the passion of a single individual who recognized the value of hybridizing among the species, resulting in a whole new plant propagation industry. With bromeliads, we can thank the efforts of Mulford Foster, a US plant explorer who mostly sought tropical plant species in Brazil. His book *Brazil: Orchid of the Tropics* is a fascinating read, packed with photographs of his intrepid travels accompanied by his

The bromeliad *Billbergia pyramidalis* produces scarlet-red pokerlike flowers, whether grown in soil or attached to a tree, in sun or light shade.

devoted wife, Racine. He spent years collecting bromeliads, and his hybridizing work inspired a new generation of breeders.

Bromeliads are tender perennials, overwintering outdoors south of Orlando, Florida, on the East Coast and parts of California on the West Coast. They can tolerate months of drought, although there are basically two kinds—terrestrial (growing in soil) and epiphyte (growing on trees). Commonly called air plants because they take their nourishment from the atmosphere through pores in their leaves and use their roots primarily as anchorage in the wild, many prefer light shade and others full sun. Generally the more prickly the leaf, the more sun it will tolerate.

Aechmea fasciata (silver vase) is the most widely grown bromeliad, mainly used as an easy-to-grow houseplant, with broad, arching, banded silvery leaves and a pink pyramid-shaped flower spike. In addition to growing in a pot with soil, it will also grow on trees. Hybrid *Aechmea* 'Blue Tango', developed by Patricia Gomez of Bullis Bromeliads, Princeton, Florida, is a remarkable plant for its large, arching flower plume composed of bright blue flowers that will last 5 to 7 months.

The terrestrial bromeliads known as *Neoregelia* form colorful rosettes of broad, arching leaves, usually variegated with a bright red or pink center and a circular depression (known as a cup) that fills with water to keep the plant alive. The tricolored variety 'Tres Colores' is my pick of the most vibrant color combinations, with glossy red at the center and stripes of ivory and green extending to the outer petal tips. Flowers form in the center of the cup. These are usually blue and resemble tiny birds with their beaks wide open clamoring for a worm. *Alcantarea* can grow to gigantic proportions, with towering flower spikes that are among the biggest in the plant kingdom, especially *A. imperialis*. At my Sanibel Island property, the most prolific bromeliad is *Billbergia pyramidalis*. Growing straplike recurved green leaves and a red flower plume shaped like a bottlebrush, it thrives in dry shade and climbs trees.

To attach an epiphyte bromeliad to a tree, spread the roots out and secure the stem section with tape or string or even wood cement; it will attach itself within a week. Bromeliads are not parasitic, though. If transferred to pots, they adapt to feed through their roots within a matter of weeks.

In gardens with frost, where bromeliads cannot survive outdoors, they can be grown as patio plants in containers and taken inside the house to provide further enjoyment as easy-care houseplants. Bromeliads mostly propagate themselves by producing offsets, called pups.

BE AWARE! For outdoor display, the bigger the bromeliad, the better. In general, the small *Cryptanthus* species known as earth star gets lost outdoors except in patio planters and desert dish gardens. Many bromeliads are grown for indoor display (as houseplants) rather than outdoors, even in frost-free areas. This includes most *Guzmania*, with what I consider the least attractive flowers. Also, bromeliads can be strictly divided between those that relish full sun and those that demand shade. Many of the sun-loving bromeliads have beautiful foliage, even orange, blue, and red, but they turn green in shade. Similarly, shade-loving bromeliads in full sun will suffer from sun scorch.

 ## PLANT PROFILE

KNOWN BOTANICALLY AS: Bromeliad species and hybrids

ZONES: The hardiest bromeliad in the United States is the native gray Spanish moss (*Tillandsia usneoides*) growing outdoors in Zones 8–11 and usually suspended from the massive, outstretched limbs of live oak trees. Most other bromeliads, however, will not survive outdoors in areas colder than Zone 9.

PROPAGATION: Mostly from "pups" around the root zone, and some from seed

SPACING: At least 12 inches apart and up to 3 feet apart for larger varieties; mostly filtered shade, but some varieties prefer full sun

PESTS AND DISEASES: Rot from boggy soil (although some varieties will tolerate a wet soil more than others), also slugs and grasshoppers

PERFECT PARTNERS: Caladiums in shade; agave and yucca in sunny locations

Calla Lilies

American-grown 'Callafornia Callas' are available in a wide color range, easily grown from bulbs that will winter over wherever the ground does not freeze.

GROW THIS! 'Callafornia Callas'

Calla lilies are known botanically as *Zantadeschia aethiopica* or *Z. sprengeri* hybrids, depending on the species used in their breeding. The former has the largest flowers, growing beside streams in boggy soil in Africa; the latter is smaller flowered and, though native to South Africa, grows among high-elevation meadow grasses in soils with good drainage and thus is sometimes called mountain calla.

At Moss Landing, south of San Francisco, Golden State Bulb Growers produce the majority of calla lilies (also called arum lilies) sold in the United States. They also maintain a breeding staff that works to create new colors. Although all their production plants are grown from seed to avoid disease, they ship the resulting tubers in clusters that can produce up to 10 flowering stems each. The brand name 'Callafornia Callas' refers to tubers produced from Golden State Bulb Growers. Choosing these means you will receive the freshest bulbs for planting.

There is a lot of misinformation published relative to hardiness, with some sources claiming that the bulbs are hardy when they are not. The ideal range for callas in the United States extends from Zone 7 to 9. In Zone 10 and warmer, there aren't enough cold nights to create a dormant period for the *Z. sprengeri* types to rest. An exception for Zone 10 is the *Z. aethiopica* series, such as 'Green Goddess', a handsome plant with white flowers tipped green. In Zone 6, frozen soil will generally rot the bulbs. However, tubers planted against the house foundation, where they benefit from house heat, may overwinter in Zone 6 (or you can dig and store tubers indoors in a frost-free location during winter).

The tubers of both kinds should be planted just below the soil surface, no more than 3 inches deep from the base of the tuber. The tubers have a smooth side and a lumpy side. The lumpy side should face up, although planting upside down will not prevent the tuber from flowering. Give them full sun. Any general-purpose organic fertilizer with a high phosphorus content, such as 5-10-5, will help keep the plants green and producing flowers.

After flowering, callas will continue to produce green leaves, and these will turn yellow before the plant goes dormant. At this stage, in areas colder than Zone 7, they should be lifted and stored indoors in a dark, frost-free location. Callas are good for garden display, and the long stems make both kinds suitable for cutting. They are also attractive grown in containers.

BE AWARE! Calla lily tubers are sold by size, from small (¾ inch) to large (3 inches). The 3-inch size is best, as it will produce a cluster of flowering stems and repeat-bloom, while the ¾-inch size may not bloom at all. Mountain callas have the widest color range, and it is the yellows, pinks, oranges, and reds that most people admire. Many bulb catalogs feature the black or maroon, but for garden display, these flowers tend to turn invisible, blending with the shadow patterns of the leaves.

 ## PLANT PROFILE

KNOWN BOTANICALLY AS: *Zantadeschia aethiopica* and *Z. sprengeri*

ZONES: All zones as a flowering houseplant; 7–9 outdoors. *Z. aethiopica* will overwinter in Zones 10 and 11 in moist soil. Use as a flowering annual elsewhere, especially as a cut flower.

PROPAGATION: Mostly dormant bulbs planted in spring for summer flowering. Lift before or soon after fall frost and store in a frost-free, cold, dark area.

SPACING: Plant shoulder to shoulder in containers; otherwise, space bulbs at least 6 inches apart in sun or light shade.

PESTS AND DISEASES: Virus diseases when plants are overwintered outdoors, and also chewing insects such as grasshoppers and slugs

PERFECT PARTNERS: Sensational planted beside a koi pond, lake, or stream with other water margin plants like arrowhead. Make sure the *Z. sprengeri* type have good drainage.

Chrysanthemums
(aka Cushion Mums)

The leading chrysanthemum breeder, Yoder, famous for its 'Prophet' series of cushion mums, is now part of Syngenta Flowers. For extra-hardiness, choose 'Minn' varieties, bred by the University of Minnesota.

GROW THIS! 'Prophet' series, 'Igloo' series, and 'Minn' series

The preeminent chrysanthemum breeder in America is Yoder Brothers (recently acquired by Syngenta Flowers). They are to cushion mums what Ecke, of Encinitas, California, is to holiday poinsettias. The best of Yoder's mum introductions is a series called the 'Prophet', noted for a compact, mounded habit, fall bloom, and a dense mass of flowers that almost hides the foliage. The 'Prophet' can be daisy flowered, button flowered, and double flowered in a wide color range that includes yellow, orange, bronze, red, pink, purple, white, and bicolors. Though they are perennials, individual varieties vary in hardiness from Zones 5 to 9 and have been bred as annuals. More reliable for winter hardiness are the 'Igloo' series of mums, also bred by Yoder, since these have been tested for extreme winter hardiness. Also, you should visit the University of Minnesota Web site for a complete list of their hardy mums. These are identified by 'Minn' in the name, such as 'MinnAutumn' (reddish bronze), 'MinnGlow' (lemon yellow), and 'MinnPink' (rosy pink).

When cushion mums survive the winter, it is best to divide them into three sections for replanting; otherwise, the mounded, cushion shape will be lost and the elongated, second-season stems may fail to hold their tidy shape. Alternatively, after plants have finished blooming in fall, remove suckers from around the base of the plant, pot up, and bring them indoors as houseplants for the winter, then replant in spring.

When growing your own plants from seed or cuttings, be sure to pinch out the lead shoot several times during the summer to force the plant to spread sideways and maintain a compact, cushion habit. After flowering, prune back the flowering stems to within 4 inches of the soil line and then mulch heavily, and they may come back to flower another season. Use a high phosphorus fertilizer to maintain flower density.

BE AWARE! The large-flowered football mums do not make good garden perennials. They need pampering, since they are bred mostly for growing under glass and winning competitions at autumn horticultural shows. There are also miniature chrysanthemums that have been specially bred for the gift market. These are unsuitable for outdoor display. They are grown under glass in miniature clay pots and sold at Easter in baskets with a bunny. There is an annual chrysanthemum, *C. carinatum*, that is sometimes sold by mail, using advertising copy that seems to suggest you are buying a cushion-type chrysanthemum. In a maritime climate like the Pacific Northwest and also in the United Kingdom, it produces beautiful tricolored daisylike flowers on tall stems suitable for cutting, but it is unsuitable for most areas of the United States, since it cannot tolerate hot summers. It is strictly a cool-season annual.

 ## PLANT PROFILE

KNOWN BOTANICALLY AS: *Chrysanthemum x morifolium*

ZONES: 3–9 as a fall-flowering annual, depending on variety

PROPAGATION: Mostly rooted cuttings, but also there are some varieties that can be grown from seed to flower the first season. Seed should be started indoors 10 weeks before outdoor planting after frost danger.

SPACING: Minimum of 12 inches apart, depending on variety, in sun

PESTS AND DISEASES: None serious, except for the usual chewing insects like slugs

PERFECT PARTNERS: For fall display, pair with Japanese anemones, New England asters, and ornamental kale.

Chrysanthemum Daisies

'Silver Princess' and 'Becky' resemble ox-eye daisies, but with a cushion habit ideal for edging flowerbeds.

GROW THIS! 'Victorian Secret', 'Becky', 'Silver Princess', 'Sheffield Pink', and *nipponicum*

In addition to cushion mums, which are used mostly for mass bedding and container displays during late summer and early fall, there are perennial chrysanthemum daisies (also known as *Leucanthemum*) such as the ox-eye daisy and its larger-flowered cousin the Shasta daisy, developed by the late plant wizard Luther Burbank. A problem with the Shasta daisy is its short flowering season, usually a few weeks in summer, so plant breeders are now focused on extending the blooming season from early summer to fall frosts. Terra Nova's best "reblooming" introduction in this extended flowering program is 'Victorian Secret'. Suitable for Zones 5 to 8, the heat-resistant plants grow to 2½ feet high, not as tall as regular Shasta daisies. They have semidouble, slightly ruffled white flowers around a button center on strong stems still long enough for cutting. 'Becky' and 'Silver Princess' are two other useful Shasta daisies, and both create a low-growing dome of white flowers with yellow eyes. They are ideal for edging and mass bedding. Give them all full sun and good drainage.

A reliable hardy chrysanthemum suitable for garden display and cutting is 'Sheffield Pink' (24 inches). The long stems explode with flowers in fall. Also don't overlook *nipponicum* (commonly called Montauk daisy) for fall bloom. The leaves are succulent and the flowers are similar to a Shasta daisy, but it flowers later—even into October and November in northern gardens.

Ox-eye daisies are smaller flowered than Shasta daisies, and they bloom a month earlier, usually in late May and early June.

BE AWARE! Many garden centers sell "tree daisies" in containers but fail to say that these are not hardy. They look hardy, like bushy Shasta daisies, with a magnificent dome of white, yellow, or pink flowers on a slender woody trunk. However, they are actually marguerite daisies (botanically known as

Argyranthemum frutescens). These grow naturally bushy and make excellent container plants. Treat them like annuals in frost-prone areas; enjoy them outdoors in summer, but move the plants indoors before frost.

 ## PLANT PROFILE

KNOWN BOTANICALLY AS: *Leucanthemum x superbum*

ZONES: 4–9 for summer flowering

PROPAGATION: By seed started indoors 8 weeks before outdoor planting; also cuttings taken before and after the plants bloom and division in fall or early spring.

SPACING: Minimum of 12 inches, depending on variety, in sun

PESTS AND DISEASES: None serious, except for usual chewing insects such as slugs and Japanese beetles

PERFECT PARTNERS: Astilbe, coneflowers, coreopsis, heliopsis, Japanese iris, monarda, and yarrow

Clematis

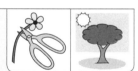

Old-fashioned 'Nelly Moser' and 'Jackmanii' still outshine other clematis varieties in my garden.

GROW THIS! 'Jackmanii', 'Nelly Moser', and *Clematis montana*

The British nursery of Jackman & Sons and the French nursery of Moser both developed clematis in the 1800s that are as popular today as they ever were because they each produce a pillar of large star-shaped flowers. They are the violet blue 'Jackmanii' (1858) and 'Nelly Moser' (1897), a pink with deeper pink petal stripes. Both bloom on new wood, so if the woody vines get too tall, they can be cut back to within 6 inches of the ground and new whiplike stems will surge upward to rebloom. And what a spectacle of bloom they can produce— 'Nelly Moser' in spring and 'Jackmanii' in early summer.

'Nelly Moser' clematis is an heirloom variety that produces record numbers of large flowers.

Clematis like their heads in the sun and their feet in the shade. Although the flowers will bloom in light shade, the roots demand a cool soil, so covering them with stones or a roof tile or an organic mulch like pine straw or shredded leaves will help them climb and bloom generously. Unlike many other vines, such as wisteria and trumpet creeper, clematis vines are lightweight and will not rot wood as quickly as the others. They climb by twining and drop their leaves in fall, surviving frozen soil.

An excellent choice for climbing up trellises, arbors, arches, and pergolas, clematis like to entwine their stems with other plants like climbing roses and honeysuckle. They may also be planted together so their flowers mingle to create a pillar of two or more clematis varieties.

Sweet autumn clematis (*C. terniflora*) comes from Japan but has naturalized throughout North America. Fast growing to 60 feet, its myriad sweetly scented white flowers can look like a blanket of snow in late summer and early autumn.

The most amazing combination planting I ever saw was at Cross Hills Gardens in Kimbolton, New Zealand, where three colors of *Clematis montana* (a white, a light pink, and a deep pink) are planted at the top of a cliff and allowed to cascade down over garden netting to create an avalanche of blossoms in spring, the flowers so closely overlapping like fish scales that they completely hide the foliage.

BE AWARE! There are many kinds of clematis with small flowers that are fine in botanical gardens as curiosities but can be disappointing for home gardeners who want big blooms and lots of them. Many of the smaller, sparse-flowering hybrids, like 'Etoile Rose' and 'Duchess of Albany', that I find lack an eye-catching display actually share parentage with a native American clematis (species *texensis*).

In addition to vining clematis that grow woody twining stems, there are herbaceous clematis that produce stiff, upright stems, often grown with perennials in mixed perennial borders. They are not nearly as desirable for flowering impact as the vining kind. These include *C. recta* (small white flowers) and *C. integrifolia* (small blue flowers).

 ## PLANT PROFILE

KNOWN BOTANICALLY AS: *Clematis* hybrids

ZONES: 4–9 for spring, summer, and fall flowering, depending on variety

PROPAGATION: Sweet autumn clematis is easily grown from seed; others are best grown from layering and stem cuttings. Three-year-old clumps can be divided.

SPACING: At least 2 feet apart to have the branches to knit together and create a flowering curtain of different varieties, in sun or light shade

PESTS AND DISEASES: Clematis wilt is the most serious problem. Usually it will affect only part of the plant, allowing the dead stems to be pruned away.

PERFECT PARTNERS: Climbing roses and honeysuckle

Coneflowers

Swedish-bred 'Magnus' is the largest purple coneflower, but new colors like 'Tomato Soup' extend the color range to red, yellow, orange, pink, white, and even green. Look for mixtures that can be raised easily from seed, such as the 'Cherokee Spirit' mixture.

GROW THIS! 'Magnus', 'Tomato Soup', 'Tiki Torch', and 'Cherokee Spirit' mixture

Coneflowers are hardy daisylike plants native to the American prairie and closely related to black-eyed Susans. For years, only two colors—purple and white—were cultivated, each with a conspicuous dark brown raised seed disk at the center of the petals. 'Magnus' is a purple variety developed by Swedish nurseryman Magnus Neilsen and has flowers that can measure up to 7 inches across. In recent years, hybridizing among a handful of species has produced some amazing colors and flower forms. Yellow was introduced from *Echinacea paradoxa* and then orange and red followed. Now there are even double-flowered kinds in red, pink, white, and green, some even available in seed mixtures. Moreover, the flower form can have flat or recurved petals. Two popular new varieties among home gardeners are 'Tomato Soup', a rich red, and 'Tiki Torch', a rich orange. A good way to grow them is in a mixed perennial border and a meadow garden.

These vegetative varieties can be expensive to purchase as transplants, so consider growing a mixture of the best colors from seed, especially the All-America Selections winner 'Cherokee Spirit' mixture, which flowers the first year. It includes purple, yellow, orange, and red in its color range.

BE AWARE! Although the original purple and white are reliably hardy from Zones 5 to 9, the newer colors are susceptible to winterkill if the flowers do not make good root development in the first year. The hardiness of all the reds, oranges, and yellows is not as good as the purples and whites because the hot colors have been developed using the southern *paradoxa* species (the least hardy of the native species).

 ## PLANT PROFILE

KNOWN BOTANICALLY AS: *Echinacea* hybrids

ZONES: 3–8 for summer flowering

PROPAGATION: By seed and root division. Plants will flower the next season from seed.

SPACING: At least 12 inches apart in sun

PESTS AND DISEASES: Mostly chewing insects such as Japanese beetles

PERFECT PARTNERS: Bee balm, black-eyed Susans, and summer phlox

Coral Bells

Mostly grown for its foliage colors, my favorite coral bells are 'Amber Waves' (orange) and 'Plum Pudding' (deep purple) for lightly shaded locations with ferns and hostas.

GROW THIS! 'Amber Waves', 'Southern Comfort', 'Cities' series, 'Plum Pudding', and 'Melting Fire'

The hardy perennial plant family *Heuchera* is native mostly to deciduous woodlands of northeastern North America from Canada to Alabama. It used to offer a very limited variety selection for gardens, principally *H. sanguinea* from the Mexico-Texas border. Its dull green, ivylike leaves form a mound, and in spring its tall stems are topped with clusters of small coral red flowers. Now, as a result of an intensive breeding program using mostly the fall-blooming *H. villosa* and other species, the most amazing foliage colors have been created, including purple, beige, and silver. When crossed with the closely related *Tiarella*—also native to North America—the resulting hybrids are called *Heucherella*, and these are especially good for light shade. Today, there are hundreds of *Heuchera* and *Heucherella* varieties available. These newcomers are the result of a breeding program that began in England and then intensified when Dan Heims of Terra Nova bred the caramel-colored 'Amber Waves' *Heuchera* from a chance mutation he spotted among a batch of seedlings. Working with another breeder, Janet Egger, other leaf colors came along, including silver, red, bronze, yellow, orange, and combinations of these colors. Today, the most popular *Heuchera* variety is 'Southern Comfort', with orange leaves year-round.

Two other breeders who have added to the wealth of varieties are an independent French breeder, Thierry Delabroye, and American Charles Oliver of the Primrose Path plant nursery. With such a dazzling assortment of leaf colors, the flowers are now considered a bonus. But for those gardeners wanting a long flowering display as well as dazzling leaf colors, look to the new 'Cities' series. These are all rebloomers (meaning they produce several flushes of bloom during a season with no pruning required). The most free flowering of these is 'Paris', which explodes with deep pink blooms starting in spring and extending well into fall.

"*Heucheras* make the best container plants in the world," according to Heims. All of the cushion forms can be mixed into dish planters, creating a beautiful rainbow effect, and new trailing *Heucherella* varieties such as 'Yellowstone Falls' and 'Redstone Falls' can be combined in a hanging basket so their 5-foot stems can create a curtain of dazzling yellow and red foliage.

BE AWARE! Although 'Palace Purple' received the distinction of a Perennial Plant of the Year Award, it has now been surpassed in sales by 'Plum Pudding' because of the latter's richer, glossier, and deeper purple leaf color. Most seed-grown *Heucheras* do not produce the vibrant leaf colors of those produced from meristem culture, with one glorious exception—'Melting Fire'. Introduced by Kieft Seeds, the ruffled chocolate-colored leaves are similar to 'Plum Pudding'.

 ## PLANT PROFILE

KNOWN BOTANICALLY AS: *Heuchera* hybrids

ZONES: 3–8 for three seasons of foliage color; flowering times vary according to variety

PROPAGATION: Species like the original coral bells can be grown from seed and division. Newer hybrids are best increased by division before or after flowering.

SPACING: 12 inches apart, preferably in light shade

PESTS AND DISEASES: None serious, except for usual chewing insects such as slugs and foraging animals such as rabbits, groundhogs, and deer

PERFECT PARTNERS: Astilbe, carex grasses, ferns, hostas, variegated English ivy, and variegated groundcover euonymus

Daffodils

At my home, Cedaridge Farm, I have more than 50 varieties of daffodils, but the fragrant double-white 'Gardenia' and mammoth 'Fortissimo' are favorites for naturalizing.

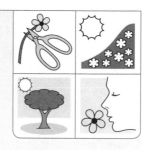

GROW THIS! 'Fortissimo', 'Ice Follies', 'Actaea', 'Pink Charm', 'Apricot Sensation', 'Tahiti', and 'Gardenia'

Daffodils are native to the Pyrenees mountains and the Swiss Alps, and there are dozens of species and thousands of daffodil varieties in spite of the fact that their basic flower color is yellow. This is because they can be classified as early, mid-season, and late, and the outer rim of petals can be a contrasting color such as white. Also, the trumpet that extends out from the middle of the flower can be large or small, frilly or cup shaped, with red, green, and pink in its composition.

To ensure they come back reliably each year, feed daffodils with a high-phosphorus fertilizer in fall, after frost, and again in spring just as the leaves emerge from winter dormancy. The three I have found most reliable for naturalizing are 'Fortissimo', a large-flowered, yellow midseason variety with an orange trumpet; 'Ice Follies', a white with a yellow trumpet that changes to all white as the flower matures; and 'Actaea', a fragrant white with a small green cup rimmed with red. Of the three, 'Fortissimo' will make the boldest display. A charming pink-cupped daffodil, 'Pink Charm' is also good for naturalizing, but of all the color combinations, my favorite is 'Apricot Sensation' because of its rich orange cup and apricot-colored background petals. In general, I don't care for double daffodils, with one exception—the delightfully fragrant 'Tahiti'. It has a beautiful symmetry and orange flecks among the mostly yellow mass of petals.

There is also an heirloom daffodil that has a heavy fragrance. In catalogs, it is usually identified as *Narcissus albus plenus* 'Odoratus', but a common name for it is 'Gardenia' because the fragrance is exactly like a gardenia. The plant blooms late, in May and June. Derived from the old-fashioned pheasant's-eye daffodils, and introduced in 1601, the petals are snow white and the flower is fully double, even resembling a gardenia.

Daffodils like to be planted in full sun but will tolerate light shade. They prefer a humus-rich soil and good drainage, though they will tolerate moist soils. After the flowers fade, allow the leaves to remain green for at least 10 weeks so they rejuvenate the bulb for a repeat flowering the following season. Hardiness range extends from Zones 3 to 8, depending on variety.

BE AWARE! Be careful when choosing so-called pink trumpet daffodils. Some, like 'Salome', are a disappointing pale pink—nothing like the vibrant deep pink of 'Pink Charm'.

Some of the double-flowered daffodils with pointed petals are ugly. In this group, I include 'Rip van Winkle', which would have been better named 'Ragamuffin', since the doubling is not symmetrical and the petal edges look ragged, as if chewed by insects. The miniature daffodil called 'Hoop Petticoat' (*N. bulbocodium*) is not reliably hardy above Washington, DC, and it doesn't give nearly the vibrant display of the larger trumpet or large-cupped daffodils. It needs a lot of miniatures to make an impact.

PLANT PROFILE

KNOWN BOTANICALLY AS: *Narcissus* species and hybrids

ZONES: 4–8 for spring flowering. In warmer areas, some gardeners will precondition bulbs for 10 weeks in the crisper section of a refrigerator in order to enjoy winter blooms. Some species and miniature varieties are not reliably hardy above Zone 7. Check with a local botanical garden or extension service for lists.

PROPAGATION: By raw bulbs planted in fall for spring flowering. After 3 years, consider dividing clumps to prevent overcrowding. Allow leaves to die down naturally after flowering.

SPACING: Plant shoulder to shoulder in containers; otherwise plant 6 inches apart in sun or light shade.

PESTS AND DISEASES: None serious. Even deer will not eat them, as the leaves contain a toxin.

PERFECT PARTNERS: Brunnera, crocus, crown imperials, hyacinths, Japanese bleeding heart, primroses, and early tulips

Daylilies

American-bred 'Siloam' daylilies come in a wide color range, many with contrasting eye zones. But for sheer size, plant the yellow 'Mary Todd' with flowers as big as an amaryllis.

GROW THIS! 'Mary Todd', 'Hyperion', 'Stella d'Oro', 'Happy Returns', and 'Siloam' hybrids

Wayside daylilies (*Hemerocallis fulva*) are a familiar sight throughout North America, their orange trumpet-shaped flowers blooming in early summer for 2 to 3 weeks in poor soils. They are a far cry from modern daylily hybrids that come in an astonishing array of colors, including yellow, lemon, red, maroon, purple, lavender blue, white, green, and bicolors. Some are miniatures like 'Pardon Me', a free-flowering cinnamon red. Others like 'Mary Todd' have flowers almost as big as Christmas amaryllis, and some are scented, like 'Hyperion'. A special series of daylilies are known as rebloomers, the most famous of which is the orange 'Stella d'Oro', bred by a Polish immigrant, Walter Jablonsky, living in Chicago. Remarkable though it is (producing 6 months of bloom), the color has become a little too common for many gardeners, and the more cheerful yellow of 'Happy Returns' (developed by Dr. Darrell Apps, a leading daylily breeder) is my preference for a rebloomer, especially for container plantings. A regular rebloomer generally will bloom for 6 weeks, but 'Stella d'Oro' and 'Happy Returns' will bloom for 6 months.

Some of the best daylilies are bicolors bred by the late Pauline Henry, a housewife and passionate gardener living in Siloam Springs, Arkansas. Her most famous daylilies have contrasting eye zones, such as yellow with a red maroon zone and pink with a red zone. Some of her most famous "eyed" varieties include 'Ethel Smith' (pink with red eye), 'Doodlebug' (white with maroon eye), and 'Royalty' (purple with red eye). Before her passing in 2000 at age 92, she developed more than 400 varieties over a period of 37 years. Although many were award winners from the American Hemerocallis Society, she did not patent any of them, so her introductions can be propagated freely by anyone. Dr. Apps, in a eulogy, stated: "Her legacy of beautiful cultivars will remain in gardens around the world for many generations to come."

Actually, the true pioneer of improving daylilies was Professor A. B. Stout. A member of the scientific staff at the New York Botanical Garden, he undertook the hybridizing of daylilies as a passion. Using crosses between Asian species such as the yellow *H. flava*, pale orange *H. aurantiaca*, yellow *H. thunbergii*, and dark orange *H. fulva* (which rarely produces viable pollen and reproduces mostly from root division), he created the first dark red daylily and went on to produce more new colors, including the first pinks and a peach-colored hybrid.

Since Stout's daylilies entered the market, his success spawned an army of professional and amateur breeders, all building on his example, so that today very few of Stout's introductions are available. However, his memory is honored by the Stout Silver Medal, an award given to outstanding daylilies by the American Hemerocallis Society.

Daylilies are virtually indestructible, even surviving long periods of heat and drought. About the only soil type they do not like is boggy soil. Although they prefer full sun, they thrive in light shade. They are called daylilies because each flower lasts only a day, but since a single flowering stem can produce dozens of flower buds, the flowering display can extend for months. With their long, strong stems, they make beautiful cut flowers, but once a flower stem is cut, the subsequent flowering from the immature buds is greatly diminished and may produce only one or two more flowers.

Plants are grown from tubers that store energy and allow them to survive even into Zone 3. These tubers normally form a cluster and at planting time should be spread out like the arms of an octopus, the crown located just 1 inch below the soil. After 3 years, mature clumps can be divided. Many garden books and catalogs claim that daylilies are deer resistant, but that is not true in my experience. In early spring, the young shoots are attractive to deer, and the flower stems with their swollen buds ready to open are also a tasty treat for deer. At these times in their growth cycle, it is best to spray the plants with deer repellent wherever deer are a potential problem.

Daylilies can be classified as deciduous and evergreen, with the evergreen varieties more suitable for southern gardens. Although daylilies are widely adaptable, many bred in the North are unsuitable for Zones 9, 10, and 11, even if the plant label says they are appropriate. In particular, Florida gardeners and those in other mild-winter areas should visit local specialist daylily growers for advice on the best kinds to grow.

BE AWARE! I never saw a double-flowered daylily that I liked (with the possible exception of 'Siloam Double Classic', which is intensely fragrant), and there are hundreds of doubles available. The doubling is rarely symmetrical, and like doubling in petunias, it destroys the trumpet-shaped flower form that is so appealing.

Also, be careful when choosing miniature daylilies. They can look attractive in containers, but in perennial borders they tend to get lost. There are also some strange flower forms like spidery petals. These are not like a spider chrysanthemum where the spidery petals take the shape of a ball and can look attractive; instead, the spidery petals tend to be sparse and twisted as if inflicted by a wilt disease.

PLANT PROFILE

KNOWN BOTANICALLY AS: *Hemerocallis* hybrids

ZONES: 3–11 for summer flowering (plant deciduous kinds for Zones 3–8 and evergreen kinds for warmer areas)

PROPAGATION: Mostly from root division, but also from seed

SPACING: Minimum of 12 inches apart in sun or light shade

PESTS AND DISEASES: None serious. In spite of daylilies appearing on "deer-resistant" lists, they are a favorite food of deer at two stages of their life cycle: as soon as the new shoots break dormancy in spring, and again when the plump flower buds are ready to open.

PERFECT PARTNERS: Asiatic and Oriental lilies, coneflowers, ornamental grasses such as variegated maiden grass, rudbeckia, Shasta daisies, summer phlox, and perennial sunflowers

Ferns

For a stunning fern garden in a shady
corner, plant upright ostrich ferns with spreading silvery
Japanese painted ferns and airy maidenhair ferns.

GROW THIS! Ostrich fern, Japanese painted fern, and maidenhair fern

Ferns are an essential part of shade gardens, and although most prefer moist soil conditions, some will thrive in dry soils. Ferns conjure up visions of delicate arching green fronds that border on boring. But one of the most beautiful theme gardens is a fernery under glass at the Morris Arboretum, Pennsylvania, where every fern shape imaginable is on display, including towering Australian tree ferns, ephemeral maidenhair ferns, glossy green holly ferns, silver Japanese painted ferns, straplike bird's-nest ferns, aerial staghorn ferns, and even a vining fern from New Zealand.

Shade-loving ostrich ferns are one of the most beautiful native ferns, growing upright, stiff fronds splayed out like a shuttlecock.

Two outstanding hardy ferns that are easy to grow are the stately ostrich fern (*Matteuccia struthiopteris*), native to the northeastern United States, and the low, spreading Japanese painted fern (*Athyrium niponicum pictum*), which has silvery fronds. Not so easy to grow, but equally coveted, is the maidenhair fern (*Adiantum* species) that not only likes shade but also requests the moist environment of a cliff, spray from a waterfall, or regular misting to keep it happy. The maidenhair fern forms beautiful dense colonies of green lace, its curved, flat fronds soft to the touch. Try it wherever moss grows in your garden.

Ostrich ferns can grow man high with their erect foliage splayed out like a shuttlecock, especially the variety known as 'The King'. Although they can be placed between other shade-loving perennials for contrast, like hosta and astilbe, ostrich ferns develop runners like running bamboo and are best planted where they can form a colony beside a stream or pond.

The Japanese painted fern is available in a wide selection of varieties, some with red stems and silvery leaf segments, and others where the fronds are almost pure white.

BE AWARE! Beware the horsetail fern or horsetail rush (*Equisetum* species). Although attractive when confined to a pot, let it loose and it can be extremely invasive, especially in boggy soils beside ponds and streams.

The curled immature green heads of the ostrich fern are called fiddleheads, and they can be gathered in the spring, steamed like asparagus, or used for stir-fries. A strong word of caution, however; there are many ferns that can be mistaken for an ostrich fern and whose fiddleheads will make you ill if eaten.

Although the Australian tree fern is often thought to be hardy (it is seen widely in English gardens), it can be difficult to grow outdoors in the United States, even in a frost-free climate, unless it can be watered frequently by irrigation.

 ## PLANT PROFILE

KNOWN BOTANICALLY AS: *Adiantum pedatum* (maidenhair fern), *Athyrium niponicum pictum* (Japanese painted fern), *Matteuccia struthiopteris* (ostrich fern), and others

ZONES: 2–7 for ostrich fern; tropical ferns extend the range to Zone 11. Check with a local botanical garden or extension office for suitable recommendations.

PROPAGATION: Mostly by offsets separated from the mother plant. Ferns also reproduce by spores (tiny dustlike organisms that develop on the underside of leaves), but this is a tedious process.

SPACING: At least 12 inches apart for ostrich ferns in light shade

PESTS AND DISEASES: None serious for ostrich ferns; tree ferns grown as a houseplant can attract aphids, mealy bugs, and spider mites

PERFECT PARTNERS: Astilbe, coral bells, foamflower, hosta, and lilies

Foxtail Lilies

'Spring Valley Hybrids' are an excellent
mixture, while 'Pinocchio' (yellow) and 'Cleopatra'
(orange) are two outstanding separate colors,
all of which make wonderful cut flowers.

GROW THIS! 'Spring Valley Hybrids' and 'Cleopatra'

Many home gardeners are seduced into buying foxtail lilies from seeing photographs of tall flower spikes studded with thousands of orange-, yellow-, pink-, and apricot-colored florets, and from books, magazine articles, and home shopping television vendors claiming that they are easy to grow. I will set the record straight. They are not easy. A golden rule with foxtails is to never plant them on flat ground. Their demand for excellent drainage requires a raised bed or a gravel slope; otherwise, they are likely to perish after the first blooming season. Above all, never water except for natural rainfall.

The dormant roots should be planted in fall with the roots splayed out like an octopus and the crown no more than 1 inch below the soil surface. Dutch nurserymen offer a mixture called 'Shelford Hybrids' involving crosses between various species native to the deserts of Afghanistan, but US-bred 'Spring Valley Hybrids', propagated by Idaho cut-flower grower Ken Romrell, has a wider color range. The variety 'Cleopatra' is an especially beautiful apricot orange variety worth purchasing separately.

BE AWARE! Named hybrids generally grow true to color, but beware of potted plants raised from seeds in garden centers, as the colors are not stable. Unnamed mixtures of foxtail lilies can be disappointing, with mostly yellow and white in the color range, and few orange or apricot to make a well-balanced mixture. One way to obtain a good mix is to buy the separate colors in equal numbers and mix them yourself, especially named hybrids like orange 'Cleopatra', deep yellow 'Pinocchio', and 'White Beauty', which is snow white with a yellow eye.

PLANT PROFILE

KNOWN BOTANICALLY AS: *Eremurus* hybrids

ZONES: 5–8 as an early-summer-flowering perennial

PROPAGATION: From bareroots planted in fall or early spring

SPACING: 12 inches apart in full sun

PESTS AND DISEASES: None serious, but highly susceptible to rot from too
   much water collecting around the roots

PERFECT PARTNERS: Asiatic lilies, tall calendulas, early daylilies, ox-eye
   daisies, and Siberian and Japanese irises

Geraniums, Perennial

Nothing among hardy geraniums can quite compare with
the old favorite hybrid 'Johnson's Blue', unless it is the
newer, longer-flowering 'Rozanne'.

GROW THIS! 'Johnson's Blue' and 'Rozanne'

Bedding geraniums are tender perennials that are mostly grown as annuals and
botanically known as *Pelargonium*. We know them as bedding geraniums, ivy-
leaf geraniums, Martha Washington geraniums, scented-leaf geraniums, and
fancy-leaf geraniums, among others.

True geraniums come from North America, Asia, and Europe. They grow
mostly mound-shaped plants and masses of small cup-shaped flowers. The color
range is similar to bedding geraniums—white and shades of pink and red, but
also blue. For years 'Johnson's Blue' has been the most popular variety of hardy
perennial geranium. A cross between an Asian and European species that originated in Holland in the mid-1950s, it is spring and summer flowering and
drought resistant. Although 'Johnson's Blue' is an Award of Merit winner from

the Royal Horticultural Society, Blooms of Bressingham has recently introduced 'Rozanne', a slightly larger-flowered blue that blooms over a longer period. Gary Doer, perennial plant expert at Blooms, declared: "Its outstanding traits are responsible for 'Rozanne' becoming the Perennnial Plant Association's 2008 Plant of the Year. Unlike most perennial geraniums, it is heat tolerant, flowering continuously from May through fall until hard frost."

Plants of both are deer and disease resistant, hardy from Zones 3 to 8, and attract butterflies. Although perennial geraniums prefer full sun, they tolerate light shade. The flowers are usually sterile, so propagation is by division.

BE AWARE! The trouble with most other perennial geraniums, such as 'Bertie Crug', 'Tiny Monster', and 'Sugar Plum', is their dwarf habit, small flowers, and short bloom period. A notable exception is the magnificent *Geranium maderense*, from the island of Madeira. Its fernlike foliage and masses of red-eyed pink flowers held in an umbrella-like cluster above the foliage put every other perennial geranium to shame. Unfortunately, it is hardy only in Zones 7 and 8.

 ## PLANT PROFILE

KNOWN BOTANICALLY AS: *Geranium himalayense, G. pretense*

ZONES: 5–8 as a summer-flowering perennial

PROPAGATION: By division of mature clumps

SPACING: 12 inches apart in full sun or light shade

PESTS AND DISEASES: Mostly chewing insects such as slugs, and also mildew diseases

PERFECT PARTNERS: Asiatic lilies, coreopsis, daylilies, gaillardia, ornamental grasses such as variegated maiden grass, and perennial sunflowers

Grasses, Ornamental

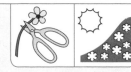

Japanese hakone grass produces a fountainlike effect in light shade. Drought-tolerant pink muhly grass produces frothy pink flower plumes like a pink mist.

GROW THIS! Zebra grass, variegated maiden grass, pink muhly grass, and hakone grass

Most perennial grasses are grown for their outstanding leaf forms. Their floral display, if conspicuous, is considered a bonus. The tender perennial pampas plume grows tall, arching, slender leaf blades that make a bold accent in mixed borders, plus a stunning display of silky white flower plumes in late summer. The hardier *Miscanthus* varieties, also known as maiden grass, don't have quite the stature of pampas plume (*Cortaderia selloana*), but they have arresting tall, arching leaves nevertheless, and silky white or red flower plumes depending on variety. The gold variegated form known as zebra grass (*M. sinensis* 'Zebrinus') has arching green leaves flecked with yellow so that a mature specimen in late spring, summer, and fall will look like a shower of sparks. Another variegated *sinensis* form, 'Variegata', also known as variegated maiden grass, has longitudinal white and green stripes and produces a distinct silvery appearance from a distance.

Pink muhly grass (*Muhlenbergia capillaris*) forms a cushion of spiky leaves and begins its spectacular flower show of misty pink flower plumes in fall when most other perennials have started to go dormant. It's an especially fine companion to plant with fall-blooming colchicums and used as an edging among beds of New England asters.

Japanese hakone grass produces a soothing fleecelike effect, especially when planted in a shady border.

Japanese hakone grass (*Hakonechloa macra*), also called Japanese woodland grass, grows in full sun and light shade. The variety 'Aureola' has green and gold stripes running the length of each leaf blade. The leaves overlap and create a cushion effect. It is particularly effective grown so the leaves cascade over rock ledges. Although the grass does not have conspicuous flowers, the attractive leaves are reason enough to grow it.

BE AWARE! Before you go wild planting carefree ornamental grasses, do a little checking locally to determine if the grasses you admire are on an invasive plant list. Fountain grasses (*Pennisetum* species), for example, are a pest in mild-winter areas like Southern California and Arizona. Japanese bloodgrass (*Imperata cylindrica* 'Rubra') is also invasive in the same general area. In the North, oat grass can be a pest. Bamboo is a type of grass, and there is nothing quite like bamboo for creating an oriental flavor to a garden. However, there are two kinds—clump forming and running. Both spread by underground roots, but the clumping type spreads much more slowly than the running kind, which can send out underground roots a distance of several feet each season.

Pampas Plume Is Not Invasive

The beautiful tall plume of pampas (*Cortaderia selloana*) is a popular accent plant in gardens with mild winters, such as California, the Pacific Northwest, and in the East south of Washington, DC. The plant produces a fountain of graceful, narrow, sawtooth leaves, and, by midsummer, gleaming white, silky flower plumes on long stems held above the foliage. I especially admire the dwarf form 'Pumila', with leaf clusters 3 feet high and flower plumes extending another 2 to 3 feet above them. Unfortunately, the pampas plume is easily confused with the similar, much more aggressive species *C. jubata,* which grows taller, displays towering dirty-white plumes, and has become invasive in arid areas of coastal California, displacing native species. Pampas plume (also called pampas grass) is a benign tender perennial, but *C. jubata* sets prodigious amounts of seed capable of being carried by the wind for miles and reproducing aggressively in the poorest soil.

Do not confuse the regal pampas plume of gardens with its loathsome cousin that should be eradicated wherever it appears.

PLANT PROFILE

KNOWN BOTANICALLY AS: *Miscanthus, Muhlenbergia, and Hakonechloa* species

ZONES: There are grasses for every zone where gardens are cultivated in North America, roughly Zones 3–11. However, be selective and choose the hardiest grasses for your zone, such as hakone grass where there is snow cover in winter (or where the ground freezes) and tender kinds like pampas plume for mild winter areas.

PROPAGATION: Mostly from root division of mature plants

SPACING: 12 inches apart for compact varieties and up to 5 feet apart for larger-grass clumps such as variegated maiden grass; sun or light shade depending on variety

PESTS AND DISEASES: None serious, except occasional chewing insects like slugs and grasshoppers, but damage is usually superficial

PERFECT PARTNERS: Mostly summer-flowering perennials like coneflowers, daylilies, Indian blanket, rudbeckia, Shasta daisies, Siberian irises, and perennial sunflowers, plus fall-flowering kinds like New England asters and sedum 'Autumn Joy'

Hellebores

Most hellebores are bought as plants, but 'Royal Heritage' is a seed mixture of the best colors, formulated to produce a wide color range from seed.

GROW THIS! 'Royal Heritage' and 'Sunshine Selections'

Hellebores are among the first flowering plants in spring, often flowering ahead of daffodil displays and at the same time as snowdrops and witch hazels. Two kinds are popular in American gardens—the white Christmas rose (*Helleborus niger*) and the Lenten rose (*H. orientalis*), both native to Europe. In appearance they look alike except that the Lenten rose has a much wider color range that includes white, pink, red, maroon, and freckled varieties. The cup-shaped flowers are mostly nodding, so the best place to display them is a slope. The leaves are evergreen, leathery, and similar to pachysandra in appearance, but in areas with severe winters the leaves can brown and look unsightly. To remedy this, simply remove all blemished leaves in late winter or spring, and this will stimulate flowering. Plants grow to 18 inches high and will form a clump up to 36 inches across. They are self-seeding; you'll find juvenile plants all around the mother plants in spring.

Some of the individual varieties look like miniature peonies, with multiple layers of petals; others resemble French anemones. Through cross-breeding, the color range has been extended to include yellow, green, and slate blue. Unfortunately, the flowers wilt quickly when cut but can be floated in a dish of water to last a week or more.

There are many species of hellebore offered by perennial growers. *H. orientalis* is the most widely adapted, overwintering from Zones 4 to 9. Numerous strains (varieties linked genetically) are available, including 'Royal Heritage', a seedling selection created by perennial plant expert John Elsley using seed collected from UK hellebore growers. These will flower within a year of starting from seed. West Virginia breeder Barry Glick offers a competing mixture as plants. Glick has accumulated more than 50,000 stock plants over a period of 12 years, many from growers in the United Kingdom, Germany, Belgium, New Zealand, and Australia. Glick's 'Sunshine Selections' are the result of hand pollination to ensure a good balance of colors and vigor. Hellebores are deerproof and thrive from Zones 5 through 9. They are best grown in light shade in a humus-rich soil.

BE AWARE! I avoid the look-alike hellebore *H. niger* because it's available mostly in white and is not nearly as forgiving of adverse soil or climate conditions as *H. orientalis*. The green hellebore (*H. foetidus*), also called stinking hellebore, with its sickly green nodding flower clusters, tends to get lost. Better to give space to more *H. orientalis* varieties and hybrids, in my opinion.

 ## PLANT PROFILE

KNOWN BOTANICALLY AS: *Helleborus* x *hybridus*

ZONES: 4–8 for early spring flowering

PROPAGATION: Difficult to divide; mostly grown from seed and seedlings

SPACING: 12 inches apart in light shade

PESTS AND DISEASES: Mostly windburn through freezing temperatures. Trim away browned leaves, and fresh new unblemished leaves will replace them.

PERFECT PARTNERS: Aconites, crocuses, daffodils, snowdrops, and early tulips

Hostas

Plant my two favorite giant-size hostas—the American-bred 'Blue Angel' and 'Sum & Substance', and you will create a beautiful blue and yellowish color combination.

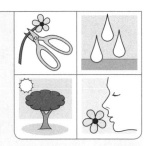

GROW THIS! 'Frances Williams', 'Blue Angel', 'Sum & Substance', 'Patriot', *Hosta ventricosa,* and 'Royal Standard'

The hosta variety 'Frances Williams' is undoubtedly the most widely planted hosta in the world. A blue-and-green bicolor, its large dinner-plate-size leaves splay out to create an immense cushion up to 2 feet high and 4 feet wide. Named for a Connecticut hobby breeder, its blue leaves are margined chartreuse green. It does have one serious fault—a tendency to burn in summer heat unless given adequate shade.

Among large-leafed hostas, a much more heat-tolerant variety is 'Blue Angel', developed by Long Island hosta breeder Paul Aden, who is responsible for some of the world's best-selling hosta hybrids. His 'Sum & Substance' (a chartreuse variety with gigantic leaves) has such large, paddle-shaped leaves it looks more like a tropical plant than a hardy one. These two hosta varieties are now such an important part of the Dutch and Japanese perennial plant industry that Aden has been honored by both countries. However, it is Paul's blue-leaved variety 'Blue Angel' that I single out as his best work, not only for its large size and handsome blistered leaves, but also for its prominent, fragrant white flower clusters with tubular florets that can be as big as foxgloves. The flowers are clustered at the top of strong stems and make exquisite cut flowers. Grow 'Blue Angel', 'Sum & Substance', and 'Frances Williams' along a shaded walk and you will experience an extraordinary tropical-looking hosta display. For a green-and-white variegated form, my choice is 'Patriot' because the variegation is at the leaf edges and consistent.

Most hostas have white or pale blue flowers. The hosta species *H. ventricosa* produces deep violet blue bell-shaped flowers in midsummer. When massed in woodlands, they can provide the same effect as bluebells in bloom. There is a variegated form with cream-edged leaves that is also striking in a shady location. Among white-flowered hostas, 'Royal Standard' is outstanding. Its chartreuse leaves are large, and the long, fragrant flower spikes, appearing in late summer, are studded with big, fragrant waxy flowers that are spectacular in flower arrangements.

BE AWARE! I would never plant the large-leaf variety 'Spilt Milk'. My youngest daughter and I were touring a hosta nursery with the owner, inspecting hundreds of varieties. She was 8 at the time, and when we came to 'Spilt Milk', she exclaimed, "Look, Dad, it has bird poop all over it!" Actually, that was the natural coloration—splashes of white against dark green heart-shaped leaves, but the white markings did indeed look like bird droppings. Nor do I like the new red-stalked hostas with ruffled leaves, like 'Miss Susie'. They look like rhubarb, and I'd rather have rhubarb in my vegetable garden than a shady perennial border.

Many of the miniature hostas like 'Little Devil', 'Teeny-weeny Bikini', and 'Hacksaw' (with its toothed leaves resembling dandelion foliage!) have poor ornamental value, except for a hosta fanatic; also many of the green-and-white variegated forms like 'Guardian Angel' have a marbled coloring that looks diseased, in my opinion.

 ## PLANT PROFILE

KNOWN BOTANICALLY AS: *Hosta* hybrids

ZONES: 3–9 as a spring, summer, and fall foliage plant

PROPAGATION: Mostly by division of mature plants

SPACING: Space large varieties up to 3 feet apart in light shade.

PESTS AND DISEASES: Mostly slugs and deer. Exposure to sun will cause sunscald on many varieties.

PERFECT PARTNERS: Asiatic and Oriental lilies, astilbe, brunnera, ferns, foxgloves, heucheras, Japanese bleeding hearts, and tiarella

Hydrangeas

'Endless Summer' blooms on new wood and produces a floral display even when the top growth is damaged by frost. 'Limelight' has extra-large greenish blooms that also bloom on new wood.

GROW THIS! 'Endless Summer', 'Limelight', 'Annabelle', and 'Pinky Winky'

One of the delights of a trip along the Brittany coast of France in early summer is the profuse flowering of mop-head hydrangeas, even used as long hedges with alternating colors of blue, pink, red, purple, and white. Along a cliff walk at Port-Blanc, I even saw an entire hillside of tall-growing pines underplanted with mop-head hydrangeas in all colors.

Many US gardeners in cold winter areas try to grow hydrangeas as foundation plants, lawn highlights, and even in whiskey half barrels; what they discover after one season is that the plant will produce healthy serrated leaves but obstinately refuse to rebloom. There can be two reasons: First, many people receive hydrangeas as gift plants at Easter. These have been specially bred for short days and greenhouse conditions, unable to bloom when daylight hours lengthen. The second reason is that older varieties of mop-heads bloom on the previous year's wood. Unless your garden is protected from harsh freezes (like beside a river or along the coast with moderating winter temperatures), the buds for the next season will be killed. The plant may still sprout new wood from the hardy roots, but this new wood will generally not bloom.

Flowers of hydrangea 'Peegee' are large, starting off white and turning pink, then bronze.

All that has changed with the introduction of 'Endless Summer', a variety that blooms on new and old wood and continues blooming all through summer until fall frost. The color of 'Endless Summer' can be pink or blue, depending on the soil pH. An acid soil turns the petals blue; an alkaline soil turns them pink. Some catalogs sell a soil amendment that will help turn mop-heads blue if you don't have acid soil.

Older hydrangea varieties, such as 'Nikko Blue', are fine near the ocean or large bodies of water like lakes and rivers where hydrangeas can survive winter. More reliable for summer flowering are varieties of *H. arborescens*, especially 'Annabelle' with its large flowers that start off lime green, turn snow white, and fade to a bronze pink.

Varieties of *H. paniculata* used to be all white, but I like the variety 'Pinky Winky', whose cone-shaped flowers open white and turn pink at the base as the flower ages. The variety commonly called 'Peegee' (*H. grandiflora*) has huge white flowers that fade to pink and bronze and is commonly trained to create a tree form. 'Limelight' resembles 'Peegee', but its flowers are lime green on long stems that weep.

Hydrangeas prefer full sun and good drainage. They will tolerate light shade and, though slow growing, can reach 10 feet high, billowing out to twice that in width.

BE AWARE! If you live in an area with a cold winter climate, you should avoid older hydrangea varieties that bloom on second-year wood because harsh winters where the ground freezes will kill the previous season's growth and buds. Rather, select varieties like 'Forever & Ever' and 'Endless Summer' so that if the previous year's growth is killed, the new growth will still bear flowers. Nor do I like hydrangeas with variegated leaves, like the 'Variegata' macrophylla type, because they look mildewed, and mildew is certainly not a good impression to make with any big leaf. Also, the variegation in a hydrangea leaf seems to hold back the plant's flowering potential, or it delays its flowering and the sparse flowers that do form occur late in the season.

 ## PLANT PROFILE

KNOWN BOTANICALLY AS: *Hydrangea* x *macrophylla, H. arborescens,* and *H. paniculata*

ZONES: 4–9 for summer flowering

PROPAGATION: Cuttings taken when flowers are not in bloom

SPACING: At least 4 feet apart in sun or light shade

PESTS AND DISEASES: Chewing insects such as slugs and deer, although they appear on many deer-resistant lists

PERFECT PARTNERS: Asiatic and Oriental lilies, astilbe, ferns, heucheras, and hostas

Indian Blanket

This is one beautiful, tough, widely
adapted member of the daisy family,
especially massed in a mixture.

GROW THIS! 'Arizona' series and 'Goblin'

There isn't a tougher, more dependable native American perennial species
than Indian blanket (*Gaillardia aristata*). One July at the Anchorage, Alaska,
airport (Zone 3), I saw sheets of them growing wild beside the runway;
another time, I discovered them growing riotously in pure sand, just yards
from the shoreline on Sanibel Island, Florida (Zone 10). Although they are a
hardy perennial with daisylike flowers that can be all red, all yellow, and a
combination of yellow and red, plant breeders have produced hybrids that
will flower strongly the first year from seed and then behave as a perennial
in successive seasons. Two hybrids from the German plant breeder Benary
have won All-America Selections awards. They are 'Arizona Sun', a red with
yellow petal tips, and 'Arizona Apricot', a yellow with an orange halo around
a yellow button center. 'Arizona Red Shades' completes a full color range.
There is also a low-growing, cushion-shaped variety 'Goblin' that covers
itself in beautiful yellow-and-red bicolored flowers, and it's ideal for edging
a perennial border.

These new Indian blankets are striking plants for the mixed border and
also containers as they bloom continuously all summer until fall frost and
branch freely from the base to create a bushy habit up to 12 inches high
and twice as wide. Flowering time from starting seed is just 11 weeks. Also
use the separate colors alone in mass plantings or mix them to create a flowering meadow.

BE AWARE! There are annual forms of gaillardia that can be direct-seeded
into the garden easily. Some of these are doubles, like the 'Plume' series in
mostly yellow and red, but the doubles never produce such a good vibrant display as the single or semidouble flowered kinds, and these doubles tend to grow
long, weak stems that sprawl about untidily.

KNOWN BOTANICALLY AS: *Gaillardia* x *grandiflora* (this is the type most often grown, a hybrid between *G. aristata* and *G. pulchella*)

ZONES: 3–10 for summer flowering

PROPAGATION: By seed started indoors 10 weeks before outdoor planting

SPACING: 12 inches apart in full sun, but will tolerate crowding in meadow gardens

PESTS AND DISEASES: None serious

PERFECT PARTNERS: Bachelor's buttons, coreopsis, daylilies, poppies, salvia, Shasta daisies, and veronica

Irises, Bearded

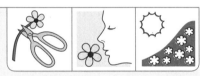

Among modern hybrids, the yellow-and-blue 'Edith Wolford' bearded iris is my favorite. Among heritage varieties, I adore the yellow and purple-lipped 'Gracchus'.

GROW THIS! 'Edith Wolford', 'Toll Gate', 'Beverly Sills', 'Red Hawk', 'Champagne Time', 'Stella Lights', and 'Gracchus'

Bearded irises are popular hardy perennials suitable for Zones 3 to 9 in a staggering range of colors that includes all shades of blue plus yellow, orange, red, ginger, pink, white, and even black. The flower of a bearded iris is composed of two ruffled upward-facing petals called standards and four downward-facing petals called falls. The standards and the falls can be contrasting colors, and it is these bicolors that help to create one of nature's most beautiful plantings—a rainbow border.

An excellent place to evaluate bearded irises is the Presby Memorial Iris Gardens in Montclair, New Jersey, where several thousand varieties are arranged chronologically by year of introduction for evaluation. The best time to visit is Memorial Day weekend, when the plantings reach peak bloom.

With such an array of varieties to choose from, it seems impossible to single out just a few varieties for special attention, but surveys among iris enthusiasts generally favor 'Edith Wolford' for the most appealing color combination—canary yellow standards and violet blue falls. Winner of a Dykes Memorial Award from the American Iris Society, the flowers have a pleasant peppery fragrance and grow to 3 feet high.

Of course, bearded irises are famous for their range of blues, but a solid blue in the landscape does not look as dramatic as a blue with a splash of white (because white always enhances a solid color). 'Toll Gate' is a gorgeous deep violet blue with ruffled petals and a prominent splash of white on the lower falls. It is one of the most eye-catching iris varieties planted today in Monet's garden. Among the pinks, 'Beverly Sills' still shines bright; among reds, I favor Schreiner's 'Red Hawk'; and among the brightest yellows, Cooley's 'Champagne Time'.

Bearded iris 'Edith Wolford' has blue lower petals and yellow upper petals, winning a Dykes Memorial Award from the American Iris Society for its exquisite bicoloration.

When choosing bearded irises from a catalog, you will note that some are labeled "rebloomers," meaning that they produce a second flush of bloom in the fall. 'Immortality' (white), 'Stella Lights' (clear blue), and 'Pure As Gold' (deep yellow) are my favorites in this series.

Don't overlook some heirloom iris varieties like 'Gracchus'. Introduced in 1884, it is a yellow with violet falls, flowering riotously and colonizing rapidly.

Bearded irises are mostly sold as sausage-shaped rhizomes for planting (two-thirds of the rhizome should be submerged in soil). They demand good drainage, and they like to bake in the sun for best flowering. Keep the beds weed free.

BE AWARE! There are miniature varieties of bearded irises, but the flowers are still large and seem out of scale with the dwarfed stems and leaves. They can look attractive as front-of-the-border edging plants and in rock gardens, but next to the regular-height bearded irises, they can look malnourished.

Varieties of *Iris* x *hollandica* grown from bulbs are not reliably hardy north of Zone 7. They may bloom the first spring after fall planting, but invariably die out completely after that first flush of bloom.

 PLANT PROFILE

KNOWN BOTANICALLY AS: *Iris germanica*

ZONES: 3–9 as an early-summer-flowering perennial, and again in fall when you plant varieties designated rebloomers

PROPAGATION: Raw rhizomes separated from mature clumps after blooming, and with the leaves cut back to an inch of the crown so the wind does not blow the transplant over when placed upright in its position

SPACING: 6–8 inches apart for a dramatic rainbow border effect, in sun

PESTS AND DISEASES: There is a borer that will tunnel into iris rhizomes, but generally damage is superficial except in commercial plantings.

PERFECT PARTNERS: Ox-eye daisies, peonies, poppies, and roses

Irises, Japanese

Although the Japanese iris color range is limited to blue, white, and purple, blue-and-white 'Lion King' is one of the largest flowered, with up to nine petals.

GROW THIS! 'Lion King', 'Crystal Halo', 'Flying Tiger', and 'Gracieuse'

Japanese irises are amazingly hardy perennials that require the complete opposite conditions from bearded irises. Whereas bearded iris want a hot, dry soil exposed to as much sun as possible, Japanese iris will thrive in a moist, boggy soil, even in light shade. They also bloom later in spring than bearded irises, and instead of the blooms facing sideways, they face up at the sky. The color range for Japanese iris is more limited (mostly blue, purple, white, and bicolors), but for planting at the edge of a water garden, there is nothing finer. Moreover, the long, slender, arching blue green leaves are decorative before and after the plants

Siberian Iris

Though their flowering display is short lived, Siberian iris (*Iris sibirica*) will thrive in moist or dry soil. Just give them plenty of sun. The flowers occur about the same time as bearded irises, in late spring. For a complete color range, choose 'Blue King' (violet blue), 'Butter and Sugar' (white with yellow center), and 'Sparkling Rose' (rose pink). Plant Siberian iris among white perennial ox-eye daisies for an especially beautiful plant partnership.

bloom, which occurs a week or two after bearded irises have faded from view. 'Lion King' is one of the biggest, measuring up to 5 inches across, its nine broad petals a deep lavender blue and white. 'Crystal Halo' is a huge sky blue iris with a white edge, and 'Flying Tiger' is blue with handsome purple veins. Plant these three varieties with a white, such as the bicolored 'Gracieuse' (ruffled white with violet edges), and you will enjoy a wide color range.

Japanese irises are often sold bareroot, but you'll have a greater chance of success if you first pot these up and allow them to develop a vigorous root system and healthy green top growth before planting in the ground. The soil should be moist; Japanese irises will even tolerate their roots permanently covered with a thin film of water. They will take fairly diverse soil conditions as long as it is not dry sand, such as a regular perennial border with good drainage.

BE AWARE! The flower of a Japanese iris can display as few as three petals and up to nine. The three-to-four petaled varieties are not as attractive as the five-to-nine petaled varieties.

Be careful introducing the yellow European flag iris (*Iris pseudacorus*) to your garden. It can be highly invasive, and if planted beside a shallow pond, invariably it will ring the pond in a few years, even seeding into areas with drainage.

I also caution against planting Louisiana iris (various southern species), as these can be equally invasive.

The Japanese water iris 'Lion King' displays lavender blue petals with splashes of white. It is among the largest in the iris kingdom and is tolerant of wet feet.

PLANT PROFILE

KNOWN BOTANICALLY AS: *Iris ensata*

ZONES: 4–9 for summer flowering

PROPAGATION: Bareroot divisions after flowering; also from seed

SPACING: 12 inches apart in sun or partial shade

PESTS AND DISEASES: None serious

PERFECT PARTNERS: Astilbe, carex grasses, hosta, and rudbeckia

Lavender, English

Deep blue 'Phenomenal' is the hardiest,
but 'Hidcote' is an equally fragrant deep violet blue.

GROW THIS! 'Munstead', 'Hidcote', and 'Phenomenal'

Lavender comes from the Latin *lavare,* meaning "to wash," because the Greeks and Romans liked to scent their bathwater with the pleasant aromatic blue flowers. Lavender oils are used in a vast range of cosmetics, including soap, shampoo, body lotion, and perfume. The dried stems and flowers are added to potpourris and hung in linen closets to deter moths. It also makes a refreshing tea, a few flower heads simply steeped in boiling water. Native to the Maritime Alps of France, vast areas of wild lavender can be seen today in the mountains around Grasse, the perfume capital of Provence.

There are two popular varieties of lavender: 'Munstead', a light blue named for the home of Victorian plantswoman Gertrude Jekyll, and 'Hidcote', a deep violet blue named for the home of an American ex-patriot living in England, Lawrence Johnston. 'Hidcote' is the more appealing color and won an Award of Garden Merit from the Royal Horticultural Society. 'Hidcote' overwinters better in Zones 7 to 9 and is generally not as hardy as 'Munstead', which will overwinter reliably in Zones 6 to 9. Both have silvery blue evergreen foliage and grow a mound of needlelike leaves up to 3 feet high. A more recent introduction 'Phenomenal' from Peace Tree Farm in Pennsylvania produces an especially impressive floral display of deep blue flowers and is hardier than 'Hidcote', to Zone 4.

The cardinal rule with lavender is to give it good drainage, because the roots are susceptible to rot if water puddles around them.

Spanish lavender is a popular purple-flowering type for frost-free locations like coastal California. Siberian sage (*Perovskia atriplicifolia*) is hardy and more commonly called Russian sage (see page 358). Unlike true lavender that flowers for a 6-week period in summer, Siberian lavender blooms continuously from midsummer to fall frost.

BE AWARE! Gardeners in northern climates (Zone 6 and colder) sometimes have problems with lavender, usually as a result of choosing the wrong kind for a cold climate. In general, the French (*L. stoechas*), Spanish or spike (*L. latifolia*), and all but English lavenders are not hardy for any climate colder than a Zone 8. For best results with any type of lavender, make a special bed of almost pure gravel and plant on a slope rather than flat ground.

 PLANT PROFILE

KNOWN BOTANICALLY AS: *Lavandula angustifolia*

ZONES: 6–9 for summer flowering

PROPAGATION: By seed sown indoors 10 weeks before outdoor planting, and from cuttings before and after the plants bloom

SPACING: At least 18 inches apart in full sun

PESTS AND DISEASES: None serious, although alternate thawing and freezing and puddling around the roots will cause rot

PERFECT PARTNERS: Asiatic lilies, coneflowers, coreopsis, daylilies, Indian blanket, roses, and other herbs

Lilies, Asiatic Hybrids

My favorites for cutting are 'Grand Cru' (an orange with maroon eye zone) and de Graaff's famous 'Citronella', which flowers early and naturalizes easily.

GROW THIS! 'Enchantment', 'Grand Cru', 'Lollypop', 'Push Off', and 'Citronella'

The late Jan de Graaff, a lily hybridizer, started the craze for breeding lily hybrids. Born in Holland, he immigrated to Medford, Oregon, to establish Oregon Bulb Farms and begin a breeding program that produced the first easy-to-grow hybrid lilies. For years his 'Enchantment', a glowing orange Asiatic hybrid with upward-facing blooms, was the most popular and a favorite among cut-flower growers serving the florist trade.

Other breeders, inspired by de Graaff's success, have taken lily hybridizing to new heights, notably in the number of bicolors, such as 'Grand Cru', with deep orange petals and a maroon eye zone; white 'Lollypop', with pink petal tips; 'White Pixels', white with myriad burgundy red freckles; and short-stemmed 'Push Off', plum red with white petal margins. However, the one Asiatic lily I have found most suitable for naturalizing is 'Citronella'. Unlike most Asiatic lilies, its yellow flowers with black freckles do not face up toward the sun but are pendent like Turk's-cap lilies. They bloom early, at the same time as roses, and they multiply faster and more reliably than any other lily I have grown.

Asiatic lilies grow in sun or light shade. Their principal demand is an organic-rich soil with good drainage. All are suitable for growing in containers such as a whiskey half barrel, but the short-stemmed 'Tiny' series is particularly suited to container growing.

BE AWARE! There is a big temptation among lily lovers to grow some of the more exotic species like the Nepal lily (*Lilium nepalense*), with its maroon petals rimmed in green, and the giant Himalayan lily (*Cardiocrinum giganteum*), with delicate, nodding bell-shaped flowers that cannot take hot summers. However, many species of lilies are susceptible to virus diseases and generally fail to bloom more than one season. The giant Himalayan lily is offered by some bulb specialists who claim hardiness in Zone 6, but it is difficult to grow anywhere in the

United States except in Zones 7 and 8 of the Pacific Northwest. Stick with the hybrids and especially mixtures that contain a balance of the best colors.

 PLANT PROFILE

KNOWN BOTANICALLY AS: *Lilium* hybrids

ZONES: 5–8, depending on variety

PROPAGATION: Raw bulbs planted in fall or early spring for summer flowering, at least 6 inches deep from the base of the bulb. Some lilies can be propagated by small black bulblets that occur in the leaf margins, especially among Turk's-cap lilies.

SPACING: Shoulder to shoulder in containers; otherwise, 6–8 inches apart in sun or partial shade

PESTS AND DISEASES: Usual virus diseases and chewing insects, such as greenfly and slugs; also foraging animals, such as rabbits and deer. Bulbs rot easily in poorly drained soil.

PERFECT PARTNERS: Bee balm, hydrangeas, roses, rudbeckia, perennial sunflowers, and yellow loosestrife

Lilies, Oriental Hybrids

My fragrant Oriental lily collection is a highlight of the summer garden, with 'Schehezerade' (a crimson, cream-edged beauty), 'Star Gazer' (strawberry red), and 'Casa Blanca' (fragrant white) the scene stealers.

GROW THIS! 'Star Gazer', 'Casa Blanca', 'Black Beauty', 'Scheherazade', and 'Dizzy'

Jan de Graaff's most beautiful garden lilies were the 'Imperial' strain of Oriental hybrids, growing large flowers with reflexed petals up to 10 inches across. In addition to a red, he produced a white and a pink—all with handsome freckles in the throat and delightfully fragrant. Using de Graaff's varieties and breeding

The heavily fragrant lily 'Star Gazer' is an American-bred Oriental hybrid that is valued for both garden display and cutting.

methods, other plant breeders have taken the Oriental hybrids to new heights of popularity with varieties such as the US-bred 'Star Gazer' and Dutch-bred 'Casa Blanca', both of which grow large, fragrant flowers on tall stems. They are among the most popular of cut flowers among florists. A single stem of either will sell for $5.

It was California breeder Leslie Woodriff who succeeded de Graaff as the world's most prolific lily hybridizer. He not only developed 'Star Gazer' (and unsuccessfully fought a legal battle with Dutch growers to earn royalties from it), but also he introduced 'Black Beauty'. Actually a dark red with black freckles, 'Black Beauty' has smaller flowers than 'Star Gazer' and the flowers face down, but it is more vigorous and reliably self-perpetuating so that a single bulb can quickly form a colony. 'Black Beauty' was the first lily ever entered in the Lily Hall of Fame.

A whole series of Oriental hybrids have pendent flowers and orange highlights, made possible by introducing genes from orange-colored trumpet lilies. My favorite is 'Scheherazade', which honors the name of the fictional Persian woman who told the story known as *One Thousand and One Nights*. It can display as many as 20 big, beautiful, deep orange-red, reflexed, nodding flowers with white petal margins, all open at one time. Another outstanding oriental is 'Dizzy', a large white hybrid peppered with red freckles and raspberry red bands along each of its six petals.

Oriental hybrids bloom in midsummer and are best massed in a raised bed all to themselves. Do not cut for flower arrangements the first year, as the stems will be short and the foliage is needed to rejuvenate the bulb. Rather, wait until the second season, when the stems will double in height and you can cut two-thirds of the stem without depleting the bulb. For use as a cut flower, trim off the powdery brown anthers, because these can stain tablecloths and clothing.

BE AWARE! There is a great temptation to wait until the garden centers have a bulb clearance sale in order to buy bargain lilies. But lilies have fleshy bulbs made up of scales that are highly susceptible to drying out or contracting a fungal disease that is not evident until you get home and open the sealed package. Since garden lilies can be planted in fall for spring blooming or early spring for summer blooming, a cardinal rule is to *buy early*, as soon as the packages go on display, usually the week after Labor Day in fall. In spring, buy no later than early March. Alternatively, buy from a catalog for delivery at those times.

The wide, flared, reflexed petal of most Oriental hybrid lilies, I believe, is a vital part of their charm, and when a hybridizer makes them produce a double row of petals, it doesn't look natural. The lily I particularly avoid planting is 'Mona Lisa', since it is described as a semidouble, but it does not always produce a second layer of petals—so you find some with and some without. It's also a weak color, a white with a flush of pale pink.

 ## PLANT PROFILE

KNOWN BOTANICALLY AS: *Lilium* hybrids

ZONES: 6–8 for summer flowering, usually 2 weeks after Asiatic hybrids

PROPAGATION: Dormant bulbs planted in early spring or early fall. Also bulb scales (each segment of an Oriental lily bulb) can be separated and planted whenever the soil can be dug; it will root, sprout leaves, and produce a flower. Some lilies (like the Turk's cap) develop bulbils at each leaf node. These can be planted to create a new plant identical to the mother.

SPACING: Shoulder to shoulder in containers; 8 inches apart in garden soil in sun or light shade

PESTS AND DISEASES: Same as Asiatic lilies—especially susceptible to deer damage and even squirrels eating the fat flower buds

PERFECT PARTNERS: Bee balm, dahlias, daylilies, gladiolus, hollyhock, rudbeckia, perennial sunflowers, and tall ornamental grasses such as feather reed grass

Lupines

*Though mixtures vary among suppliers,
the old-established 'Russell Hybrids' are still
my favorites, with up to 50 flower spikes on a plant.*

GROW THIS! 'Russell Hybrids' and 'Gallery Hybrids'; *Baptisia australis*

George Russell (1857–1951), a railway worker and gardener for hire, rented two allotments (in a community garden) in York, England, and, as a hobby, collected species of lupines (called lupins in the United Kingdom) from all parts of North America. Crossing mostly the blue perennial tree lupine, *Lupinus polyphyllus* (from California and the Pacific Northwest), with other species, he created a magnificent series of colors, the plants displaying tall flower spikes above a bush of fan-shaped leaves. At the Chelsea Flower Show, held in London each spring, they are always the center of attention, outshining everything else on display with spires of yellow, orange, pink, red, blue, mauve, maroon, purple, white, and bicolors.

Russell guarded his plants zealously and refused to sell the seed until finally he granted Baker's Nurseries, near Wolverhampton, the rights to propagate and sell them. Introduced at the Chelsea Flower Show in 1937, they gained the highest honor—a gold medal—from the Royal Horticultural Society. Russell continued to inspect the production fields, and it is said that his demand for quality was so strict that he once removed more than 4,000 plants from a production field of 5,000 so only the best colors and strongest plants would cross to set seed. They grow to 4 feet tall.

Today's Russell lupines are best treated as biennials, allowed to grow a green crown of leaves the first season and flower the second. They are hardy, flowering in late spring during cool weather, and are best massed as a rainbow mixture in beds and borders and as a meadow planting. In parts of the Pacific Northwest, coastal Maine, Scotland, and New Zealand, they have naturalized. The seed has a hard coat and is best soaked overnight in lukewarm water to start germination. They tolerate a wide range of soils (including sandy soils with good drainage and moist soil) in full sun.

BE AWARE! Many who see the great sweeps of blue lupines (called blue-bonnets) across meadows in the Texas Hill Country aspire to create a similar planting in their gardens. However, bluebonnets (*Lupinus texensis*) like an alkaline soil, and since most soils of the northeastern United States are acid, they are likely to fail. A much more reliable relative of the Texas bluebonnet for naturalizing is the hardy perennial *Baptisia australis* (*australis* means "southern," since the plants are native mostly to Arkansas and Texas). The plants grow taller and bushier than Texas bluebonnets, but the blue color is almost as intense; providing they have good drainage, they are reliably hardy in a wide range of soils.

Several breeders have introduced dwarf varieties of lupine, such as 'Lulu' and 'Minarette', but it is the taller Russell hybrids, such as the 'Gallery Hybrids' mixture, that are more likely to please.

PLANT PROFILE

KNOWN BOTANICALLY AS: *Lupinus polyphyllus* hybrids

ZONES: 5–8 (some varieties to Zone 4) for early summer flowering

PROPAGATION: Mostly from seed, some as annuals started indoors 8 weeks before outdoor planting; others as biennials, dying after flowering

SPACING: 12 inches apart in sun

PESTS AND DISEASES: Mostly mildew disease, rust, and southern blight

PERFECT PARTNERS: Asiatic lilies, coreopsis, daylilies, Indian blanket, and poppies

Peonies, Herbaceous

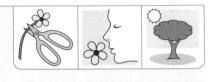

American-bred 'Estate' peonies are outstanding,
but old-fashioned 'Bowl of Beauty' is my favorite for cutting.

GROW THIS! 'Bowl of Beauty', 'Festiva Maxima', 'Cytherea', and 'Barrington Belle'

There are basically two kinds of peonies popular with home gardeners: the perennial herbaceous peony that has soft stems and large cup-shaped or double flowers, and tree peonies that grow woody stems. Most modern herbaceous peonies are crosses between European kinds (*Paeonia officinalis*) and Chinese kinds (*P. lactiflora*). They drop their leaves in fall and go dormant, surviving by underground roots.

Tree peonies (*P. suffruticosa*) are deciduous shrubs, and although they also drop their leaves in fall, the woody stems remain exposed (see Peonies, Tree, on page 342).

Herbaceous peonies are more popular because they are easier to grow and much less expensive, capable of surviving for generations. The creams of the crop in my experience are 'Bowl of Beauty' (a single, cup-shaped, deep rosy red with a magnificent dome of powdery yellow-and-red stamens) and 'Festiva Maxima' (a huge double white with flecks of red at the base of the petals).

Significant advances in peony breeding were made by the late Professor A. P. Saunders, a chemistry teacher at Hamilton College in Clinton, New York. A Canadian by birth, he is considered to be the father of the modern peony. Working to improve both herbaceous and tree peonies, he registered more than 200 herbaceous varieties. "The Saunders peonies constitute one of the country's greatest horticultural legacies," wrote Tom Fischer, former editor of *Horticulture* magazine. One of his most popular is 'Cytherea', an award-winning, large-flowered double pink.

Another outstanding selection of large-flowered hybrids called 'Klehm's Estate Peonies' has been developed by America's leading peony breeder, Roy Klehm and other family members, in a popular range of colors that includes white, all shades of pink, and red. 'Barrington Belle', a deep shimmering red with a glorious golden dome of stamens at its center, is one of the more famous.

Herbaceous peonies can be delightfully fragrant, and they make good cut flowers. They are heavy feeders and benefit from a high-phosphorus fertilizer applied around the roots in spring, as the new leaves emerge, and in fall after frost.

BE AWARE! I do not like some of the newer peonies with twisted petals, as though they survived a plague of ravenous slugs: varieties like 'Bric a Brac', 'Salmon Jazz', and 'Daisy Coronet' that look like Edward Scissorhands shredded them to pieces.

Peonies can be propagated two ways—from root division and seeds. Not all peonies will set seed, and it can take 3 years for a peony plant to bloom from seed. However, some nurseries used to go through their production fields at the end of the season and harvest seeds. The resulting flowers can be unpredictable, some small and some large and all sizes, shapes, and colors in between, but the advantage of growing from seed is the low cost of production compared to root division. These seed-grown peonies are usually sold as potted plants and not advertised as seed grown, but simply some fanciful name like 'Peonies on Parade' or 'Peonies All Sorts, Mixed Colors.' I have not seen these offered in recent years, but there is the chance that these seed-grown peonies will return.

 PLANT PROFILE

KNOWN BOTANICALLY AS: *Paeonia officinalis*

ZONES: 4–8 for spring flowering

PROPAGATION: Mostly from root division after flowering, but also from seed

SPACING: Minimum of 2 feet apart in full sun or light shade

PESTS AND DISEASES: Mostly nematodes. Also the leaves are susceptible to mildew disease.

PERFECT PARTNERS: Bearded iris, lupines, Oriental poppies, and roses

Molly the Witch

The most highly prized peony species among peony enthusiasts is *Paeonia mlokosewitschii*, commonly called Molly the Witch. The only true yellow herbaceous peony, it is highly regional in its performance, fairly reliable in the Pacific Northwest but difficult elsewhere. Plants grow bushy, 3 feet high, and bloom early with yellow cup-shaped flowers up to 4 inches across. Native to a small area of the Caucacus Mountains, award yourself a blue ribbon if you can flower it.

Peonies, Tree

You cannot consider yourself a connoisseur gardener until you have grown the fabulous 'Joseph Rock', a large white with bold maroon blotches.

GROW THIS! 'Joseph Rock', 'Alhambra', 'Canary Brilliants', 'Roman Gold', and 'Marchioness'

The late Joseph Rock was an explorer and was on an expedition sponsored by the National Geographic Society to Tibet when he discovered a magnificent large-flowered tree peony growing at a monastery in an area of tribal warfare. He collected seed, and back in the United States it produced flowers identical to the parent: ruffled white with maroon blotches at the base of each petal, the flowers measuring up to 10 inches across.

Rock revisited the monastery, hoping to collect more seed of this unique peony, but he discovered the monastery in ruins and the plant destroyed. Using the progeny of his original plant, peony hybridizers have been able to cross it with other peonies to create a series of 'Rock' hybrids that include red and pink, all with handsome maroon blotches. However, it is the original maroon and white that never fails to bring gasps of amazement in home gardens.

A unique feature of the tree peony is the number of yellow-flowered varieties available (a color lacking in herbaceous peonies). Using *P. lutea* from China, Professor A. P. Saunders developed a whole series of yellow-flowered kinds. These include 'Alhambra', a large semidouble golden yellow with maroon flecks; 'Canary Brilliants', a bright yellow; and 'Roman Gold', a single-flowered sulfur yellow with a dark red center zone. Another color found in Saunders tree peonies is peach. His 'Marchioness' is a single-flowered peach with raspberry red inner flares and ruffled petals and an unusually heavy bloomer. Many Saunders tree peonies are offered by Klehm's Song Sparrow mail-order catalog.

Tree peonies are best planted in spring or fall, using root cuttings with at least three "eyes" (growing points). They like a cool, well-drained soil such as at the base of a rock wall that's mulched with pine straw or shredded leaves. Tree peonies are heavy feeders and need more room than their smaller-flowered herbaceous counterparts. After severe winters, parts of the plant may winter-kill, but any dead or damaged branches can be pruned away.

BE AWARE! Advice given for herbaceous peonies grown from seed also applies to tree peonies. Collected from production fields, seed-produced seedlings often are variable and undependable. I think much of the allure of growing a tree peony is to see flat layers of petals surrounding a golden dome of stamens and a dark center. When a tree peony is fully doubled like many herbaceous peonies, it loses its appeal, as is the case with 'Madame André Devillers', a deep rosy-red French hybrid. 'Joseph Rock Double' is another double tree peony that is not nearly as beautiful as the single-flowered original; its handsome maroon petal markings are hidden, and the normally mounded dome of powdery yellow stamens is all but undetectable, too.

 ## PLANT PROFILE

KNOWN BOTANICALLY AS: *Paeonia suffuticosa*

ZONES: 5–8 for spring flowering

PROPAGATION: Mainly from root division before or after flowering; also from seed

SPACING: At least 3 feet apart in sun or light shade

PESTS AND DISEASES: Partial winterkill of individual branches is common after a severe winter. Prune away the dead parts.

PERFECT PARTNERS: Late-flowering azaleas, bearded irises, Oriental poppies, ox-eye daisies, rhododendron, and Siberian irises

Itoh Hybrid Peonies

The magnificent Itoh series of hybrid peonies are crosses between herbaceous peonies and tree peonies. This has resulted in flowers that are similar to tree peonies in appearance, but with fragrance (which tree peonies lack), and more blooms (up to 50 on a low, mound-shaped plant). Their improved flowering performance is due to their ability to develop both primary and secondary buds. Named for Toichi Itoh, the first hybridizer to successfully cross a tree peony with an herbaceous peony, these hybrid peonies display a color range that includes some spectacular yellows with red bicoloration. My favorite varieties are the yellow-and-red 'Misaka', the copper-and-red 'Kopper Kettle', and 'Cora Louise', a ruffled white with dark red eye zone.

Persian Buttercups

Grow the American-bred strain called 'Tecolote'
for the best spring-flowering mixture.

GROW THIS! 'Tecolote'

The name "Tecolote" (pronounced tek-oh-low-tay) is an American Indian name
for a small desert owl that builds its nest inside giant saguaro cacti in the
Sonoran Desert and is often seen at dusk against glorious desert sunsets. It is
those desert sunset colors that you will see in the 'Tecolote' mixture of Persian
buttercups, a flowering perennial bulb that blooms in spring wherever winters
are mild, such as Zones 8 to 10. The 'Tecolotes' can be purchased in a hot-color
mixture called 'Island Sunsets' and a cooler-color mixture called 'Pastel'. The
former includes red, yellow, and orange; the later includes white, pink, peach,
and bicolors of soft tones. Both mixtures are composed of fully double flowers
with black poppylike centers. The petals shimmer like satin in full sun.

Plants grow to 2 feet high, with stems long enough to make it a popular cut
flower among florists.

BE AWARE! In spring, florists and garden centers often sell a large-flowered
mixture called 'Bloomingdale', specially bred to grow under glass for the cut-
flower trade. For outdoor garden display, however, choose the more robust
'Tecolotes', available in single colors as well as the two mixtures. They are fan-
tastic massed in beds and borders and whiskey half barrels on a deck or patio.

PLANT PROFILE

KNOWN BOTANICALLY AS: *Ranunculus asiaticus*

ZONES: 8–11 for spring flowering; all zones as a houseplant

PROPAGATION: Raw bulbs planted in fall for spring flowering

SPACING: 6 inches apart in full sun

PESTS AND DISEASES: Slugs, spider mites, and aphids

PERFECT PARTNERS: Freesias, French anemones, harlequin flowers
(*Sparaxis* spp.), and other tender spring-flowering bulbs

Phlox, Summer

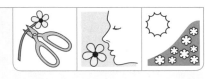

'Volcano' phlox is almost mildew immune. 'Natasha' is a mildew-resistant, earlier-flowering pink-and-white bicolor.

GROW THIS! 'Volcano', 'Intensia', 'Shortwood', 'Alpha', and 'Natasha'

Summer phlox is a hardy prairie wildflower that blooms riotously in summer with masses of cone-shaped, fragrant flower clusters on strong stems. Color selections began in France in the 1870s, and plant breeders (notably the Dutch) have extended the color range from mostly pink to vivid red, purple, white with a red eye, and almost blue.

Now gardeners can plant summer phlox with confidence that powdery mildew will not discolor and cause the plants to turn brown and die. The variety 'Volcano', developed in Holland and introduced by the international Australian plantsman Anthony Tesselar, is almost immune to powdery mildew. Moreover, the flower clusters can grow to twice the size of older phlox varieties.

The 'Intensia' series of hybrid summer phlox has similar mildew resistance and a wider color range that includes 'Star Brite', a rose pink and white, as well as 'Blueberry', a stunning violet blue with a purple eye zone. Also for good mildew resistance, Blooms of Bressingham recommend their 'Shortwood' variety, featuring pink flowers with a dark red eye.

A closely related species, *Phlox maculata* comes from the Carolinas and blooms early in late spring. The variety 'Alpha' is a beautiful pink, while 'Natasha' produces columns of lavender flowers with white stripes, an attractive bicolor that is valued for cutting. *P. maculata* has the advantage of being resistant to nematode damage and powdery mildew, problems that can occur with *P. paniculata*.

Use phlox in the cutting garden and massed in mixed perennial borders. Give them full sun and good drainage. They make good companions with Oriental lilies.

BE AWARE! The rule for growing beautiful summer phlox is simple—avoid mildew-prone varieties. Mildew disease is so prevalent in summer over most areas of the United States that the plants become afflicted and die before a decent flower display can be enjoyed. I also avoid dwarf varieties like 'Pinafore Pink' (clear pink flowers), as they look unnaturally top-heavy with bloom compared to the taller kinds.

 ## PLANT PROFILE

KNOWN BOTANICALLY AS: *Phlox paniculata* and *P. maculata*

ZONES: 5–8 for midsummer flowering

PROPAGATION: By seed and root division

SPACING: At least 12 inches apart in full sun

PESTS AND DISEASES: Powdery mildew

PERFECT PARTNERS: Coneflowers, daylilies, Oriental lilies, ornamental grasses such as maiden grass, and rudbeckia

Pincushion Flowers

Most pincushion flowers are short-lived summer-flowering plants, but 'Butterfly Blue' is everblooming until fall frost.

GROW THIS! 'Butterfly Blue'

The great French Impressionist painter Paul Cézanne painted wonderful landscape and floral arrangements and declared that his favorite flower was scabiosa, commonly called pincushion flower, although we do not know whether his preference was for the annual or the perennial kind. There is little difference between the two visually, except the annual kind (*Scabiosa atropurpurea*) is slightly smaller flowered but has a greater color range, including red, pink, blue, and even black. The perennial pincushion flower is mostly blue or white. Both bloom in summer and grow long stems suitable for cutting.

'Butterfly Blue' differs from both in that it is an everblooming perennial. It has an outer circle of spoon-shaped sky blue petals and a high dome (the pincushion) composed of blue and white parts. An old variety that was once thought to be lost to cultivation, it was discovered in an Irish garden and reintroduced. Botanically known as *S. columbaria*, such has been its popularity that it was declared Perennial Plant of the Year in 2000.

Scabiosa likes full sun and soil with good drainage. 'Butterfly Blue' is low growing, to 8 inches high, and looks best planted in drifts in the forefront of mixed perennial borders.

BE AWARE! One scabiosa species—*S. stellata*—has tiny white flowers that dry to make an everlasting cut flower, quite charming in dried-flower arrangements, but these flowers are inconspicuous in mixed borders. A yellow species is sometimes offered in seed catalogs, but it is a rangy, weedy-looking plant with too-tall stems and widely spaced small flowers. Botanically known as *S. ochroleuca* and commonly called the giant pincushion flower, it will grow to 10 feet high with sparse, pale yellow flowers on long stems. Its untidy appearance restricts its ornamental value to providing a tall, staked highlight at the back of mixed perennial borders.

'Butterfly Blue' pincushion flower was named Perennial Plant of the Year in 2000 because of its ability to bloom continuously all season, which is rare for a flowering perennial.

 ## PLANT PROFILE

KNOWN BOTANICALLY AS: *Scabiosa* species

ZONES: 3–8 for summer flowering

PROPAGATION: Annual kinds from seed, perennial types by root division

SPACING: 12 inches apart in full sun

PESTS AND DISEASES: None serious

PERFECT PARTNERS: Coreopsis, daylilies, gaillardia, and yarrow

Poppies, Oriental

I never saw a poppy I didn't like, but the gigantic *Papaver bracteatum* is amazing. It displays crimson flowers up to 10 inches across on poker-straight stems.

GROW THIS! 'Turkenlouis' and *Papaver bracteatum*

Oriental poppies are from the Himalayas, and they are scene-stealers even in poor soil, especially the crimson reds with their enormous satinlike petals. In Giverny, Monet's garden in France, red Oriental poppies are partnered with bearded irises and herbaceous peonies for a stunning display in early June.

The variety 'Turkenlouis' is especially beautiful, because the large red flowers have fringed petal tips and a black eye zone around a powdery black seedpod, each petal resembling the wing of a bird. However, if it's extra-large size you desire, then grow *Papaver bracteatum* from seed. Native to Persia, each red poppy head has smooth petals, the flower shaped like a saucer, with black markings at the base of each shimmering petal. I've grown individual flowers up to 10 inches across. Moreover, the stems are strong, standing poker straight, and the leaves are serrated, resembling ferns when not in bloom. They differ from regular Oriental poppies by having stiff, thick stems covered in hairy, indented leaves, rather than the leafless flower stems on regular Orientals. Red is the most prevalent color among Oriental poppies, but there are several shades of pink, a white, and purple, most with black petal markings.

Oriental poppies demand full sun and good drainage. They prefer a location sheltered from strong winds. In addition to mixed perennial borders, grow them in meadow gardens.

BE AWARE! Many kinds of annual opium poppy—also called bread-seed poppy (*P. somniferum*)—resemble Oriental poppies, and local laws differ on growing them in home gardens. In Monet's garden, a pale pink opium poppy is direct-seeded among all the flowerbeds to flower in June, and invariably the seedpods (the source of the opium) are harvested by tourists thinking they can extract the opium, which occurs in a milky sap when the mature seedpod is cut. However, I'm told that the opium poppies grown in Monet's garden are a nonnarcotic type, so it's best to enjoy the show of flowers and forget the illegal activities.

 ## PLANT PROFILE

KNOWN BOTANICALLY AS: *Papaver orientale* and *P. bracteatum*

ZONES: 3–9 for spring flowering

PROPAGATION: By root division and root cuttings (2-inch segments with a node) taken in fall; also from seed that can be direct-sown to flower the following season

SPACING: 12 inches apart in full sun

PESTS AND DISEASES: Powdery mildew and root rot in poorly drained soil

PERFECT PARTNERS: Bearded irises and herbaceous peonies

The Scoop about Blue Poppies

I am quite confident in saying that the most coveted—and the most challenging—perennial plant to grow is the blue poppy (*Meconopsis betonicifolia*) from Tibet. From seed, it is quite easy to germinate in a peat-based potting soil and to raise seedlings to transplant size, but it is difficult to nurse them through the summer because they resent heat and humidity. Cool-summer locations like the Pacific Northwest and coastal Maine are better suited to growing the blue poppy. I have grown it in my Pennsylvania garden, but I raised the seed during summer in an air-conditioned conservatory and transplanted 4-inch potted plants to the garden at the onset of cool nights in September. The plants survived winter in a lightly shaded location with a mulch of shredded leaves and then flowered in spring, but perished in July with the onset of heat and humidity.

Plants are often listed as biennials, but some hybrids are perennial if grown in an organically rich, cool soil with good drainage. In locations where they will survive summer heat, prune away flower stems that form the first season so all the plant's energy goes into building a big root system. A healthy root system will then allow the plant to behave as a perennial. Good luck!

Primroses

Most people think primroses are tender
and sensitive to summer drought, but most American-bred
'Barnhavens' are extremely hardy and drought tolerant.
I never lost one from heat or cold.

GROW THIS! 'Barnhaven'

*"Beware! I warn you! Primroses cast a spell. The only way to avoid
it is to have nothing to do with the plants. Once you start growing
primroses you are lost. You want more and more...."*

—DORETTA KLABER, *PRIMROSES AND SPRING*

The primroses most commonly sold at garden centers in the spring are 'Pacific Giant Mix' or similar hybrids. Although their beautiful large flowers look spectacular in a bold color range that includes yellow, orange, red, blue, and pink, they are not hardy and were bred specifically as short-lived bedding plants or potted plants to last until the end of spring. They are so susceptible to extremes of cold and hot weather that they are best treated as annuals for early spring displays.

The hardiest perennial primroses are called 'Barnhavens', developed by a concert pianist and housewife, the late Florence Bellis, working from her home near Medford, Oregon. During the Depression, she decided to improve her impoverished life by investing in a packet of mixed primroses from Suttons Seeds in England. They contained primroses called "bunch-flowered" that had been developed by the famous Victorian plantswoman Gertrude Jekyll. In her spare time, Florence began crossing them, and she collected plants from neighbors to augment her gene pool, so that today there are more than 160 distinct varieties available. 'Barnhaven Blues' resemble wild English primroses but in a mixture of blue shades; they won an Award of Garden Merit. The 'Marine Blues' are in a similar blue mixture, but the flowers are held in clusters high above the foliage. The 'Grand Canyon' mixture includes copper, bronze, brick red, and rusty red in its color mix—the colors of a desert sunset—all with yellow centers. 'Spice Shades' are unbelievable—chocolate, coffee, tawny brown, ginger, and cinnamon, often scented. The 'Gold Laced' strain—also an Award of

Garden Merit winner—displays dainty flowers with black or rusty red petals edged in gold. The alpine auricula primroses are almost indescribable, they are so stunning. Like precious jewels, many are tricolored with a frosted green edging to the petal tips. The auriculas are divided into garden-worthy kinds for home gardeners and exhibition types for collectors, the latter best grown in a cool greenhouse.

The 'Barnhavens' are the finest strains of primroses the world has ever seen. They are not only hardy but also drought resistant, surviving hot, humid summers and coming back faithfully year after year. They are early flowering—as early as daffodils—in spring, their cheerful blooms often appearing before the last snowfalls of winter.

It is a miracle the 'Barnhavens' ever survived after Florence's death. When she retired, she sent her stock seed to a British couple, Jared and Sylvia Sinclair in the English Lake District, with a note that said: "Yours to keep or kill." After their retirement, the Sinclairs entrusted production to Angela Bradford, an English lady living in Brittany, France. After her retirement, she handed over the reins to another English couple living in Brittany, Mr. and Mrs. Daniel Lawson. Before her passing, Florence Bellis wrote a book about her breeding work and love of gardening titled *Gardening and Beyond*. It explains how she would find one or two viable pollen grains to work with, among flowers that were supposed to be sterile.

Plants of 'Barnhaven' primroses are rarely seen at garden centers, but seed and plants are available by mail from info@barnhaven.com, or you can visit the Web site www.barnhavenprimroses.com.

Primroses like a humus-rich soil in sun or partial shade and a mulch of shredded leaves to control weed growth. Be aware that the seed is miniscule, like specks of dust. It should be pressed into a peaty soil mix sufficient to anchor the seed, but not enough to exclude light, and the soil should never be allowed to dry out. Germination is inhibited above 70°F. Start the seed at least 10 weeks before outdoor planting. Established plants can be divided to increase your collection.

BE AWARE! Most of the primroses sold in garden centers during spring are potted plants intended for one season of color for planting outdoors when daffodils are in bud. These have been specially bred for greenhouse culture to be used as annuals and generally will not survive a freezing winter. The 'Pacific Hybrids' belong to this group. Fairy primroses (*Primula malacoides*) and German primroses (*P. obconica*) also are not reliably hardy where the ground freezes during winter. They are sensitive to high heat and are mostly used for massed bedding and window boxes in mild maritime climates, such as coastal California.

 PLANT PROFILE

KNOWN BOTANICALLY AS: *Primula* hybrids

ZONES: 4–7 for spring flowering, depending on variety

PROPAGATION: By seed started indoors 10 weeks before outdoor planting; also from root division after flowering. Barely cover seed with soil, as it needs light to germinate.

SPACING: 6 inches apart in sun or light shade

PESTS AND DISEASES: Mostly root rot from poor drainage

PERFECT PARTNERS: Crown imperials, daffodils, small ferns, hakone grass, heuchera, hyacinths, pansies, tulips, and violas

Rainbow Plants

I recommend 'Frieda Hemple' and strap-leafed 'Florida Sweetheart' as my favorite Florida-bred caladiums; the best way to plant these colorful foliage plants for summerlong color is massed in a rainbow mixture.

GROW THIS! 'Frieda Hemple', 'Rosebud', 'Florida Sweetheart', and 'Moonlight'

Commonly called rainbow plant because their heart-shaped leaves produce myriad colors (and no two leaves are ever identical), caladiums are tropical plant species from South America and sensitive to frost. Except in frost-free areas like Zone 10, the bulbs must be dug up in fall and overwintered indoors when grown in areas with cold, wet winters.

Sebring, Florida, is the caladium capital of North America, the location for Caladium World, a company that produces one of the most extensive selections of fancy-leaf varieties, including strap-leaf, lance-leaf, and dwarf varieties. At my frost-free garden on Sanibel Island, I have tested them all, and my pick for cream of the crop are the following: 'Frieda Hemple', a red with purple leaf margin; 'Rosebud' for its large tricolored leaves that are pink in the middle, white around the pink leaf veins, and bright green around the leaf margin; and 'Florida Sweetheart', displaying a lancelike ruffled leaf that is white with striking red leaf veins, similar in appearance to a series known as 'Thai' hybrids, but larger. Caladiums produce a beautiful white flower similar to a calla lily, but usually it is hidden below the large leaves.

Use rainbow plants in containers, several colors planted side by side, or grow the colors separately. Also use them informally, massed beside woodland paths and on the shady side of a house foundation.

The one condition rainbow plants detest is cold, wet soil. They relish the heat and humidity and can be combined with other shade-loving plants like coleus, tuberous begonias, and impatiens for a stunning display.

The bulbs (or corms) are shaped like a doughnut without the hole and should be planted with the smooth side facing down. Cover with at least 2 inches of soil. Give them good drainage and a humus-rich sandy soil for leaves that can be 12 inches long and 8 inches wide.

BE AWARE! No two leaves of a rainbow plant are ever alike, and sometimes you will see mail-order advertisements that imply one bulb will produce myriad colors. Photographs showing a pot crowded with different colors make it appear as if they all come from one bulb, but in fact these container mixtures are possible only by crowding a number of different varieties in a pot. That's actually a good way to grow them—shoulder to shoulder, as if they were one plant.

In general, the bigger the leaf, the bolder your rainbow plant display will be. Check whether the catalog description says the variety is suitable for sun (and therefore a good patio plant), since the majority prefer shade.

In general, the strap-leaf kinds do not produce as bold a display as the fancy-leaf types. With strap-leaf kinds, stay with the pinks and the reds, and steer clear of the whites like 'White Wing' and 'White Wonder'; you will get a better display of white from two outstanding white fancy-leaf types: 'Moonlight' and 'Candidum'.

KNOWN BOTANICALLY AS: *Caladium* hybrids

ZONES: All zones as a houseplant. Zones 3–11 as a summer-flowering annual; Zones 10 and 11 as a spring- and summer-flowering tender perennial

PROPAGATION: Bulbs planted in spring after frost danger; lift in fall before frost and store indoors

SPACING: 12 inches apart for shady flowerbeds; shoulder to shoulder for container plantings

PESTS AND DISEASES: Mostly chewing insects such as slugs and grasshoppers

PERFECT PARTNERS: Tuberous begonias, ferns, hostas, impatiens, wishbone flower, and shade-loving ornamental grasses like varieties of carex

Roses

Where to start? Truthfully, the 'Knock Out' series of shrub roses is disease resistant and everblooming, but German-bred 'Veilchenblau' is a sensational climber with masses of unique violet blue flowers.

GROW THIS! 'Climbing Blaze', 'Meidiland Bonica', 'Red Meidiland', 'Flower Carpet', 'Double Knock Out', 'Sub Zero', 'Iceberg', 'Veilchenblau', and 'Abraham Darby'

There are so many roses in cultivation, from hybrids and old garden roses to climbers and shrub roses, it's difficult to know where to begin. My own garden, Cedaridge Farm, is an excellent place to test roses since we have lots of disease like black spot and lots of rodent damage, especially during winter when mice will tunnel to the roots and eat them or gnaw at the trunk. In general, our best success has been with climbers, because they have vigorous root systems that withstand rodent damage. These are particularly notable: 'Climbing Blaze'; selections of the 'Meidiland' landscape roses, especially pink 'Bonica' (the first shrub rose to win an All-America Rose Selections award) and 'Red Meidiland' (both bred in France by Meilland rose growers); and the original carmine red 'Flower Carpet' rose, which became the most popular rose in North America before it was unseated by the 'Knock Out' rose series.

A typical cluster of 'Knock Out Pink' rose blooms shows the beautiful swirling petal arrangement. Red and yellow are also popular colors in this disease-resistant, everblooming series.

Introduced by rose growers Conard-Pyle of Pennsylvania, the original 'Knock Out' is a free-flowering, disease-resistant, single-flowered, and semidouble red, and since then it has been offered in other colors. The sheer quantity of bloom, the mounded shrubby habit, and the dark-green-almost-bronze leaves endear this to most people. From a distance, in peak bloom, it doesn't look like a rose but more like a red azalea. It was developed by independent Wisconsin rose breeder William Radler, whose objective was to "breed the maintenance out of roses—[with] greater cold tolerance to save time, giving them winter protection and [greater] disease resistance to eliminate the need to spray." Kyle McKean, rose expert at Conard-Pyle, when asked to describe 'Knock Out's' phenomenal success, responded: "Simply put, the 'Knock Out' family of roses totally revolutionized the way we think of roses. Never before has such a rose bloomed so long with so little effort."

Another spokesman for Conard-Pyle told me that if they had seen 'Double Knock Out' before introducing the original 'Knock Out' rose (with its single blooms), they would have waited for the double because it's such a big improvement.

Conard-Pyle also introduced the hardy 'Meidiland' landscape roses. I cannot praise 'Red Meidiland' or 'Bonica' enough, as they are the most free-flowering roses in my garden. They are repeat-blooming, first producing an extraordinary display in June on bushy plants. One of my 'Red Meidilands' has grown to the top of a mature dogwood tree.

Of the thousands of hybrid teas available, the most suitable for severe winter conditions are the 'Sub Zero' series. Developed by Dr. Herbert Brownell, deep in New England's snow-covered mountains, they not only are among the hardiest roses you can grow but also exhibit good disease resistance. The four most popular are 'Arctic Flame', a velvety deep red with a fruity fragrance; 'Maria Stern', a rich orange red; 'Senior Prom', a deep pink with sweet fragrance; and 'Helen Hayes', a golden yellow with a heavy fruity fragrance.

In my experience, the 'Flower Carpet' series is variable in its performance, but the original carmine red 'Flower Carpet' remains a favorite at Cedaridge Farm, creating a low, shrubby mound of semidouble blooms and being disease resistant.

The floribunda hybrid 'Iceberg' (bred in Germany and winner of a Gold Medal from the National Rose Society) is without question the most desirable white, available not only as a shrub rose but also as a free-flowering climber, ideal for covering arbors and gazebos.

No garden should be without some old garden roses or heirloom varieties. My two favorite heavily fragrant doubles are 'Belle de Crecy' for its deep pink color and swirl of heavily fragrant petals surrounding a button center; and 'Reine des Violettes' for its plum color, fruity fragrance, and swirling flower form. Another favorite heirloom, 'Veilchenblau' (German for "violet blue"), is a unique vigorous climber introduced in 1909. Although the cup-shaped flowers lack fragrance, they are almost blue and are held in generous clusters. The stems are thorn free. June flowering, it is one of the most free-flowering heirloom roses you can grow. "Why would you want to grow any other rose?" questions an admirer on the Internet. The English rosarian David Austin has made a name for duplicating the look of old garden roses in new sizes and colors. Some are region-specific, but the apricot 'Abraham Darby' is my favorite and seems widely adapted.

BE AWARE! The species rose, *Rosa multiflora*, should be avoided as it is invasive and difficult to eradicate. Some rose growers use *R. multiflora* as a hardy rootstock for hybrid tea and floribunda roses, so be sure to prune away any suckers that occur beneath grafts of grafted roses. Even small pieces of a *R. multiflora* root left in the soil can regenerate. In many states, this wild rose is banned as a menace to farmland.

A list of roses to warn against could fill a book. In general, be careful with hybrid teas, as these are generally not long lived without high maintenance. Many are susceptible to black spot disease and rodent damage. Rodents are a serious problem, because they will either girdle the main trunk or burrow beneath the snow during winter to eat the roots. Check with a local botanical garden or extension office for a list of carefree roses recommended for your area.

PLANT PROFILE

KNOWN BOTANICALLY AS: *Rosa* hybrids and species

ZONES: Basically there are roses to grow in every US gardening zone from 3 to 11

PROPAGATION: Mostly from tip cuttings after flowering, although many can be grown from seed

SPACING: 3 to 6 feet, depending on variety, in full sun

PESTS: Too numerous to name, but black spot is the major disease that defoliates plants (there are resistant varieties), while Japanese beetles will disfigure the flower buds and blooms. Also, aphids are a problem, colonizing the tenderest parts: stems and flower buds.

PERFECT PARTNERS: Bearded irises, clematis, coreopsis, daylilies, gaillardia, honeysuckle, lavender, and lilies

Sage, Blue

Transplants of deep violet blue
'May Night' always seem to outshine other perennial blue sages, although the lighter blue 'Merleau' will bloom within 10 weeks from seed.

GROW THIS! 'Merleau' and 'May Night'; also Siberian sage

Perennial salvias consist of a large number of species that offer a wide color range including red, yellow, blue, pink, purple, and white. Although they are perennials, breeders have coaxed some of them into performing as annuals, notably *Salvia* 'Merleau', with spires of violet blue florets that bloom within 10 weeks from seed and continue blooming all summer through high heat and humidity until fall frost. Plants grow to 3 feet high with spear-shaped, aromatic silvery leaves.

Among perennials, *S. nemorosa* (and its hybrids) is outstanding for long-lasting flower spikes and sheer quantity of blue spires. Developed by a German nursery,

'May Night' is the preferred choice for intensity of blue and longevity of bloom over older varieties. Siberian sage (*Perovskia atriplicifolia*) is taller growing (to 4 feet) and presents a misty appearance from a distance. These blue salvias require full sun and good drainage. Use them with yellow-flowering plants in combination planters.

Californians should look to many of their own native blue salvias for garden display, notably 'Allen Chickering', a cross between *S. clevelandii* and *S. leucophylla* introduced by the Rancho Santa Ana Botanic Garden.

BE AWARE! The wild species of *Salvia nemorosa* are beautiful plants with blue flower spikes, but they are short lived compared to named varieties of hybrids. Choose drought-resistant varieties such as 'May Night' (deep violet blue) for the longest-lasting display.

 ## PLANT PROFILE

KNOWN BOTANICALLY AS: *Salvia* x *sylvestris* and *Perovskia atriplicifolia*

ZONES: 5–9 for summer flowering. California has some excellent native blue salvias suitable for Zones 7–9.

PROPAGATION: Mostly by root division

SPACING: 12 inches apart

PESTS AND DISEASES: None serious

PERFECT PARTNERS: Bearded irises (especially yellows), coreopsis, daylilies, gaillardia, Shasta daisies, and perennial sunflowers

Agastache: The Hummingbird Sage

The hardy flowering perennial *Agastache* (also called hummingbird sage or hummingbird mint because it attracts hummingbirds in droves) is native to the Southwestern United States and Mexico. Not only does it resemble sage in appearance, it has aromatic leaves that smell like sage. However, the tubular flowers have a more diverse color range, not only in shades of blue and red but also in orange. The species *A. aurantiaca* has spires of orange tubular flowers, while the hybrid 'Blue Fortune' won an Award of Garden Merit from the Royal Horticultural Society. The plants are mostly hardy and everblooming, with a hardiness range that can extend from Zone 3 to 10 depending on variety. Just give the plants good drainage in a sunny position. They look especially attractive when planted among ornamental grasses, and they'll attract butterflies as well as hummingbirds.

Stonecrops (aka Sedums)

For dry slopes where other perennials have difficulty growing, plant 'Autumn Joy'. Its dusky pink flower clusters turn bronze and stay ornamental well into winter months.

GROW THIS! 'Brilliant', 'Autumn Joy', 'Class Act', and 'Mr. Goodbud'

Sedums are succulent plants with fat, fleshy leaves that store water, making them tolerant of drought. Many are low-growing alpine plants suitable for groundcover, such as 'Dragon's Blood'. Varieties of *Sedum spectabile*, such as 'Brilliant' (a rosy red), grow taller, up to 2 feet, and form domed clusters of star-shaped flowers resembling a cauliflower head. The variety *S. telephium* 'Autumn Joy' begins its flowering display by producing light green flower clusters in midsummer. These turn a rusty red by fall and then dry to a parchment brown, retaining their decorative flower form well into winter. At the dried stage, the stems can be cut to make beautiful dried arrangements.

Even though many garden experts think that 'Autumn Joy' is overused, I still believe it's an indispensable part of perennial borders for fall display. Two newer, similar-height sedum varieties that have won Royal Horticultural Society Awards of Garden Merit are 'Class Act', a stunning rosy red selection of 'Brilliant'; and 'Mr. Goodbud', with unique mauve flowers.

Sedums demand full sun and good drainage and neutral or slightly alkaline soil for full flowering effect. They are effective in rock gardens, especially using a collection of different species and heights.

BE AWARE! In general, the bronze-leaf sedums (such as 'Chocolate Drop' and 'Matrona', with its broccoli-like flower heads) will not give you as good of a flower display as the blue green stonecrop sedums. Their dark flowers tend to get lost among the foliage, and they will fall apart after heavy rains.

 PLANT PROFILE

KNOWN BOTANICALLY AS: *Sedum* species and hybrids

ZONES: 4–9 for late summer and fall flowering

PROPAGATION: Any stem section can be rooted in a moist, sandy potting soil.

SPACING: At least 18 inches apart in full sun

PESTS AND DISEASES: None serious, except for deer eating the stems to the ground before the plants even have a chance to bloom

PERFECT PARTNERS: Fall asters, cannas, black fountain grass, and flowering kale

Tickseed (aka Coreopsis)

Flowers of most new tickseeds are too small for my liking, but 'Early Sunrise' blooms the first year from seed, and cheerful lemon yellow 'Moonbeam' is everblooming.

GROW THIS! 'Crème Brulee', 'Zagreb', 'Heliot', 'Fruit Punch', 'Pineapple Pie', and 'Early Sunrise'

Coreopsis used to be a minor player in perennial borders until 'Moonbeam', a lemon yellow, showed how conspicuous and long lasting it could be at the front of the border, where it will form a cushion of flowers on delicate threadlike foliage, blooming for several months until fall frosts. However, the introduction of 'Crème Brulee' by Blooms of Bressingham has put a big dent in sales of 'Moonbeam'. According to Blooms' perennial plant expert Gary Doerr, "The flowers are larger, a deeper yellow, and they appear further down the stems as well as on top of the plant." The leaves are mildew resistant, and it flowers all summer from June into October on neatly mounded, robust plants. 'Zagreb' (to 3 feet) is a taller version of 'Crème Brulee' suitable for cutting.

A taller, larger-flowered yellow variety, *Coreopsis grandiflora*, is often used as a background, flowering for several weeks from midsummer. Now both kinds have been altered by plant breeders to perform reliably as annuals, flowering the first season from seed. 'Heliot', a bright golden yellow with red eye zone, won a gold medal in the Fleuroselect trials for its everblooming quality and first-year flowering from seed.

The small-flowered *C. verticillata* kinds have undergone an amazing transformation at the hands of plant breeders like Dan Heims of Terra Nova Nurseries.

Working with native species from all parts of the United States, breeders have consiserably enlarged the color range of the dwarf coreopsis, resulting in a spectacular array of bicolors such as 'Fruit Punch', a red with white petal tips, and 'Pineapple Pie', a yellow with a red eye zone. These all make wonderful mounded edging plants and look terrific massed in containers.

The grandiflora-type 'Early Sunrise' won an All-America Selections award for its ability to flower within 10 weeks from seed. It is especially beautiful planted with blue larkspur and blue lavender, with 2-foot stems suitable for cutting.

BE AWARE! New varieties of *C. verticillata* have flooded the market, and all look dazzling in close-up photographs, especially those varieties with a contrasting eye zone, such as red on a yellow background. However, some of the solid color rusty reds and bronze varieties often become invisible in the garden because their petal color blends with the surrounding soil or brown mulch. Stay with the brighter colors for the best displays, especially the white-and-red and yellow-and-red bicolors.

Coreopsis can be a solid color or bicolored like this 'Heliot' variety, winner of a gold medal in the Fleuroselect trials.

 ## PLANT PROFILE

KNOWN BOTANICALLY AS: *Coreopsis verticillata* and *C. grandiflora*

ZONES: 6–9 for summer flowering

PROPAGATION: By seed sown indoors 10 weeks before outdoor planting; also by root division

SPACING: 12 inches apart in full sun

PESTS AND DISEASES: None serious, although all coreopsis require excellent drainage to avoid root rot.

PERFECT PARTNERS: Blue sage, daylilies, gaillardia, scabiosa, and yucca

Tulips

With hundreds of colors to choose from,
it's hard to pick a favorite, but 'Gavota'
(a yellow-and-maroon bicolored triumph type)
always seems to stand out in tulip trials.

GROW THIS! 'Red Emperor', 'Stresa', 'Gavota', and 'Cairo'

Most people want their tulips to come back after the first season. Unfortunately, few of them do, because the majority of home gardeners plant hybrids that generally disappear after their first season. The majority of hybrid tulips—such as the parrots and peony-flowered classes and even the famous Darwin hybrids—either rot during cold, wet North American winters with alternate freezing and thawing, or the bulbs split into smaller nonflowering bulbs. To increase the chance of a repeat performance year after year, it's best to choose among the species (or "botanicals"): the water lily tulips (botanically called *kaufmanniana*); the peacock class (called *greigii*), with striped leaves; or the Foster types (*fosteriana*), of which 'Red Emperor' is the most famous. Though fleeting, 'Red Emperor' is early flowering, with large, shimmering blood red petals, naturalizing in soil with good drainage. All three open their petals out flat on sunny days and retain an urn shape under cloud cover. I like to see the peacocks planted as a mixture, because many of them are bicolors. The water lily tulips are the earliest flowering of all; if I had to choose only one tulip variety for my garden, it would be the award-winning 'Stresa', a shimmering yellow with red eye zone that not only comes back faithfully each year but can multiply.

Also repeat-blooming for me are the viridiflora tulips (with green petal markings), which are my favorites for arrangements—though many of the triumph, cottage, and lily-flowered tulips also make satisfying cut flowers. Varieties of triumph-type tulips include some unique colors, such as 'Gavota' (a yellow with maroon stripes) and 'Cairo' (a stunning bronze).

BE AWARE! Do not buy anything other than Dutch tulips, since the Dutch will not allow the export of bulbs that are not flowering size, capable of blooming in spring after fall planting. Some mail-order bulb merchants will sell tulip culls (discarded tulip bulbs too small to flower).

There is no such product as a blue tulip, even though some bulb catalogs describe and picture them as blue. The closest to blue is lilac or shades of purple. Also, there are no true black tulips. The closest is 'Queen of the Night', which is a deep maroon or eggplant purple depending on how it is lit.

I have a personal dislike for most Darwin hybrid tulips even though they are spectacular in flower. The problem is their flowering period is too brief, often no more than a week, whereas a more traditional class of tulip—such as the lily-flowered, triumph, and cottage types—will put on a display that can last 3 weeks. Miniature tulips, like miniature daffodils, don't give much bang for the buck. They can look lovely planted as drifts in a rock garden or in containers on a patio, but they become lost in a larger landscape.

 ## PLANT PROFILE

KNOWN BOTANICALLY AS: *Tulipa* hybrids and species

ZONES: 4–8, depending on variety, for early spring flowering

PROPAGATION: Raw bulbs planted in fall for spring flowering in sun or light shade

SPACING: Shoulder to shoulder in containers; 5 inches apart in garden soil, planted 5 inches deep from the base of the bulb

PESTS AND DISEASES: Tulips, after they have emerged from dormancy, are a favorite food of deer, and also of rodents and squirrels that will unearth them to eat.

PERFECT PARTNERS: Crocus, crown imperials, daffodils, hellebores, hyacinths, Japanese bleeding heart, and primroses

Water Lilies

French-bred Marliac hybrids such as
orange 'Comanche' and rosy red 'James Brydon' are
my pick among the hardies. Among tropical kinds, the
peach-colored 'Albert Greenberg' never disappoints.

GROW THIS! 'Comanche', 'James Brydon', 'Atropurpurea', 'Sunny Pink', 'Helvola', and 'Albert Greenberg'

The late Joseph Bory Latour-Marliac established a nursery specializing in water plants at Le Temple-sur-Lot in the south of France. He focused on improving hardy water lilies, using as parents the common white species that grows wild throughout Europe, a red he found in Sweden, a pink from Cape Cod, and a yellow from Mexico. From these, he developed a strain of sterile hybrids known as Marliac hybrids to include varieties such as 'Comanche' (a color-changing orange), 'Chromatella' (a yellow), 'James Brydon' (a deep rosy pink and a Plant of the Year selection in 2006 by the International Water Lily Society), and 'Atropurpurea' (an even darker red than 'James Brydon').

The Impressionist painter Claude Monet was so impressed with Latour-Marliac's water lilies he dug a special pond to start a collection. Their fame soon spread to England, where the Royal Horticultural Society invited Latour-Marliac to give a lecture about his breeding methods. It is said that he was so protective of his success, and so reluctant to share his secrets with British nurserymen, that when he gave the lecture, he deliberately misled them into believing he used tropical water lilies in his breeding. We now know this is impossible, as the tropicals and hardies are incompatible and will not cross.

Since Latour-Marliac's lead, other breeders have made some amazing improvements, including 'Sunny Pink', which is a similar color to 'Comanche' but twice the size.

Don't overlook hardy miniatures, the best of which is undoubtedly the bright yellow 'Helvola'. It produces a generous quantity of flowers all season among mottled leaves and can be grown in a water-filled container, such as a whiskey half barrel.

Hardy water lilies flower mostly during summer months, from June through September. They are best planted in submerged pots of clay soil with pebbles over the top to hold in the plants (the lip of the pot should be placed 12 inches to 2 feet below the water surface). Although a single tuber will make a 6-foot-wide expanse of floating circular leaves in one season, a more impressive cluster of flowers can be achieved by planting three to a minimum-size 10-gallon pot. Feed at 3-week intervals using special water lily tablets that are high in phosphorus. You press the tablets down into the clay soil around the inside edge of the pot.

In winter, before the water in the pond freezes, the pots can be lowered below the ice line. If frozen, the tubers will die. Generally, it is advisable not to have fish (like koi) and water lilies together, as the koi may eat the new shoots and discourage the plant from spreading. However, at Cedaridge Farm, I do have the two together without problem. I just feed the koi daily to keep them from chewing on the water lilies.

BE AWARE! First, let's explode a myth: It is true that tropical water lilies are larger flowered than hardies and come mostly from Africa and Australia, where magnificent blues exist (a color missing from the hardies), but it is not true that hardies bloom longer than tropicals. The fact is that you will get another month of bloom from tropicals after the hardies have stopped. But tropicals are sensitive to cold temperatures and must be taken indoors to survive the winter. For my money, the large-flowered pink tropical 'Albert Greenberg' is dramatic with its extra-decorative mottled foliage. Some tropicals are night bloomers, so be sure you check the label to distinguish them apart.

If not confined to a pot, hardy water lilies can be invasive, excluding light for the survival of fish. Particularly invasive is the sacred lotus water lily, with its aggressive spreading root system. It can take over the shallow parts of an entire pond or lake. Many kinds of other aquatic plants are invasive, the worst of which is the water hyacinth that has escaped into the wetlands of the South (especially Florida), completely covering the surface of canals and lakes. Parrot feather (*Myriophyllum aquaticum*) is hardy from Zones 6 to 11, and it can crowd out every other kind of water plant. My advice is to buy from reputable water garden nurseries and preferably from a local water garden nursery so you can buy live plants rather than dormant roots.

PLANT PROFILE

KNOWN BOTANICALLY AS: *Nymphaea* hybrids

ZONES: Hardies 3–11 for summer flowering; tropicals 10 and 11

PROPAGATION: From root division before or after flowering

SPACING: At least 6 feet apart in full sun

PESTS AND DISEASES: Aphids that colonize the flower stems that protrude above water; also fish that eat the new shoots

PERFECT PARTNERS: Arrowhead, Japanese irises, lotus, pickerelweed; also pond margin plants such as astilbe, goatsbeard, hostas, and scarlet lobelia

Yarrows

'Summer Pastels' is a mixture that is easily raised from seed to flower the first year.

GROW THIS! 'Moonshine', 'Summer Pastels', 'Tutti Frutti', and 'Pomegranate'

This common wayside weed in many parts of the United States and Europe has undergone an amazing transformation at the hands of plant breeders. Displaying white flat flower clusters in the wild, in Grandma's day there were basically three choices—yellow 'Coronation Gold' and the more refined lemon yellow 'Moonshine' (developed by Blooms of Bressingham) and a pale pink. There is hardly a perennial border in England where you will not find one or all of these planted in drifts beside tall blue delphinium. But today, the color choice is astonishing, culminating in a seed-grown variety 'Summer Pastels', which will flower the first season. It won an All-America Selections award for its unique color mixture. This includes all shades of yellow, orange, pink, and mauve plus creamy white.

A mixture with more intense colors has been introduced by Blooms of Bressingham, called 'Tutti Frutti'. According to Blooms' Gary Doerr, the company receives rave reviews about one of its colors, 'Pomegranate', for its glowing red flower clusters and bushy habit, with stems that stand erect and don't easily flop over.

Yarrow is an aggressive hardy perennial that should be divided every third

---

Some Choice Everblooming Perennials

Although annuals are famous for their longevity of bloom, most perennials—like Oriental poppies, bearded irises, and peonies—have a relatively short bloom period. These perennials can be considered everblooming because they hold their flowers for so long or because they create a season-long foliage effect.

Begonia 'Nonstop' (flowers)

Bromeliads (foliage)

Coral bells (foliage)

Coreopsis 'Moonbeam' (flowers)

Daylily 'Stella d'Oro' and 'Happy Returns' (flowers)

Geranium 'Rozanne' (flowers)

Hibiscus moscheutos 'Luna' (flowers)

Hosta (foliage)

Hydrangea 'Endless Summer' (flowers)

Indian blanket (flowers)

Ornamental grasses (foliage)

Rainbow plant (foliage)

Rose 'Knock Out' (flowers)

Scabiosa 'Blue Butterfly' (flowers)

Water lilies (flowers)

---

season to prevent it from becoming invasive. Plants prefer full sun and a well-drained soil and may need staking to prevent their heavy flower stems from falling over. Plants grow to 4 feet high. The flowers are especially good for cutting and are suitable for meadow gardens.

BE AWARE! The white varieties used alone and massed in a perennial border tend to punch a hole in the landscape. Used sparingly in a mixture, white yarrow is fine but otherwise tends to look weedy. The dwarf, spreading variety *Achillea tomentosa* should be avoided, as it can be invasive, spreading quickly into unwanted areas.

 PLANT PROFILE

KNOWN BOTANICALLY AS: *Achillea* hybrids

ZONES: 3–9 for summer flowering

PROPAGATION: By seed started indoors 10 weeks before outdoor planting, and by root division

SPACING: At least 12 inches apart in sun

PESTS AND DISEASES: None serious

PERFECT PARTNERS: Coneflower, daylilies, delphinium, hollyhock, larkspur, naked ladies, and Oriental lilies

Yuccas

Pass up the common green-leaf kinds for distinctive variegated selections, such as 'Color Guard'. Golden yellow along the midrib and green at the margins, its asparagus-like spears open out into a candelabra of white bell-shaped flowers.

GROW THIS! 'Color Guard' and 'Sapphire Skies'

Native to arid parts of North America, yuccas are tough desert wildflowers that grow spiky foliage and a tall, white flower cluster. The hardy species *Yucca filamentosa* will grow from Canada to the Florida Keys, coast to coast. Poor soil, even pure gravel, on dry slopes in full sun is like the Hotel Ritz to a yucca. It eventually creates a weed-suffocating colony through offsets.

'Color Guard' is a hardy yucca that has gold stripes down the center of the stiff, pointed leaves, and it's more brightly colored than others with gold stripes on the leaf edges.

The wild species has dark green leaves, but several new variegated kinds considerably enhance its ornamental value, especially when planted among drought-tolerant ornamental grasses like fountain grass and the hardy prickly pear, *Opuntia humifusa*. Discovered by hosta breeder Paul Aden in Japan, the variety 'Color Guard' displays green leaf margins and wide yellow stripes along the leaf midrib. 'Sapphire Skies' is a selection from another hardy yucca, *Y. rostrata*. Suitable for Zones 4 through 9, it exhibits an explosion of slender, blue, spiny leaves and, in time, will form a trunk—the hardiest yucca species to do so.

BE AWARE! 'Golden Sword' is similar to 'Color Guard' but does not have such bright variegation. In areas with frost, don't confuse yuccas with agave (another American desert plant), most of which are tender, or with the look-alike African aloes, which are also tender. Some make attractive patio plants, but they will need to be moved indoors to survive the winter.

 ## PLANT PROFILE

KNOWN BOTANICALLY AS: *Yucca filamentosa* and other species

ZONES: 4–11 for early summer flowering

PROPAGATION: Offsets called pups that crowd around the mother plant. Unlike agaves, yucca plants do not die after flowering.

SPACING: At least 2 feet apart in full sun

PESTS AND DISEASES: Mostly carefree, although scale can be a problem

PERFECT PARTNERS: Foxtail lilies, hardy prickly pear, and lavender

BEST CHOICE LAWN GRASSES

M y first introduction to lawn grass varieties was in England when a seed company I worked for introduced zoysia grass plugs under the name 'Emerald Velvet'. It was promoted as a tough lawn grass that would crowd out weeds, and it sold a lot of product on that basis, but with England's frosty winters, the grass would turn brown and not color up until late in spring, as happens over much of North America (except in frost-free areas).

I was later responsible for introducing to the gardening public a new turfgrass seed variety, from Penn State University turfgrass experts, called 'Pennfine'. An improved perennial ryegrass, it became a good substitute for bluegrass because of its improved drought tolerance, hardiness, and clean-cutting ability when mowed. Though 'Pennfine' has been super-seded by newer, improved perennial ryegrasses, like 'Manhattan II' from Rutgers University, these newer grasses are making lawns easier to grow and longer lasting.

The following listing of popular lawn grass varieties is not all-inclusive, as there are so many, but it does cover the varieties most popular among homeowners. Most importantly, before you plant a lawn, you need to know your region's climate, and you should solicit advice from a local USDA extension office. You'll see a lot of television ads promising perfect lawns if you use a particular company's fertilizer, weed killer, or turf-growing mix, but I'd like you to treat these commercials with skepticism; these prod-ucts are mostly chemical based, and the seed mixtures are cheap annual grasses that have no endurance to establish a hard-wearing, perennial, ever-green lawn.

CHECK THE LABEL

When you go to a garden center, you may be confronted with a dozen or more choices in lawn grass seed, usually beautifully packaged in a colorful box or bag. You should check the label, read the ingredient list, and decide whether the mix is a superior improved perennial ryegrass mixture or an inferior annual mix. If you buy off the Internet or through the mail, make sure you know what's in the lawn grass mix before you purchase it.

Packages with improved perennial ryegrass are the best for overall quality and durability over a wide range of climates. The various lawn grass varieties will be given as a percentage, and mixes may contain a minimum of three dif-ferent kinds of grass seed. In addition to an improved perennial ryegrass, a stan-dard mix may contain bluegrass; that's because if any of the ryegrass fails to germinate in 3 to 5 days, the bluegrass will come up and fill in the bare spots within 10 days. The mixture may also contain a fescue because certain fescues are shade tolerant, so if any parts of the lawn area are shady, the fescue will grow. This type of mixture, with various (and appropriate) seeds, will make a picture-perfect lawn.

The ideal time to establish a new lawn from seed is either spring (as soon as a warming trend begins after snow has melted) or fall, usually after the middle of August, when nights begin to turn cool again.

SEED, PLUGS, OR SOD?

With most lawn grasses, you have a choice of seeding a lawn, using plugs (usually 4-inch square transplants), or buying sod (usually tilelike rectangles of mature grass). Seeding is the least costly but the most time consuming because you need to prepare the bare soil, be sure it's free of weeds, and seed at the rate recommended on the label. You will need to cover the seed (or press it into the soil surface with a roller), water immediately unless rainfall is predicted, feed after emergence of the leaf blades, and mow when the grass is established and thick (usually when the grass blades are more than 4 inches high). To keep the grass knitted together and lush, fertilize in fall with a fall-specific fertilizer (usually high in phosphorus for good root development) and again in spring with a spring-specific product (usually high in nitrogen for good leaf blade development).

Plugs are equally high maintenance and are used mostly for warm-season "tillering" grasses like zoysia. These grasses are very slow growing, and it takes a long time to establish a lush lawn. The plugs are planted into bare soil in a checkerboard pattern, usually 8 to 12 inches apart, watered, fertilized, and weeded rigorously until the plugs send out tillers and knit together to create a dense mat of green leaves. Once established, a plug lawn is lower maintenance than a seeded lawn because it requires less mowing and watering and creates an effective weed barrier.

Sodding is the most expensive way to establish a lawn because you are literally buying a section of mature grass that can create an instant green carpet. However, you still need to create an area of bare soil, water, and fertilize until the planting is established.

Packages of seed, flats containing plugs, and piles of sod can all be found at garden centers. Sod for large areas can also be purchased from local sod farms. One thousand square feet of lawn seeded with improved perennial ryegrass can cost $12.98 for the seed; that same area of sod may cost about $90, but you might consider the cost of sod worth it when you consider that the result is an instant green lawn.

There is also a technique called patching, where you buy a seed mix with a distributing agent that allows you to reliably seed bare spots in an established lawn.

Whichever method you choose, start with bare soil free of obstructions like weed roots, stones, and debris, and realize that if you have poor sandy soil or hard clay soil or stony soil, you must improve it by adding a layer of topsoil or by mixing in lots of good compost. When seeding a new lawn, consider whether you need a grass seed suitable for full sun or shade and choose the right mix by reading the labels on the seed package. On sloping ground, you may need to stabilize the soil by using a biodegradable net that allows the grass to grow through but keeps the soil from being washed away.

COOL-SEASON AND WARM-SEASON GRASSES

Lawn grasses can be classified as cool-season and warm-season kinds. Cool-season grasses include Kentucky bluegrass (a widely adapted turfgrass), fine fescues (for the finest lawns—like a putting green, but it's so high maintenance that it's unsuitable for most homeowners), improved perennial ryegrass (similar in appearance to bluegrass but more widely adapted and the preferred grass for most gardens where there is frost), and tall or red fescue (the best kind for shade).

Warm-season grasses include Bermuda grass, Saint Augustine grass, Bahia grass, zoysia, and buffalo grass. They are all tough, heat-, and drought-resistant varieties most suitable for southern states. The first four warm-season grasses are similar, being coarse-bladed grasses requiring little maintenance that are grown mostly from plugs. Buffalo grass is a fine-textured grass not suitable for hard wear but good cosmetically for arid areas like Texas, Arizona, Nevada, and parts of Colorado.

Be wary of choosing zoysia and other warm-season grasses if you live in an area that sees cold weather; these warm-season grasses turn brown at the onset of frost and remain brown all winter until late spring. Generally, these grasses are sold as plugs or 4-inch squares and need to be spaced 8 inches apart to allow them to send out "tillers" (side roots) and knit together. Once established, a zoysia lawn can be an effective weed barrier, but it is recommended mostly for frost-free areas.

GRASS SUBSTITUTES

Because most lawn grasses need mowing to keep them from looking weedy, consider certain hardy perennial groundcovers that look like grass and never need mowing. Two of my favorites are dwarf variegated bamboo (*Sasa nipponica*—

Dwarf variegated bamboo, a no-mow perennial substitute for turfgrass

a running bamboo that is easily controlled by mowing around the edges) and lily turf (*Liriope muscari*), both suitable for sun or light shade.

DEALING WITH COMMON LAWN PROBLEMS

Depending where you live, there are many problems that can afflict lawns, some more prevalent in the South and others more in the North. Every extension office can provide localized recommendations for dealing with problem diseases like brown patch, dollar spot, and leaf spot or an invasion of insect pests or weeds.

Lily turf, a no-mow perennial that looks like turfgrass

Bentgrass, Creeping

When I lived beside Morecambe Bay in the north of England, I used to go for cliff walks and see along the tide line hundreds of acres of a very fine-bladed grass called creeping bentgrass. At times, fishermen would come with their carts and dig up sections of it to sell to local golf courses for putting greens and to landscapers who wanted a lawn with a billiard-table look for wealthy clients or homeowners willing to fuss with a fine-bladed lawn grass. As you can guess, it is extremely high maintenance. During hot weather, it often needs irrigating every day to keep it green and mowing twice a week to keep it short enough for lawn sports.

 PLANT PROFILE

KNOWN BOTANICALLY AS: *Agrostis stolonifera*

ZONES: 4–8

PROPAGATION: Seed or sod

SPACING: Read label directions for seeding.

PESTS AND DISEASES: Susceptible to common lawn problems like brown patch and dollar spot

USES: Best for the finest textured lawns in full sun; also putting greens, croquet courts, bowling greens for boules or bocce, and grass tennis courts. Usually confined to small areas due to high maintenance.

Buffalo Grass

This drought-resistant North American lawn grass isn't hard wearing, but it will stay green and produce a lawn effect when other plants are dying from thirst. Although it's native to North America's prairies, breeders have produced a number of widely adapted varieties suitable for as far north as Canada and as far south as the Mexico border. Selections are especially suitable for arid areas like Texas, Nevada, and Arizona. The leaf blades stay short and require little or no mowing. It spreads by stolons to create a dense, fine-textured weave.

 ## PLANT PROFILE

KNOWN BOTANICALLY AS: *Buchloe dactyloides*

ZONES: Best for 6–9

PROPAGATION: Seed and plugs, also sod

SPACING: 6 inches between plugs in full sun

PESTS AND DISEASES: Usual lawn blights such as brown patch and dollar spot

USES: Lawns in arid or desertlike areas

Fescue, Red

Also known as creeping red fescue, this is one of the best fine-textured grasses for shade. As a consequence, it is often combined with bluegrass and improved perennial ryegrass mixtures as insurance—to fill in wherever there is too much shade for the other two. It is generally suitable for areas where bluegrass is recommended and often is included as an ingredient in bluegrass lawn mixes to fill in where the bluegrass fails to grow.

 ## PLANT PROFILE

KNOWN BOTANICALLY AS: *Festuca rubra*

ZONES: 4–9, wherever bluegrass grows

PROPAGATION: Seed and sod

SPACING: Read label directions.

PESTS AND DISEASES: Brown patch, dollar spot, leaf spot, and other common lawn diseases

USES: Mostly used for shady lawns and shady grass paths

Kentucky Bluegrass

This beautiful soft-bladed, dark green grass is what most people consider the ideal lawn variety. It is comfortable to walk over with bare feet and to sunbathe on. It has lost some appeal in recent years with the popularity of improved perennial ryegrass varieties, but it is still included in mixtures featuring improved perennial ryegrass since the two grasses look so much alike. If the lawn suffers from drought or cold, bluegrass can quickly recover after the return of favorable growing conditions. Bluegrass is a widely adapted grass with fairly good drought tolerance and winter hardiness, though it tends to be more popular in areas like the Pacific Northwest, coastal California, mountain states, the Midwest, and the northeastern United States.

 ## PLANT PROFILE

KNOWN BOTANICALLY AS: *Poa pratensis*

ZONES: 4–9

PROPAGATION: Seed germinates in 10 days; also widely available as sod.

SPACING: Read label directions.

PESTS AND DISEASES: Common lawn diseases such as brown patch and dollar spot. Is damaged by dog urine.

USES: Lawns, parks, grass paths, and wherever a lush, green, dense turf is desired

No-Mow Grass

Remarkably, there are certain lawn grasses—such as prairie dropseed (*Sporobolus heterolepis*), buffalo grass, and some fescue mixtures—that are so slow growing or so low growing that they can go a whole season without any mowing whatsoever or with only one or two cuts. I saw my first no-mow lawn at Chanticleer Gardens in Wayne, Pennsylvania. They have pioneered the idea of creating lawns with a prairie grass called prairie dropseed. These form clumps with tufts of arching leaf blades. As the leaf blades elongate, they create a fountain effect and look beautiful, like wavy sedge grasses across a marsh. Although the grass is difficult to walk through as it matures, it is attractive—a dark glossy green in spring and summer, golden yellow in fall, and bronze in winter. It does need cutting once a year in early spring before new leaf blades sprout (with the mower blade set high so it clears the leaf crowns); this removes the previous season's growth. After cutting, the lawn will look like a lot of sleeping hedgehogs surrounded by bare soil, but the grass quickly grows from each cluster to form a new dense cover that requires no further cutting until the following early spring.

For arid areas like Arizona and Texas, buffalo grass can make a fine no-mow grass since it is extremely slow growing. For northern states, mixtures of fescue grasses are sold as no-mow grasses, mostly to grow in orchards and transition areas between lawn and woodland.

 PLANT PROFILE

ZONES: There are no-mow grasses suitable for all zones.

PROPAGATION: Although a no-mow lawn can be established from seed, it is better to use plugs and transplant them in a checkerboard pattern, or you can purchase sod.

SPACING: Plant plugs 12 inches apart in full sun.

PESTS AND DISEASES: Common lawn blights such as brown patch and dollar spot

USES: Lawns where there is little or no traffic, orchards, vineyards (between rows), pasture, and transition areas between manicured lawns and informal areas

Perennial Ryegrass, Improved

Note the qualifier "improved." There are crucial differences between regular perennial ryegrasses and improved varieties, and not all books on lawn grasses point out the difference. I wouldn't have a regular perennial ryegrass lawn if you gave it to me. I do, however, have beautiful lawns featuring the latest advances in "improved" perennial ryegrass, pioneered by turfgrass experts at Penn State University.

First, the old regular perennial ryegrasses were not as hardy as bluegrass and not as attractive, and the leaf blades had a tendency to shatter after mowing, giving an untidy cut. Then, on a Friday morning 20 years ago, I was photographing a garden near Philadelphia and saw a groundskeeper seeding some bare soil to create a new lawn. When I returned on Monday afternoon, I was amazed to see that the grass had germinated over the weekend and the bare soil had turned green with newly sprouted grass blades from a high germination rate. I asked the groundskeeper what kind of grass he had used, and he told me about a new improved variety of perennial ryegrass called 'Pennfine' produced by turfgrass specialists at Penn State University. It was fast germinating, indistinguishable from bluegrass, more heat and drought tolerant than bluegrass, hardier than bluegrass, more hard wearing, and less disease prone. In the Philadelphia area, it didn't brown out like other turfgrasses during winter, and even after a covering of snow, the grass would be as green as a billiard-table top when the snow melted.

I was garden editor of *Woman's Day* at the time and decided it would make a good article. I contacted one of the turfgrass specialists at Penn State, and he suggested a special formula for the majority of households in America, consisting of 20 percent 'Pennfine', 60 percent bluegrass, and 20 percent fescue. "Why the low percentage of 'Pennfine'?" I asked. He explained that if the formula contained any more 'Pennfine' than 20 percent, it would turn into a 100 percent 'Pennfine' lawn because the 'Pennfine' was so much more aggressive and faster germinating than the other two grasses, and that's not what a homeowner should have—because a mixture of several varieties will ensure a lush green lawn if conditions are not suitable for one of the grass seed varieties taking root (such as dry conditions following germination, or part of the site being shady). So, for *Woman's Day*, I had a grass seed company make up the formula under the name 'Quicklawn', and it was offered exclusively to *Woman's Day* readers. It was such a huge success that the grass seed company decided to offer the 'Quicklawn' mixture through retail outlets nationwide. And it is still available through Internet sources.

Over the years, 'Pennfine' has been improved upon by other turfgrass breeders, notably at Rutgers University. Their best equivalent of 'Pennfine' (still an improved perennial ryegrass) is 'Manhattan II'. The grass is fine textured, a pleasure to walk on in bare feet, and the leaf blades are dark green and shiny. Its lush appearance is deceptive, as it stands up to hard wear and crowds out weeds. It is used for lawns and playing fields and does not require as much fertilizer or water as bluegrasses.

The success of 'Quicklawn' produced many imitators, advertised in full-page magazine advertisements and even on television; but instead of including an improved perennial ryegrass in the mix, they invariably use cheap, unsuitable annual grasses and still make the same claims. Look for the original 'Quicklawn' product by doing an Internet search, and be sure it contains improved perennial ryegrass in the mix.

 PLANT PROFILE

KNOWN BOTANICALLY AS: *Lolium perenne*

ZONES: 4–9, wherever bluegrass grows

PROPAGATION: By seed, direct-sown. Under ideal conditions, the seed germinates in 3–5 days.

SPACING: Broadcast according to package label instructions.

PESTS AND DISEASES: Susceptible to brown spots from dog urine and other common lawn diseases such as brown patch and dollar spot

USES: Lawns, playing fields, golf courses, and grass paths

Zoysia and St. Augustine

Most books on lawn grasses do not recommend zoysia for northern gardens or anywhere except frost-free zones since zoysia is a tropical grass that turns brown at the slightest hint of frost. However, during a visit to Japan, I saw a lot of zoysia used for lawns in frosty areas. And sure enough, the grass had turned brown, but my Japanese guide pointed to the surrounding ornamental grasses and deciduous trees that had also turned russet colors associated with fall. The fact that the lawn was brown instead of green during fall, winter, and early spring didn't seem to bother Japanese landscapers at all.

In spite of my Japanese friend's lesson in Japanese lawn aesthetics, I still wouldn't feel comfortable with a zoysia lawn at my Pennsylvania property (where I want to photograph my daffodils against a lush green carpet, not a brown one), but at my frost-free property on Sanibel Island, Florida, I have a zoysia lawn that stays green all year and I love it. Although there are fine-bladed zoysia varieties, mine has a broad leaf blade and is not ideal for bare feet, but it is extremely drought resistant, hard wearing, and good looking. There isn't a weed in the lawn (the knit of leaf blades won't permit weeds to enter), and it requires much less mowing than any other type of warm-season turfgrass because it is so slow growing.

For northern gardens, 'Meyer Amazoy' is a popular hardy strain propagated in Maryland. 'Cashmere', propagated in Florida, is a fine-bladed strain recommended for southern gardens.

St. Augustine grass is native to the Gulf of Mexico region and resembles a broad-leafed zoysia. Best for Zones 8 south, it thrives during high temperatures, creating a dense mat of dark green leaves that will crowd out weeds. It tolerates a wide range of soils, including salty and alkaline sandy soil but not boggy soil.

 ## PLANT PROFILE

KNOWN BOTANICALLY AS: *Zoysia* species

ZONES: 10 and 11 for an evergreen groundcover; in Zones 4–9, the grass blades will brown after fall frost and stay brown until the last frost date in spring.

PROPAGATION: From plugs, or better still, from 4-inch squares sold at garden centers, or by using larger rectangles of established turf. However, when you purchase by mail, you might get a 4-inch-square plug with instructions to divide it into smaller pieces, but that's not the way to go since zoysia is naturally slow growing and anything smaller than a 4-inch-square transplant could take two seasons or more to fill in.

SPACING: Usually 12 inches apart in a checkerboard pattern so the plugs produce tillers (side-spreading roots) that will knit into their neighbors and provide a dense foliage cover

PESTS AND DISEASES: Highly disease resistant but still susceptible to common lawn problems like brown patch and dollar spot

USES: Southern lawns and southern golf courses

SOURCES

There are hundreds of seed, plant, and bulb companies, and you'll find most of them online. And there are thousands, if not hundreds of thousands, of dedicated seed savers and amateur plant breeders working around the nation and the world to help preserve wonderful plants and the genetic diversity of the seed supply, and you may find them online, too.

Many companies build a fine reputation. Some stay small and continue to offer one-on-one customer service. Other companies grow and change and are often acquired by another company, and their business practices can change.

I've also listed plant societies that may offer expert advice on planting and growing your favorite plants. Some of them have local chapters if you'd like to get more involved with other people who share your interest.

If you see an asterisk behind a company's name, it means the company also offers seeds (and in the perennials category, it means the company offers bulbs).

VEGETABLE AND HERB SEEDS AND PLANTS

Baker Creek Heirloom Seeds*
2278 Baker Creek Road
Mansfield, MO 65704
www.rareseeds.com

Bunton Seeds*
939 East Jefferson
Louisville, KY 40206
http://buntonseed.com

Burpee Seeds*
300 Park Avenue
Warminster, PA 18974
www.burpee.com

The Cook's Garden*
PO Box 5030
Warminster, PA 18974
www.cooksgarden.com

Dixondale Farms
PO Box 129
Carrizo Springs, TX 78834
www.dixondalefarms.com

Dominion Seed House*
Box 2500
Georgetown, Ontario L7G 5LS
Canada
www.dominion-seed-house.com

Gurneys Seed & Nursery Co.*
PO Box 1478
Greendale, IN 47025
www.gurneys.com

Harris Seeds*
355 Paul Road
Rochester, NY 14624
www.harrisseeds.com

Henry Field's Seed & Nursery*
PO Box 397
Aurora, IN 47001
www.henryfields.com

J. L. Hudson, Seedsman*
PO Box 337
La Honda, CA 94020
www.jlhudsonseeds.net

Johnny's Selected Seeds*
955 Benton Avenue
Winslow, ME 04901
www.johnnyseeds.com

J. W. Jung Seed Co*
335 South High Street
Randolph, WI 53957
www.jungseed.com

Park Seeds*
1 Parkton Avenue
Greenwood, SC 29647
www.parkseed.com

Pinetree Garden Seeds*
PO Box 300
New Gloucester, ME 04260
www.superseeds.com

Rohrer Seeds
2472 Old Philadelphia Pike
Smoketown, PA 17576
www.rohrerseeds.com

Seed Savers Exchange*
3994 North Winn Road
Decorah, IA 56101
www.seedsavers.org

Seeds of Change*
PO Box 1570
Sante Fe, NM 87592
www.seedsofchange.com

Shumway, R. H.*
3344 West Stroud Street
Randolph, WI 53957
www.rhshumway.com

Stokes Seeds*
PO Box 538
Buffalo, NY 14240
www.stokeseeds.com

Territorial Seed Company*
PO Box 158
Cottage Grove, OR 97424
www.territorialseed.com

Thompson & Morgan*
PO Box 4086
Lawrenceburg, IN 47025
www.tmseeds.com

Tomato Growers Supply Co.
PO Box 60015
Fort Myers, FL 33906
www.tomatogrowers.com

Totally Tomatoes
West Shroud Street
Randolph, WI 53956
www.totallytomato.com

Vesey's Seeds*
PO Box 9000
Calais, ME 04619
www.veseys.com

W. Robinson & Son (Seeds & Plants) Ltd.*
Sunny Bank
Forton
Nr. Preston
Lancashire PR3 0BN
UK
www.mammothonion.com.uk

HERBS

Garden Harvest Supply
2952 West 500S
Berne, IN 46711
www.gardenharvestsupply.com

Nichols Garden Nursery*
1190 Old Salem Road
Albany, OR 97321
www.nicholsgardennursery.com

Well-Sweep Herb Farm
205 Mount Bethel Road
Port Murray, NJ 07865
www.wellsweep.com

BULBS

Brent & Becky's Bulbs*
7900 Daffodil Lane
Gloucester, VA 23061
www.brentandbeckysbulbs.com

de Jager Bulb Co
188 Asbury Street
PO Box 2010
South Hamilton, MA 01982
http://dejagerflowerbulbs.com

John Scheepers
23 Tulip Drive
PO Box 638
Bantam, CT 06750
www.johnscheepers.com

Van Bourgondien*
PO Box 309
Cleves, OH 45002
www.dutchbulbs.com

Van Engelen
23 Tulip Drive
PO Box 638
Bantam, CT 06750
www.vanengelen.com

PERENNIALS

Andre Viette Farm & Nursery
994 Long Meadow Road
PO Box 16
Fisherville, VA 22939
www.viette.com

Bluestone Perennials
7211 Middle Ridge Road
Madison, OH 44057
www.bluestoneperennials.com

Plant Delights Nursery
9241 Saul's Road
Raleigh, NC 27603
www.plantdelights.com

Song Sparrow Nursery
13101 East Rye Road
Avalon, WI 53505
www.songsparrow.com

Wayside Gardens*
1 Garden Lane
Hodges, SC 29695
www.waysidegardens.com

White Flower Farm*
PO Box 50
Litchfield, CT 06759
www.whiteflowerfarm.com

SPECIALTY PLANTS

B&D Lilies
330 P Street
Port Townsend, WA 98368
www.bdlilies.com
Garden lilies

Gilbert H. Wild & Son
Sarcoxie, MO 64862
www.gilberthwild.com
Peonies, irises, daylilies, hostas

Kurt Bluemel
2740 Greene Lane
Baldwin, MD 21013
www.kurtbluemel.com
Ornamental grasses

Lilypons Water Gardens
6800 Lilypons Road
Buckeystown, MD 21717
www.lilypons.com
Water lilies

Schreiner's Iris Gardens
3625 Quinaby Road
Salem, OR 97303
www.schreinersgardens.com
Bearded irises

SPECIALTY PLANTS—CONT.

Siskiyou Rare Plant Nursery
2825 Cummins Road
Medford, OR 97501
http://siskiyourare plantnursery.com
Alpines

Wildseed Farms
100 Legacy Drive
Fredericksburg, TX 78624
www.wildseedfarms.com
Wildflowers

NATIONAL PLANT SOCIETIES

American Begonia Society
33 Kintyre Lane
Bella Vista, AR 72715
www.begonias.org

American Gourd Society
PO Box 2186
Kokomo, IN 46904
www.americangourdsociety.org

American Hemerocallis Society
PO Box 10
Dexter, GA 31019
www.daylilies.org

American Hydrangea Society
PO Box 53234
Atlanta, GA 30355
www.american hydrangeasociety.org

American Iris Society
PO Box 177
DeLeon Springs, FL 32130
www.irises.org

American Peony Society
713 White Oak Lane
Gladstone, MO 64116
www.americanpeonysociety.org

American Primrose Society
3524 Bowman Court
Alameda, CA 94502
www.american primrosesociety.org

American Rose Society
PO Box 30,000
Shreveport, LA 71130
www.ars.org

Cactus & Succulent Society
PO Box 1000
Claremont, CA 91711
www.cssainc.org

Herb Society of America
9019 Kirtland Chardon Road
Kirtland, OH 44094
www.herbsociety.org

International Waterlily and Water Gardening Society
PO Box 546
Greenville, VA 24440
http://iwgs.org

Perennial Plant Association
3383 Schirtzinger Road
Hilliard, OH 43026
www.perennialplant.org

ACKNOWLEDGMENTS

First, a big thanks to my wife, Carolyn, who has worked with me designing and planting the test gardens at Cedaridge Farm and who has accompanied me to many of the test gardens featured in this book. Also, to the late Harry Smith, who taught me to photograph gardens; the late O'Dowd Gallagher, who taught me to write; and the late David Burpee, dean of American seedsmen, who taught me how to evaluate both flowers and vegetables for home gardens.

INDEX

Boldface page numbers indicate photographs or illustrations. <u>Underscored</u> references indicate boxed text, charts, and graphs.

'Diamond Frost', 153,
222, 252
Eustoma grandiflora (Texas
bluebells), 189–90
'Echo' series, 189
'Forever Blue', 189
'Forever White', 189
'Mariachi' series, 189
'Mariachi Blue', **265**

F

False spirea. *See* Astilbes
(*Astilbe* × *arendsii, A.
chinensis*)
Fell, Derek, **ix, x, 6, 213**
Ferns (various species and
hybrids)
fiddleheads, 315
horsetail (horsetail
rush) (*Equisetum*
species), 315
Japanese painted
(*Athyrium niponicum
pictum*), **276**, 314,
315
maidenhair (*Adiantum*
species), 314
ostrich (*Matteuccia
struthiopteris*),
314–15, **314**
'The King', 314–15
Fertilizer
compost as, 26
Derek's Compost Tea,
43
organic, 25–26
Festuca rubra (red fescue),
377
Flower of the hour
(*Hibiscus trionum*),
158
Fountain grass (*Pennisetum*
species), 320

Foxtail lilies (*Eremurus*
species and
hybrids), **276**,
316–17

G

Gaillardia (Indian
blanket)
'Arizona Sun', **279**
Gaillardia × *grandiflora*
(Indian blankets),
327–28
'Plume' series, 327
Garden basics
drainage, 27, **27**
fertilizer, 25–26, 43
insect and pest control,
28–31
light, 26
soil, 24–25
compost and, 24, 26
hydrogel and, 37
importance of good,
24–25
testing of, 24–25
watering, 28
weed control, 27–28, **27**
Garden sites
container gardening,
36–37
raised beds, 33–35
vertical gardening,
35–36
Garlic-pepper spray, 30–31
Gazanias (*Gazania
hybrids*), 154–55
'Kiss' strain, 154, **253**
'Big Kiss', 154–55
'Sunbather Totonaca',
155, **252**
Geraniums, bedding
(*Pelargonium
hybrids*), 156–57

'Calliope' variety, 156,
253
'Designer' series, 156
'Multibloom', 156, 157
seed-raised, 156, 157
Geraniums, ivy-leaf
(*Pelargonium
peltatum*)
seed, 157
Geraniums, Martha
Washington (regal)
types (*Pelargonium
domesticum*), 157
Geraniums, perennial
(*Geranium
himalayense, G.
pretense*), 317–18
'Johnson's Blue', **276**,
317–18
'Rozanne', 317–18
Gerbera (Transvaal daisy),
149–50
Gloriosa daisies (*Rudbeckia
hybrid*), 136, 137
Grasses, lawn. *See also*
Lawns
Bahia grass, 374
bentgrass (*Agrostis
stolonifera*), **291**, 376
Bermuda grass, 374
buffalo grass (*Buchloe
dactyloides*), 374,
376–77, 379
cool-season, 374
fescue, red (*Festuca
rubra*), 377
Kentucky bluegrass (*Poa
pratensis*), 374, 378
no-mow grass, 378–79
buffalo grass, 374,
376–77, 379
prairie dropseed
(*Sporobolus heterolepis*),
291, 378–79

ABOUT THE AUTHOR

Few people are better qualified than the author to write about choosing plant varieties. At age 19, Derek Fell began working with Europe's biggest and oldest-established seed house, Hurst Seeds Ltd., in London. At that time, Hurst was the only British seed house that still maintained a breeding program for home garden vegetables and flowers. Fell was responsible for producing Hurst's seed catalog, and from their test gardens in Essex, he helped their breeders launch their new vegetable and flower seed introductions to the general public. After winning first place in Britain's Best Seed Catalog Contest, Fell was invited by the dean of American seedsmen, David Burpee, to move to the United States and work on his mail-order seed catalog. After 6 years as Burpee's catalog manager, Fell was appointed executive director of All-America Selections (the national seed trials) and the National Garden Bureau (an information office sponsored by the American seed industry). During this period, Fell traveled the world, meeting with plant breeders and persuading them to enter their best new introductions in the All-America Selections trials. He also worked as a consultant to the White House during the Ford administration on programs to fight inflation through home vegetable gardening.

Fell left All-America Selections and the National Garden Bureau to write garden books, serve as a consultant on mail-order marketing to seed and nursery companies, and build up a photo library of horticultural subjects. In 1989, to aid him in this work, he purchased Cedaridge Farm, a Zone 6 garden in Bucks County, Pennsylvania, for the purpose of testing new varieties of mostly flowers and vegetables and also of different organic growing techniques such as deer control, irrigation systems, and composting. In 2008, he also purchased a frost-free property, Karamea, on Sanibel Island, Florida, to create a Zone 10 facility for the growing of coconuts, banana trees, citrus, mangoes, and other tropical plants.

Fell is experienced at the art of selling live plants through the medium of television. For 6 years, he was host of *Step-by-Step Gardening* on the QVC shopping channel. His was the first successful garden show on QVC to sell live plants.

Fell visits the California Pack Trials annually to keep abreast of the latest developments in flower seed production, and he visits the independent test plots of numerous institutions such as the Michigan State University plant trials in addition to test plots run by seed and nursery companies such as Burpee's Fordhook Farm, the Landisville Farm Museum heirloom test plots, and others.